THE ALBANIANS

THE ALBANIANS

A MODERN HISTORY

Miranda Vickers

I.B.TAURIS
LONDON · NEW YORK

To my mother, Barbara Kathleen Blake

Published in 1995 by
I.B.Tauris & Co Ltd
45 Bloomsbury Square
London WC1A 2HY
175 Fifth Avenue
New York NY10010

In the United States of America
and Canada distributed by
St Martin's Press
175 Fifth Avenue
New York NY10010

A CIP record for this book is available from the British Library

A full CIP record is available from the Library of Congress

ISBN 1 85043 749 1

Typeset in Monotype Ehrhardt
by Lucy Morton, London SE12

Printed and bound in Great Britain by WBC Print,
Bridgend, Mid-Glamorgan

Contents

Preface

Since the end of the one-party state in 1990, and the country's gradual re-emergence from total isolation, interest in Albania has been growing. However, images of this unknown corner of Europe are for the most part grim, bleak and often misleading. In order to comprehend the ruthless character of the Albanian regime and the complex series of alliances and splits with other Communist states in the period following the Second World War, it is necessary to recall the Albanian people's long history of subjugation and humiliation.

Because of the country's geographical position, its political and historical evolution has been shaped by the Ottoman Empire, and the five hundred years of Ottoman occupation provide the key to understanding Albania today. The period of Ottoman rule had a profound influence on the evolution and character of Albanian society which accounts for many of its distinctive features, such as why so many Albanians chose to convert from Christianity to Islam. In examining Ottoman rule from the time of the rise of the great Albanian pashaliks in the middle of the eighteenth century it is possible to detect the first stirrings of an Albanian national consciousness, which gradually developed into a national movement.

The Albanian-inhabited regions of the Balkan peninsula were at the very centre of what became known as the Eastern Question, and as a consequence suffered Great Power rivalry and interference. These regions were claimed either wholly or in part by Serbs, Montenegrins, Greeks and Bulgarians as part of their historical territories. The Albanian state came into being at the close of 1912, as the collapse of

the Ottoman Empire became imminent. The fledgling country immediately found itself drawn into the Balkan Wars and the First World
War, as Balkan armies marched deep into Albanian territory with the
hope of dividing the state between them. The debate over the final
delimitation of Albania's frontiers after the war dragged on until 1925,
by which time half a million Albanians found themselves included
within the new Kingdom of Serbs, Croats and Slovenes. The dictatorship of Ahmed Zogu was unable to stop Albania becoming a mere
Italian colonial dependency, occupied by Italy and then by Germany
during the Second World War. The victory of the Communist-led
partisans in the Second World War and the subsequent rule of Enver
Hoxha sealed Albania's fate for the next 45 years.

These topics provide the general focus of the text, which concludes
with a look at how Albania fared during the heady days of 1990–91
and the emergence of political pluralism within the country. The
euphoria following the election victory of the Democratic Party in
1992 already seems to belong to a past era, as Albania struggles to find
its place in a Balkans seething with unresolved tensions, mistrust and
insecurity. In looking at the Albanian question, four issues in particular
arouse the most curiosity: why the Albanians were the last Balkan
people to develop a national consciousness; how the Albanian state
came into existence; why half the Albanian nation was excluded from
that state; and why Albania remained for so long one of the world's
most isolated, closed and repressed societies. If this book helps even
partially to answer these questions, it will have achieved its objective.

I am greatly indebted to the following people for their specific contri-
butions to this work. To James Pettifer, whose enthusiasm for Albania
gave me often needed encouragement; to Geoffrey Stern, for his helpful
suggestions and a careful, informed reading of the text; to Dr Mark
Wheeler, for his brief but useful comments; to Harry Hodgkinson,
who let me use his unpublished correspondence with Edith Durham
and enlightened me with many informal discussions about her work in
Albania and the life and times of King Zog. The British Academy and
the Historical Association provided financial assistance. I am also
grateful to the British Council; to Dr Marenglen Verli; to Ihsan
Toptani; to the Koca family, for letting me share their home in Tirana;
to Emma Sinclair-Webb for her patience, good humour and useful
ideas; and especially to Gerard Rosato, who read and commented on
the text despite having heard the word Albania perhaps once too often.

Glossary

Arberesh	Albanians who left for Italy following the defeat of Skenderbeg and the Ottoman conquest of Albania.
Ayan	Provincial notables.
Bashibazouk	Irregular Ottoman soldier.
Bashkimi	'Unity', in Albanian.
Besa	Word of honour, used extensively in Albania.
Cheta	Guerilla band.
Devshirme	Levy of Christian children trained for the elite Janissary corps of the Ottoman army.
Dhimmi	A protected, Christian or Jewish inhabitant of a Muslim state.
Fis	Tightly-knit clan or family grouping.
Ghegs	Albanians who live north of the Shkumbi river and in the Albanian-inhabited areas of the former Yugoslavia.
Hakmarrje	Blood feud.
Han	Inn.
Kanun of Lek	Unwritten law used in north Albania.
Katchak	Guerilla movement.
Kavass	Armed constable, servant or courier in the Ottoman Empire.
Komitadjis	Guerilla fighters.
Kosova	Predominantly Albanian-inhabited region of the former Yugoslavia. Known as Kosovo-Metohije by the Serbs, and as Kosova by the Albanians.
Millet	Community of Christian and Jewish inhabitants of the Ottoman Empire; Ottoman system of grouping its subjects according to their religion.
Megali Idea	Plan of expansion to include all Greeks within Greece.

Pashalik	Land coming under the authority of a pasha or bey.
Philiki Etairia	Secret society founded by Greeks in Odessa in 1814, which aimed for the reconstruction of the Byzantine Empire.
Porte	Title of the central office of Ottoman government.
Sanjak	Administrative district, sub-division of a vilayet.
Sipahi	Member of a semi-feudal cavalry.
Tanzimat	Reforms, specifically the centralizing and Westernizing reforms of 1839–73.
Tekke	Lodge of a mystical Islamic (Sufi) order of fraternity.
Timar	Landed estate or fiefdom.
Tosk	Albanian who lives south of the Shkumbi river.
Vilayet	Ottoman province.

Vienna

Budapest

Tisza R.

HUNGARY

TRANSYLVANIA

MOLDAVIA

RUSSIA

Odessa

CROATIA

BOSNIA

Belgrade

WALLACHIA

Sarajevo

SERBIA

Vidin

Bucharest

Danube R.

Niš

BULGARIA

BLACK

Adriatic

Sofia

SEA

MONTENEGRO

Sea

Plovdiv

Skopje

Adrianople

Ohrid

MACEDONIA

Constantinople

ALBANIA

Thessaloniki

Janina

Aegean

Sea

IONIAN ISLANDS
(British, 1809-1863)

GREECE

Athens

0   100   200

Miles

CRETE

MAP 1   The Ottoman Empire in 1815

MAP 2 Albania in 1913

MAP 3   The Balkan States in 1914

Introduction

Anon from the castle walls the crescent banner falls,
And the crowd beholds instead, like a portent in the sky,
Iskander's banner fly, the Black Eagle with double head...
And the loud exultant cry that echoes wide and far is:
'Long live Skenderbeg!'
Henry Wadsworth Longfellow, 'Skenderbeg',
4 February 1873, *Tales of a Wayside Inn*,
London, 1886, p 244

Since 1945 it has been the policy of Albanian archaeological exploration to establish the link between the ancient Illyrians and modern
Albanians, thereby proving the continuity of Albanian settlement not
only in the modern state of Albania but also in the disputed territory
of Kosova in Serbia. There are numerous theories as to the exact
origins of the Illyrians, and whether or not they are the ancestors of
the modern Albanians. It is now generally accepted that by the seventh
century BC certain tribes sharing a common Illyrian language and
culture had settled in the territory now known as Albania. Contemporary scholars describe the number of tribes who at one time occupied
much of the Balkan peninsula as far north as the Danube as 'Illyrian'.
But whether Greeks or Illyrians inhabited much of the southern region
of present-day Albania, known as Epirus, remains a highly controversial issue. Most probably both Greeks and Illyrians were originally
interspersed in this area much as they are at the present day.

From the seventh to the sixth centuries BC Greek traders established colonies along the Albanian coast at Durrachium, Butrint and
Apollonia. These cities gradually developed trading links with the

Illyrian tribes who lived further inland, and other towns – such as Lissus (Lezhe), which eventually became part of the Illyrian state of the Ardiaeans – grew up. From the third century BC Shkoder was the Ardiaean capital, and remained as such until after 168 BC, when Illyria succumbed to the Roman conquest.[1] The Ardiaei were a large grouping of tribes who since the fourth century BC had been noted as pirate raiders along the coast of the Peloponnese. At this time there was no definite geographic or ethnographic Albanian entity: the Ardiaean kingdom was divided up, and what is now central Albania constituted part of the Roman province of Macedonia. The Romans built what was to become one of their most famous roads, the Via Egnatia, the two branches of which started from Apollonia and Durrachium, joined near Elbasan, followed the Shkumbi river, rounded Lake Ohrid and continued on to Thessalonika and eventually to Byzantium. Early in the fourth century, the Prefecture of Illyricum was divided into eleven provinces, the four southernmost of which were Praevalitana, Dardania, New Epirus and Old Epirus. Modern Albania consists of New Epirus (which had its metropolis at Durrachium) much of Praevalitana and parts of the other two provinces. When the empire was split into eastern and western sectors in 395 AD, southern Illyria went to the Eastern Empire and the Eastern Church, whilst northern Illyria went to the Western Empire, under the ecclesiastical authority of the Pope.[2]

Throughout the third and fourth centuries AD, the Illyrian regions suffered numerous invasions from the Huns, the Visigoths and the Ostrogoths. The dispersal of Slavs in the southern Balkans following the unsuccessful siege of Thessalonika in 586 resulted in the Slav occupation of Praevalitana and the region south of the Shkumbi river, a distribution now indicated by place-names of Slav origin.[3] These invasions weakened the Byzantine Empire, and by the end of the sixth century, following further invasions by Slav tribes, the indigenous tribes began to move their settlements from the exposed lowland plains to the comparative security of higher ground. Following the collapse of the Roman Empire and the weakening of the Byzantine Empire, the Illyrian-speaking peoples expanded once again into the Mat valley and the Muzeqe plain. By then they were known to their southern neighbours as Albani, and their language as Albanian.[4] During the tenth century the central Balkan regions became the scene of conflict between the Byzantines and the Bulgarian tsars Simeon and Samuel. By the end of the century the Empire of Samuel comprised most of the land between the Black Sea and the Adriatic, including all the

Albanian regions. However, in 1018 the Bulgarians were defeated in a battle on the outskirts of Beligrad (Berat) by the Byzantines, who then reestablished their rule over the Albanian-speaking regions.

After the religious schism of 1054, when the Eastern and Western churches split, the Albanian regions were divided into a Catholic north and an Orthodox south. Catholicism began to spread through the pastoral tribes of what is now northern Albania, and Latin was reinstated where Greek had formerly dominated as the cultural and ecclesiastical language. Caught in the East–West struggle, the local Albanian lords and bishops tried to adapt themselves to the changing situation, wavering between Eastern Orthodoxy and Roman Catholicism according to their momentary interests. These oscillations, however, and the mixed populations of cities such as Durrachium, prevented the Orthodox–Catholic conflict from taking a violent form on Albanian territory.[5] The eleventh and twelfth centuries saw the continual weakening of Byzantine influence in Albania, due to a succession of Norman campaigns along the coast. In 1081 Valona (Vlore) and other coastal cities fell to the Normans, who with their sights set on Constantinople continued to press onward along the Via Egnatia. Following the death of the Emperor Manuel Comnenus in 1180, Byzantium sank into such political chaos that one Illyrian tribe, the Arbanon, was able to proclaim an independent principality of Arbania, which included much of present-day North Albania, with its capital at Kruja. After the collapse of Byzantium under the fourth crusade in 1204, Arbania had next to defend itself from the state of Venice. Throughout the twelfth century the Venetians had been trading along the Albanian coast, and in 1205, following the renunciation of Byzantine territories to Venice, Durrachium, by then known as Durazzo, passed to Venetian control.

The first rulers of separatist Epirus in the thirteenth century had made treaties and alliances with the Albanian chieftains to the north of their domain. The Byzantine emperors had regarded them as a threat to the peace, and granted them privileges to buy them off. But in the fourteenth century they began to infiltrate into Epirus and Thessaly. Many found their way down into the Morea, where by 1400 there were reckoned to be about 10,000 Albanians, and by 1450 as many as 30,000. The history and the demography of Epirus were to be permanently affected by the invasion and settlement of the Albanians.[6] The civil wars in Byzantium in the mid fourteenth century had destabilized the European provinces of the empire, opening the

way in the Balkans for the conquest of the most powerful of all the
Serbian kings, Stefan Dushan; conquests easily accomplished with the
aid of the local nobility. The Serbian conquest of the Albanian-
speaking lands within the area formed by Antivar (Bar), Prizren, Ohrid
and Valona (Vlore) was mainly accomplished during the year 1343,
when Dushan launched a massive invasion of Albania, and by 1348
Epirus and Thessaly were completely under Serbian control. Thereafter Dushan declared his imperial aims and assumed the imposing
title of Emperor of the Serbs and the Greeks. However, the Serbian
Empire lacked uniformity and cohesion, being composed of small
semi-independent states under such powerful families as the Dukagjin,
Balsha, Thopia and Kastrati.

The Arrival of the Ottomans

As the Byzantine Empire was losing control of its Balkan possessions,
Ottoman forces were conquering Asia Minor, and by 1354 they had
crossed the Dardanelles and entered the Balkan Peninsula. The gravity
of the Ottoman danger had not been accurately estimated by either
the Byzantine or the Balkan rulers, whose main efforts were absorbed
in wars among themselves. None realized the imminence or extent of
the Ottoman threat. After the death of Dushan in 1355, northern
Albania came under the control of local chieftains, the most important of which were the Balsha (Balsici) family, led by their chief,
Balsha I. At the same time another local state was formed in central
Albania under the most powerful member of the Thopia clan, Charles,
who reigned from 1359 to 1388. In the south, the then Serbian Despot
of Epirus, Symeon Uros, soon decided that he preferred the plains of
Thessaly to the mountains of Epirus, and divided his realm into two.
In other words, as the Chronicle of Ioannina (Janina) puts it, he
abandoned 'the whole of Aitolia' to the Albanians. It was an admission
of defeat born of the realization that the Albanians had become too
numerous and too powerful to be moved, a pact proved by their
victory over the despot Nikephoros at Acheloos in 1359. Symeon
calculated that they were less dangerous organized as a client state of
his own empire, behind the barrier of the Pindus mountains, than
allowed to run free all over northern Greece. His decision was to have
important consequences for the future of Epirus.[7]

After establishing military bases in Macedonia the Ottoman forces
began their incursions into the Balkans. This caused alarm among the

local feudal lords, and precipitated a number of Serbian, Hungarian, Bosnian, Bulgarian and Albanian nobles into forming a coalition under the leadership of the Serbian Prince Lazar. On 28 June 1389 the coalition armies marched onto the vast plain of Kosova to confront the Ottoman troops led by the Sultan, Murad I. During the battle, despite the death of Sultan Murad at the hands of a Serbian soldier, the Balkan armies were totally crushed, and Prince Lazar was among the thousands slain. The Ottoman victory at Kosova effectively sealed the fate of the Balkan peninsula for the next five hundred years. The weak Byzantine Empire and the small insignificant Slav states were now unable to hinder the advance of the Ottomans, who under their new sultan, Mehmet I, swept down through lowland and central Albania, encountering little opposition. In 1415 they captured Kruja and in 1417 the cities of Vlore, Kanina, Berat and Girokaster. Having secured these strongholds, military garrisons were then established and colonists brought from Asia Minor were settled in the plains of Kruja and Girokaster. In 1421 Mehmet I was succeeded by Murad II, and under his rule new districts fell under Ottoman rule.

Natural barriers had divided the Albanian people into two distinct groups with different dialects and great variations in their social structures. Those who lived in the mountainous regions to the north of the Shkumbi river were Ghegs (amongst whom are included the Albanians of Kosova). The social organization of the Ghegs was tribal, based upon a tightly knit clan system connecting various isolated homesteads. Those who lived south of the Shkumbi in the lowlands and plains were Tosks, and constituted the bulk of the landless and subsistence-level peasantry. By the time of the Ottoman conquest, the Tosks had abandoned the tribal clan system in favour of a village-based social organization. By 1426 only those tribes in the more inaccessible mountain regions of Albania remained free of Ottoman control. There the population continued to preserve its own self-administration by paying the Albanian lords fixed tributes. By fulfilling this obligation, they were then free to live by the rules of their common law. This was known as the *Doke*, and later as the Kanun of Lek, and remained in widespread use until as late as the 1930s. Although this law is said to have been laid down by the chieftain Lek Dukagjin (1410–1481), the laws and customs ascribed to him for the greater part date from far earlier than the fifteenth century.

Dukagjin was responsible for classifying the unwritten laws enshrined in the Kanun, a form of primitive constitution which outlined the social customs and organizing principles of northern Albanian society, inherited from the Illyrians. Its decrees regulated all aspects of life, including such matters as the arrangement of marriages, the boundaries of fields and the payment of taxes. It was transmitted orally down through the generations and arbitrated by a council of elders. The Kanun had a highly complex legal code which attempted to regulate the *hakmarrje* or blood feud, a system of revenge killing widespread in Albania. Dukagjin could not prevent the endemic feuds, as families set great store by using the *hakmarrje* to regain their honour, but he did prescribe strict rules in an attempt to contain and discourage these feuds. For instance, the Kanun of Lek decreed that if a man was seriously insulted, his family then had the right to assassinate the offender, but in undertaking this the family would then be liable to a revenge assassination by the victim's family. The original victim's nearest male relative was then obliged to assassinate his relative's murderer.

And so a pattern of revenge killing was established that ran through generations of families and spelled the death of countless young men. Serious social and economic hardship was caused not only by the death of so many able-bodied young men, but also because so many others had to go into hiding with distant relatives, often for several years, in order to escape a revenge killing. Women, however, were held in such low esteem that they were exempt from all feuds, as was a potential victim caught while in the company of a woman. Children of both sexes were also immune from the *hakmarrje*. The *besa*, or oath, could be used to cover a certain period or purpose, and during its duration the feud became dormant. The moment it expired, however, the blood feud resumed. Due to the ferocity of the vendettas most north Albanian houses resembled fortresses, built in stone with just half a dozen little holes about a foot square to serve as windows. By the Law of Lek, if all the men of a family were killed in a feud, then the eldest unmarried daughter must become the man of the house.

Infant betrothal was an important aspect of Albanian society. As soon as a female child was born, a part of her purchase price was immediately paid by the family of her prospective husband. The balance was paid once she had reached puberty and had been sent to her unknown husband. On the rare occasions when a girl refused to marry the intended man her purchase price was refunded, but she was forced to swear a vow of lifelong virginity. Having done so, she could wear male attire, inherit land and live as an equal with men. However, should she renege on this vow, she would dishonour her family, who could only avenge themselves through her murder. The Kanun of Lek was the most widely practised of many ancient codes of customary law used throughout Albania.

In 1428, when Sultan Murad began his war against the Venetians for control of Thessalonika, the Sublime Porte (the central office of Ottoman government in Constantinople) also began to extend its military operations towards the coastal regions of Albania, which were then still under Venetian command. Ottoman troops had already subdued Greece and Epirus and had captured the important town of Janina. The subjugated Albanian territory south of the river Mat and north of Epirus was embraced in a single sanjak (province) with its administrative centre in Girokaster. The sanjak of Albania was but a part of the Ejalet of Rumelia, which embraced all the sanjaks of the Balkans. In 1432 the Porte carried out a land registration whereby the territory of Albania was divided into 335 timars or fiefs, usually comprising two or three villages, which were then distributed among the leaders of the civil, military or religious administration. Dibra and its surroundings became a separate sanjak, while the region of Kosova was included in the sanjak of Shkup (Skopje). In order to evade the Ottomans, thousands of Albanians retreated into the mountainous regions, or else they migrated to Greece where they settled in Thessaly, Attica, and as far south as the Peloponnese. Others left for Italy and Dalmatia. Thus many small towns and villages that could not defend themselves were abandoned.

Skenderbeg Forges Albanian Unity Against the Ottomans

Nonetheless, the Ottoman conquest of central and southern Albania was not fully completed, and desultory warfare continued as the larger and more powerful Albanian clans fought to retain their autonomy. The most important of these independent Albanian domains was that led by Gjon Kastrioti, who by 1420 had extended his boundaries from Prizren in the north down to Lezhe in the south. Gjon died in 1437 and was succeeded by his son Gjergi, who was born around the year 1405. As a young man Gjergi was sent to the Sultan's court at Adrianople as a hostage against any further Albanian insurrections. Having nominally renounced his Christian faith and adopted the Muslim name of Skender he joined the army, and appears to have

given proof of his ability in several Ottoman campaigns. He reached
the rank of general, for which reason the Sultan bestowed on him the
title of 'bey' or 'beg'. Despite his military successes as an Ottoman
general, he maintained connections with the domain of the Kastriots,
occasionally receiving emissaries from there asking him to return to
lead them in a revolt against the Porte. Now known as Skenderbeg,
Gjergi decided to bide his time before deserting the Ottoman army.
His chance finally came when the Hungarians defeated the Ottoman
forces at Nis in 1443. Skenderbeg was able to recapture his father's
citadel at Kruja, and after massacring those in the Kastrati domains
who refused to renounce Islam he set about establishing himself as an
independent lord.

To secure his independence from the advancing Ottomans,
Skenderbeg needed the assistance of other Albanian forces. In March
1444, having realized that the major weakness of the Albanian people
lay in their disunity, Skenderbeg organized a meeting of nobles in the
Venetian town of Alessio (Lezhe). At this meeting, which became
known as the 'League of Lezhe', the participants agreed to forget
their differences and to form a united front to resist the Ottomans.
The League voted Skenderbeg commander-in-chief of the Albanian
forces which now carried the war, with renewed vigour, into the
eastern regions of Dibra and Ohrid. For the next twenty-five years
Skenderbeg led the Albanian forces, which when combined rarely
exceeded 10,000 men, to successive victories over the far larger and
better equipped Ottoman armies. By the second quarter of the
fifteenth century the Ottoman campaign against central Europe and
Italy had gathered momentum. The threat posed by the Porte spread
alarm throughout Europe – especially in Hungary, where Ottoman
attacks were increasingly devastating. Skenderbeg's military successes
evoked a good deal of interest and admiration from the Papal state,
Venice and Naples, themselves threatened by the growing Ottoman
power across the Adriatic. Hoping to strengthen and expand the last
Christian bridgehead in the Balkans, they provided Skenderbeg with
money, supplies and occasionally troops.[8]

On 14 May 1450, a huge Ottoman army arrived at the walls of
Kruja and laid siege to the castle. According to the Chronicles of
Ragusa (Dubrovnik), the siege lasted four months, leaving thousands
dead beneath the ramparts, until the Albanian armies managed to
force the Ottoman army to withdraw before the onset of winter. The
fall of Constantinople in 1453 prompted Pope Pius II to try to raise

another crusade against the Porte. By now the Albanian regions were suffering from ever more devastating Ottoman military expeditions. In June 1466 Mehmet II himself led an army of approximately 150,000 men to Kruja which laid the country to waste as they passed. Unable to muster adequate foreign assistance, the Albanian forces were hopelessly outnumbered and were eventually forced to surrender the city to the Ottoman troops. After a severe illness Skenderbeg died at Lezhe on 17 January 1468, and was buried there in the Cathedral of Saint Nicholas. Even after his death resistance continued, and it was not until 1479 that all the Albanian-inhabited regions were fully subjected to Ottoman rule. Skenderbeg's most significant achievement was his ability to weld the various Albanian tribes together, for the first time, into a force capable of checking the Ottoman advance towards the Adriatic and Italy. Over four hundred years later the name of Skenderbeg was to become a symbol of unity and strength to Albanians as they struggled to confirm their national identity.

Skenderbeg's son Gjon was too young to command a following. He therefore chose to settle in the Kingdom of Naples. A large number of Albanians also followed him across the Adriatic, where they settled in numerous colonies and became known as Arberesh. In the conflict over control of the Kingdom of Naples between the Aragon King, Alfonso I, and the Angevins, the Albanians sided with Alfonso, who rewarded them by allowing Albanian settlement in seven regions of southern Italy – Campania, Apulia, Molise, Abruzzi, Basilatica, Calabria and Sicily. Many years later, in the 1770s, an Englishman, Walter Swinburne, saw some Arberesh villages in Calabria and noted how they had preserved the Albanian language and customs. They then amounted to some 100,000 persons living in about a hundred villages, the chief of which was Bora, thirty miles from Reggio.[9] The Arberesh went on to play an important role in the nineteenth-century Albanian national awakening, and have managed with some difficulty to retain their own language and traditions in present-day Italy, where, in 1981, they numbered around 200,000.

By 1480 the Sultan had concluded a peace with Venice and begun earnest preparations for the conquest of Italy. In August of that year Christian Europe was thrown into a state of alarm as Ottoman troops landed in the Kingdom of Naples, capturing the castle of Otranto. However, the death of Mehmet II the following year allowed the Neapolitans to retake the city, and the seriousness of the revolt in Albania which began during that winter deterred the Ottoman commanders from continuing their campaign in Italy. They were quite unprepared to deal with the revolt, and had underestimated the danger that the mountain areas of Albania still presented to their rear. They had therefore to keep troops and supplies in Albania, which would otherwise have been sent to relieve their garrison at Otranto.[10] Nevertheless, the Albanian uprising ultimately failed, because the country had been at war almost continuously throughout the fifteenth century. The population was seriously reduced not only by constant warfare, but also by famine, plague and emigration. The region's economy was all but destroyed, as villages were devastated and abandoned. In the depopulated countryside vast tracts of land gradually reverted to their natural state. The once flourishing cities of Durres, Vlore, Shkoder, Berat, Kruja and Lezhe went into rapid decline, and the area now known as Albania became a decaying and isolated backwater of the Ottoman Empire.

I

The Nature of Ottoman Rule and the Rise of the Great Pashaliks

For around five hundred years the Balkan peninsula was governed, to varying degrees, by the Ottoman Empire. In general, up until the end of the eighteenth century, the Ottoman state was remarkably tolerant towards its diverse, multi-ethnic and multi-lingual population. The empire was not always the stagnant oriental despotism it became known as in its closing years. In fact, the Ottomans managed to devise an extremely complex but effective social structure, combining established Muslim socio-political traditions with Turkic and Byzantine elements. Throughout the long years of Ottoman domination, Christian Orthodox, Catholic and Muslim societies lived side by side in relative peace. The main concern of the Porte at this time was the recruitment of support to maintain peace along a lengthy and vulnerable frontier. It was therefore in the interests of the Porte to practise a degree of tolerance towards the variety of religious and ethnic groups that comprised the European regions of the Ottoman Empire.

Following the establishment of Ottoman rule, no effort was made either to destroy or to unify all the diverse elements of the Balkan peninsula. Instead, national and local particularisms were enforced and deepened. In some localities Muslim, Serbian, Bulgarian and Greek villages existed side by side for centuries with little or no cultural or personal intermixing. Any monotheist who accepted the theoretical political supremacy of Islam and was willing to live in a Muslim state under stipulated conditions became a *dhimmi*, a 'protected' person. This protection extended beyond religious freedom; it involved a form of self-government that became institutionalised and

known as the millet system. This was basically a minority home-rule
policy based on religious affiliation. All Ottoman subjects were divided
into groups, or millets, not according to their ethnic origin or language
but according to their religion. By this system it was hoped a barrier
would be created between the empire's Christian and Muslim elements.
The Porte did not want a national consciousness to be formed in any
part of the Muslim world, which might then challenge Ottoman rule.
The millet system therefore provided a degree of religious and cultural
continuity among the various ethnic groups, but also permitted their
incorporation into the Ottoman administration. The first millet, the
Orthodox (the others were the Armenian and Jewish), was established
in 1454, as Mehmet II regarded the Papacy and Venice as his main
enemies and sought, by granting rights and freedoms, to neutralize
their influence among the Balkan Christians. The Byzantine Empire,
although instrumental in extending Orthodox Christianity throughout
much of the Balkans, had collapsed because, among other reasons, it
had been unable to deal with the ethnic and religious diversity that
characterized the region. Thus Sultan Mehmet II used the millet
system to counterbalance these differences and secure a degree of
harmony.

The land became the economic base of the cavalry, the Sipahis,
which won the first great Ottoman military victories. In return for
military or administrative services, an individual, almost always a
Muslim, received a grant of land, a timar, which he held on a non-
hereditary basis. The timar system remained effective as both an
economic and a military support for Ottoman power until gunpowder
was introduced, when the infantry soldier with a musket became a
more efficient instrument of war than the horseman. Thereafter, the
Janissary corps became the chief arm of the state.[1] The elite Janissaries
were renowned as highly efficient troops. They were originally composed mainly of boys from rural Christian families, who were required
periodically to donate one healthy male child to be converted to Islam
and trained either for the Ottoman administration or the Janissaries.
This practice, known as the *devshirme* or child levy, often proved a
severe loss to peasant families, as infant mortality was extremely high
and surviving healthy sons were rare. That all nationalities could rise
to high office provided they adopted the Islamic faith was an important
aspect of Ottoman rule. Muslims were accorded highest status: they
stood a far better chance in courts and paid lower taxes. The restrictions on the Christian population, on the other hand, were many.

They were not allowed to bear firearms, to wear conspicuous clothing, or to wear the colour green, which was sacred to Muslims. They were to dismount when passing a Muslim on horseback, their churches could not have bells and new ones could not be built. Although Christians were not encouraged to join the military forces they were expected to provide taxes in support of them, together with the *devshirme*. Christian peasants thus paid taxes on the produce of their land and home industry, and on all their personal possessions, as well as a special head tax levied on all male Christians in place of the military service required of the Muslims.

The Beginning of Ottoman Decline

Towards the end of the seventeenth century the fortunes of the Porte began to wane. The defeat of the Ottomans at Vienna in 1683 had marked the beginning of the decline of the Ottoman Empire. From then on the Porte was confronted by a succession of wars with either Venice, Austria or Russia. As the Ottoman forces suffered defeat after defeat, they found themselves constantly on the defensive in their European territories. War was no longer a lucrative source of revenue for the Sipahis and, later, the Janissaries, and so they frequently ignored the Porte's call to arms. Most of the Janissaries by this time were in fact shopkeepers who held paper appointments in one of the regiments and only showed up at musters to receive pay. The Sipahis, who during the heyday of the empire had been paid indirectly by the granting of fiefs (timars), had been driven off the land by inflation.[2] Unsure of the loyalty of its Christian subjects, the Porte encouraged conversions to Islam. In sensitive regions such as Bosnia, Slav conversions occured, whilst Muslim Albanians were encouraged to expand into lands vacated by Christians in the plain of Kosova–Methohija. Many former Albanian Catholics were resettled in the northern Kosova area. In 1690, unwilling to convert and fearing a massacre if they remained, the Orthodox Patriarch of Pec (Peja), Arsenije IV, led some thirty thousand Serbian families to migrate from Kosova to Hungary. This considerably altered the ethnic composition of the region, the departure of the Serbs leading to large-scale immigration of Albanians into Kosova, which thus acquired an Albanian majority.

By the eighteenth century, therefore, the Albanian-inhabited areas presented a complex religious picture. The Catholics, by then the weakest group, were concentrated in an enclave centred on Shkoder, whilst the Orthodox were to be found principally south of the Shkumbi river, in the districts around Korca and Girokaster. Muslims lived throughout the country, but chiefly in the centre and the Kosova region. As a Muslim, the Albanian was the ally and equal of the Ottoman, who protected him from Slavic and Greek encroachment, offered him employment and paid him well for his military service. To those Albanians who chose to convert to Islam there were many opportunities to serve in high administrative positions. During the sixteenth and seventeenth centuries, a number of Ottoman governors and administrators were of Albanian descent. Among the most celebrated of these was Sinan Pasha, possibly the greatest architect of the Islamic world. He was born in about 1500 in the region of Topoyani, in central Albania, and rose to importance through the *devshirme* system. Five times appointed Grand Vizir, he could be ruthless and harsh (he allegedly destroyed the holy relics of Saint Sava, patron saint of Serbia), but he was also a major builder of caravanserais, bridges, baths and mosques. These included the town of Kacanik in Kosova, important buildings in Thessalonika and Belgrade, as well as in Istanbul and the countries of the Arab world.[3]

In the stifling climate of later Ottoman domination, commerce and manufacture stagnated, and Albanian-inhabited areas remained by far the most backward region of Europe. During the mid eighteenth century, however, there was one notable exception to the general rule of decline. The town of Voskopoje in southern Albania, known in medieval times as Moskhopolis, enjoyed an exceptional cultural development, becoming a significant commercial and intellectual centre. Although the population was primarily Albanian and Vlach, the town became a centre of Greek culture.[4] It was endowed with numerous richly decorated Orthodox churches, as well as the first printing press in the Balkans, which printed a large number of books in the Greek language. In 1744 a group of intellectuals founded an academy to provide higher education for Orthodox students. Nevertheless, despite its success Voskopoje could not withstand the comparative primitiveness of the surrounding districts, and the town suffered repeatedly from raids by itinerant robbers. The constant feuding caused Voskopoje to be plundered three times: in 1769, 1772 and 1780. Twenty years later, the French consul F. Pouqueville, who visited the town, wrote – 'After ten years of devastation, rape and warfare, Voskopoje disappeared from the surface of Albania. A couple of hundred huts inhabited by poor shepherds is all that remains of this town and misery will soon bury these among the ruins where you can still detect its former splendour.'[5] The tragic end of Voskopoje, a town of 40,000 inhabitants, is but one example of the feudal anarchy that plagued Albania in the latter half of the eighteenth century.

During the nineteenth century the growth of nationalism among the empire's Balkan and Asiatic peoples was to prove the most important factor in the destruction of the Ottoman state. It is difficult to say, however, to what extent, if at all, national feeling had developed amongst the Albanians by the early nineteenth century. To all the Balkan peoples, religion was synonymous with a person's ethnic and social identity. Religion also served to shape a linguistic national consciousness. Orthodox and Catholic Christians adopted the script of their respective churches. Thus the Serbs and Bulgarians used the Cyrillic alphabet; the Romanians, the Latin; and the Greeks used the Greek alphabet of their church. The religious diversity of the Albanians, on the other hand, resulted in the Catholic Albanians using the Latin script, Orthodox Albanians using the Greek alphabet, and the Muslim Albanians using the Arabic script. These religious divisions helped to deprive Albanians of a solid foundation for the development of any national awareness. By adopting the Islamic faith an Albanian was automatically classified a Turk. Bearing all this in mind, it is interesting to note that Lord Byron's travelling companion, J.C. Hobhouse, found a willingness among Albanians to emphasize the fact that they were Albanian; he wrote,

> There is a spirit of independence and a love of their country in the whole people, that in a great measure, does away with the vast distinction, observable in other parts of Turkey between the followers of the two religions. For when the natives of other provinces, upon being asked who they are will say 'We are Turks' or 'We are Christians', a man of this country answers 'I am an Albanian'.[6]

We can assume then, that for many Albanians the fact that the Ottoman administration classified them as either Catholics, Orthodox or Turks, had little meaning to a people who lived on the fringes of the empire in tightly knit tribes or clans known as *fis*. The *fis* was primarily a family grouping, headed by the oldest male of the parental or grandparental generation. In general the Albanians were perceived by the Ottoman administration as wild and lawless. Because of their distinct individuality, which appeared to defy control, the Ottomans were originally forced to modify their system to suit the peculiarities of the Albanians. Thus the Gheg highlanders and the Christian communities around Himara and Suli enjoyed virtual autonomy in return for the payment of a small, but regular, tribute to the Porte's administrators. In the north, each tribe, Catholic or Muslim, was obliged to elect from among the Muslims of Shkoder a representative, a sort of consul, who mediated between the tribe and the Porte and acted as its advocate in case of any dispute. He was known as a Boulim-bashi, a well respected figure. This situation, however, contributed to the growth of rivalry and jealousy between the different clans and tribes – a state of affairs that was carefully fostered by the Porte in order to secure its own position in the area. Nevertheless, the majority of Albanians continued to view the Ottoman administration as providing security from their Slav and Greek neighbours. What struggles the Albanians did pursue at this time were concerned with the preservation of their traditional privileges, or the pursuit of local advantages. There is no evidence that nationalist impulses lay behind such struggles.

During the eighteenth and nineteenth centuries, Ottoman society underwent a profound transformation that altered the land tenure system, the army and the leadership of the millets. These fundamental changes were embodied in the rise of the *ayan* (notables). These were influential people (or more often families) of diverse origin. Some were Ottoman governors who had established a local power base, others were landowners or religious dignitaries.[7] At the same time the towns witnessed the birth of new commercial elites and the rise of a secular intelligentsia. This structural differentiation acquired social and political significance as the latter two groups rose first among the non-Muslims. Islamic pressure on the Christian population began to increase with the Russo-Ottoman wars of the eighteenth century and the accelerating decline of the Ottoman Empire. This resulted in a notable decline in the previous Ottoman policy of religious tolerance, as Islamic pressure on the Christian population intensified. The Russo-Ottoman war of 1768–74 almost led to the expulsion of the Ottoman administration from Europe, and the threat posed by this war encouraged the Porte to levy increased taxes on all non-Muslim subjects, whilst those who converted to Islam had their taxes lowered and were given grants of land.

Throughout their turbulent history Albanians had shifted with relative ease from one religion to another: Catholic, Orthodox or Muslim according to momentary interests. During the late middle ages, their country had become the battlefield between the Catholic West and the Orthodox East: whenever the West was advancing, the Albanian feudal lords – often followed by their populations – espoused Catholicism; whenever Byzantium was the victor and the West retreated, they embraced Orthodoxy.

A notable example was Skenderbeg's father, Gion Kastrioti, who had changed religion several times. He was a Catholic as an ally of Venice, and turned Orthodox as an ally of Stefan Lazarevic of Serbia.[8] The Albanian saying 'Ku eshte shpata eshte feja' – 'Where the sword is, there lies religion' – is directly related to this history. Of all the Balkan subject peoples, the Albanians were most inclined to convert to Islam. The majority of converts, however, were men, whilst women often retained their Christian beliefs even when married to Muslims, and were a factor in maintaining goodwill between the members of the two faiths.[9] At various times whole villages voluntarily renounced the religion of their forefathers for political advantage. The ability to gain a timar or avoid donating a precious healthy son to the *devshirme* were but two of many reasons for abandoning Christianity. The majority of conversions took place in the lowlands, around the Shkumbi river, where direct Ottoman pressure could most easily be exerted. Amongst the Albanians of Kosova there appears to have been a far greater readiness to accept Islam, perhaps because of the pressure of their close proximity to the Serbs, who by the 1830s had achieved their own autonomous state. Albanians who wished to retain their Christian faith after the Ottoman conquest often found it difficult to compete with those who had converted. To make their already difficult lives easier, therefore, many Albanians gradually adopted at least the outer signs of the Islamic faith, thus obtaining such privileges as the right to bear arms.

In 1809, Hobhouse quoted an observer of Albanian religious practices:

> These people, living between Christians and Mahomadens, declare that they are utterly unable to judge which religion is best but to be certain of not entirely rejecting the truth, they very prudently follow both. They go to the mosques on Fridays and to the church on Sundays, thus making sure of the protection from the true prophet.[10]

A characteristic instance is the story of the Karamurtads, or inhabitants of 36 villages near Pogoniani, which was related to an English traveller by an Albanian in 1899:

Till about a hundred years ago these people were Christians but, finding themselves unable to repel the continual attacks of the neighbouring Moslem population of Leskoviki, they met in a church, solemnly swore that they would fast until Easter and invoke all the saints to work within that period some miracle which would better their miserable lot. If this reasonable request were not granted they would all turn Mohammedan. Easter Day came but no sign from saint or angel and the whole population embraced Islam. Soon afterwards they obtained the arms which they required and had the satisfaction of massacring their old opponents of Leskoviki and taking possession of their lands.[11]

The Great Pashaliks of Shkoder and Janina

An effect of the extreme decentralization of the Ottoman administration was the emergence of certain native vested interests able to exploit their privileged position. The gradual but continuous weakening of Ottoman authority allowed the Albanian feudal lords, or beys, to rely more on their own personal power than on central Ottoman rule. These beys extended the limits of their pashaliks (land coming under the authority of a pasha or bey) thus increasing their revenues and influence. The beys were the practical rulers of their districts, except in the vicinity of large towns. This, however, led to wars and rivalries between the smaller and larger beys, plunging the Albanian regions into feudal anarchy. This situation prevailed until the middle of the eighteenth century, when the mass of small feudal estates were merged into two huge pashaliks. The first, in northern Albania, had Shkoder as its capital and was ruled by the Bushatis; the second, in southern Albania, had Janina as its capital and was ruled by Ali Pasha of Tepelene. In 1757, inspired by the achievements of the Albanian founder of modern Egypt, Muhammad Ali Pasha,[12] the feudal lord Mehmet Bey Bushati appointed himself overlord of the region of Shkoder. However, it was under his son, Kara Mahmoud, that the Pashalik of Shkoder achieved its distinction. Behaving more like an independent prince, the ambitious Kara Mahmoud extended his rule into Kosova to the north and as far south as Berat. In 1785 he launched an attack on neighbouring Montenegro, during which he captured the pirate stronghold of Dulcingo (Ulcinj) and burnt the pirate fleet. He then negotiated with the Habsburgs for arms and money with which to fight the Porte. In scenes reminiscent of Skanderbeg's time, Kara successfully fought off a succession of Ottoman armies ranged against him, finally forcing the Ottomans to abandon their three-month siege of Rozofat castle in November 1787. The victories of Kara Mahmoud, and his disregard for the authority of the Porte, attracted the attention of both Austria and Russia, both wishing to make use of him in their own plans against the Ottomans.

The Habsburg government was willing to recognize Kara Mahmoud as the independent ruler of Albania in return for his support against the Porte. Under these circumstances, the Sultan was forced to offer Kara a full pardon in return for his renewed allegiance. In June 1788 an Austrian delegation went to Shkoder to negotiate with Kara, who, influenced by the fact that the Ottoman armies were winning at the time, massacred the Austrian agents and sent their heads to the Sultan. Back in favour in Istanbul, Kara was appointed governor of Shkoder, but his ambitions were still unsatisfied. Kara wished to extend his territorial control yet further. He therefore seized the opportunity to attack Montenegro again in 1796, but was thoroughly defeated and later beheaded. Kara Mahmoud had nevertheless managed to turn the Pashalik of Shkoder into an important commercial centre within an autonomous Albanian principality. Upon the death of Kara, his younger brother, Ibrahim Pasha, who had always opposed his brother's policies and remained loyal to the Sultan, was made governor of Shkoder, which he administered until his death in 1810.

The second great pashalik was ruled by Ali Pasha of Tepelene, who was appointed Governor of Janina in 1788 in return for services rendered to the Porte. At that time, Albania was governed roughly on the principle of 'divide and rule'; local pashas were appointed by the Porte to act as governors of the major commercial centres such as Janina and Shkoder. Under their sway the various districts and towns were allowed a degree of independence on condition they paid regular tributes. Janina, in Old Epirus, was at this time the most important town in Albania, if not the whole of Greece, with a population of 30,000. Ali Pasha was born in Tepelene in 1740. He left home at the age of nine, after the death of his father, whereupon he became the leader of a band of brigands and spent almost twenty years as a robber in southern Albania and Thessaly. Towards the middle of his life, he turned his knowledge of brigandry to his advantage in order to appease the Sultan, who was alarmed at the bands of robbers plaguing Thessaly at that time. Knowing their whereabouts, Ali was able to suppress his brigand friends and thus gained the confidence of the Sultan, who rewarded him with the Pashalik of Trikkala. As local beys battled for control of Janina, Ali took the town in 1788 with the Sultan's blessing. Under the control of Ali Pasha, Janina flourished as a major cultural and economic centre, accessible to all the important markets of southern Albania and western Greece. At the time, as in the past, no hard and fast geographical line could be drawn between Albania and Greece.

Towards the end of the century, Ali showed considerable diplomatic skill in negotiating alliances alternately with France and England. For Napoleon, with his new acquisitions of southern Italy and Dalmatia, Albania was significant because of its proximity to both of these countries and the entrance it commanded into the Balkan peninsula. Albania was, therefore, to be considered in whatever plans Napoleon might make for intervening in the affairs of the Near East. In 1797 France occupied the Ionian islands and hoped to weaken the Porte by fomenting trouble in the Balkans. An Ottoman alliance with England and Russia and a declaration of war on France followed. In 1799, however, the Ionian islands fell to Russia, with whom Ali had failed to establish friendly relations. The Russians stirred up Ali's rivals, including the Suliot people who had left their homeland of Himara many years before for the steep mountains of Suli in Epirus.[13] The Suliots, then numbering around 12,000, were Christian Albanians inhabiting a small independent community somewhat akin to that of the Catholic Mirdite tribe to the north. The Suliots dwelt in a wild, inaccessible cluster of villages on a plateau near Arta, about two thousand feet above the river Acheron. In 1797, Ali Pasha ordered an attack on the town of Himara, which had supported the Suliots against him, and more than 6,000 unarmed civilians were slaughtered. For this exploit the Porte awarded him the title 'Arslan', or Lion. But the Suliots persistently thwarted Ali, and in the autumn of 1799 he decided to mount an expedition against them. Once again defeated and humiliated, Ali was determined to break the Suliots. Finally, at the end of 1803, after a prolonged and bloody war, the Suliots were forced to surrender and were, in return, promised safe passage to Corfu. Ali immediately, and characteristically, violated this assurance by mercilessly attacking the Suliot refugees. It was during this attack that the dramatic episode occurred in which the Suliot women threw themselves and their children over a precipice in the Zalongue mountains rather than fall into Ali's hands.

In the autumn of 1805 Napoleon appointed a political mission to promote good relations with Ali Pasha. Ali had good reason for cultivating such a friendship while the Russians occupied the Ionian Islands and their fleet cruised in the Adriatic. On the other hand, Ali did not intend to throw himself into Napoleon's arms. He was not unaware of the favourable position he occupied for making himself politically important to both sides in the European struggle, so far as it concerned the Balkans, and he intended to take advantage of it to realize his ambitions for territorial expansion.[14] Assisted by his sons, Ali extended his authority throughout southern Albania and a large part of the Greek mainland, maintaining his pashalik by regular tributes and bribes to Istanbul. Although Ali was by now regarded as the most powerful man in the European part of the Ottoman Empire, the continued successes and obvious ambitions of Napoleon made Ali uneasy, and so he sought an ally in the English. He found a ready supporter in the poet Lord Byron, who was then travelling throughout both old and new Epirus and was entertained by Ali Pasha at his palace. Byron admired the Albanians, for they reminded him of the highlanders of Scotland. He wrote, 'Their mountains seemed Caledonian, with a kinder climate. The kilt, though white, the spare active form, their dialect, Celtic in its sound, and their hardy habits; all carried me back to Morven.'[15]

Since Albania had become important to Napoleon by reason of his new possessions in southern Italy and Dalmatia, it was certain also to acquire significance for the allies, Russia and Britain. It would become a necessary link in a chain of defences that they were seeking to establish along the western frontier of the Ottoman Empire in order to check Napoleon's plans for expansion eastward.[16] British diplomacy, however, found it difficult to improve relations between Ali Pasha and the Russians. Ali had appealed for British assistance to enable him to expand southward to the predominantly Greek towns of Parga and Preveza. Not only was Ali deeply suspicious of Russian activity in the Adriatic, but the Russians would find it hard to support Ali's subjugation of the Greeks. To do so would violate religious feeling among the Orthodox Christians and also weaken the political influence of Russia among the Orthodox and subject Slav peoples in the Balkan peninsula, an influence that had since the 1805 Treaty of Pressburg been Russian policy to strengthen.[17] As the British laboured to prevent Ali from forming an alliance with Napoleon, French interests were quietly being promoted in Janina by their agent, François Pouqueville. It was very much through his efforts at the Porte that Ali secured the appointment of his two sons, Mouktar and Veli, to the pashaliks

respectively of Morea and Lepanto.[18] Both the French and the British
wooed Ali with occasional consignments of munitions, cannon and
artillery, which he promptly utilized to expand his territorial boundaries.
Ali had long coveted the fortress city of Berat, which was of
great strategic as well as practical value to him, as it was the centre of
the district that was known as the 'granary of Albania'. In 1809 Ali
seized Berat, where he installed his eldest son Mouktar as governor.
The following year he captured Vlore, and the year after that Delvina
and Girokaster.

Around this time, Ali was converted to Bektashism by Baba Shemin
of Kruja, and with Ali's backing Shemin reestablished the sect at
Kruja and founded the *tekke* of Melcani at Korca. The Bektashis are
a Dervish, that is Sufi (and mendicant), order and their mother
monastery was originally at Pir-evi, in Asia Minor. The Bektashi
(Baktashiyya) movement began to take root in the Balkans at the time
of the Ottoman conquest. It did so peacefully, slowly and without
serious opposition. Those who preached it came in tiny groups, often
just three – a Baba and two Dervishes. Among the earliest preachers
who allegedly reached Albania and its borders were Pir Abdali in
Kosova and Shah Kalenderi in Elbasan. This was a period when small
cells of the order were not established in geographically fixed *tekkes*.[19]
According to one scholar, the monastic order of the Bektashis was
planted in Albania by the middle of the sixteenth century at the latest.
This is already indicated by the numerous Albanian Bektashi saints
who can with certainty be identified during that century.[20]

The Bektashis were a pantheistic sect, finding God within nature
and animals, as well as man. They called for Shi'ite retaliation against
the (Sunni) Ottoman power, and preached tolerance of all non-Islamic
creeds. This explains, in part, why the sect grew steadily in Albania
as it made easy their cooperation with the northern Catholics and
southern Orthodox alike. The close connection between the Janissaries
and the Bektashi groups attached to them contributed to the spread
of the sect within the Ottoman Empire. The great expansion of Bektashism
in Albania occurred at the beginning of the nineteenth
century, when *tekkes* were established at Girokaster, Tepelene and
Janina. Many of the conversions of the southern, Christian Tosks can
be attributed to the Bektashi influence promoted by Ali Pasha. It was
then the Sultan began to suppress the Bektashis as a threat to his
authority, eventually ordering the massacre of all Bektashi Janissaries.
The Bektashis were regarded as a danger by the Ottoman government

because they challenged the official religion of the State, Sunnism. Various *tekkes*, many containing priceless Arabic and Persian philosophical manuscripts, were razed to the ground upon the Sultan's orders. Following the massacre of the Janissaries in 1826, the Bektashis were compelled to withdraw from military and administrative centres, and started building their *tekkes* in mountainous regions for security.[21]

By 1820, Ali had reached the height of his power, and together with his sons he controlled the whole of southern Albania, Epirus and Thessaly. His pashaliks were maintained at vast expense by means of tributes and bribes, and through aiding and reinforcing a local administration which recognized his authority. Ali also financed the building of fortifications, mosques, and even churches to appease his Christian subjects. Inevitably Ali's success and audacity had long attracted the unfriendly attention of the Porte, and his continued desire for autonomy and designs on the north eventually caused the Sultan to take measures to curtail his power. Ali was abruptly dismissed from office and ordered to hand his pashaliks over to the nominee of the Sultan. Realizing that any further cooperation with the Ottoman administration was impossible, he therefore openly espoused the cause of the Greeks. When he formed ties with the Philiki Etairia, a Greek revolutionary organization, the Ottoman authorities became concerned that mass Christian support might be given to Ali. By 1821, some five to seven thousand Greek fighters had joined Ali. The Sultan finally ordered Ali to Istanbul to give an account of his activities. Ali refused the invitation, but his army gradually surrendered to the Porte. Abandoned by all but a few followers, Ali held out for the next 17 months against the siege of his citadel at Janina, where he was finally killed by Ottoman agents and his severed head sent to Istanbul. Victor Hugo, writing in the 1820s, called him the only colossus and man of genius of his time, worthy to be compared with Napoleon.[22]

Ali no doubt aided the cause of Hellenic independence by his support of the Philiki Etairia, but had he lived longer the weakness of his ties with the Greeks would no doubt have become apparent. He can, nevertheless, be credited with promoting, for the first time, the notion of an Albanian identity for the domains under his control. Upon nearing Tepelene nearly forty years after Byron's and Hobhouse's visits, the painter Edward Lear described how the area left the most lasting impression on him: 'Even now, after the lapse of so many years, a foreigner perceives that the awful name of Ali Pasha is hardly pronounced without a feeling akin to terror. My curiosity had

been raised to the very utmost to see this place.'[23] Lear sat and mused
in the crumpled ruin of Ali's once splendid palace, where he wrote:
'The poet Byron is no more, the host is beheaded, his family nearly
extinct, the palace is burned. War, change and time have perhaps left
but one or two living beings who, forty years back, were assembled in
these gay and sumptious halls. Of all the scenes I have visited, the
palace of Ali Pasha at Tepelene will continue most vividly imprinted
on my recollection.'[24]

The Continuing Disintegration of the Ottoman Empire

Throughout the eighteenth century, Ottoman prestige in international
politics had gradually weakened. A series of military defeats testified
to the technological and economic as well as military inferiority of the
Porte. The beginning of the nineteenth century saw a series of insurrections against the Ottomans by their Balkan subjects. The Serbs
revolted in 1804 against the excesses of the Janissaries, but following
a new war between Russia and the Porte from 1806 to 1812, the
Treaty of Bucharest restored Serbia to Ottoman control. In 1821 the
Greeks began their war of liberation, which lasted until the destruction by the combined fleets of Russia, England and France of an
Ottoman–Egyptian armada in the bay of Navarino on 20 October
1827. One of the main consequences of the careers of Kara Mahmoud
and Ali Pasha was that they instilled in the Porte a profound distrust
of the Albanians. During the domination of Albania by the Bushatis
and Ali Pasha, the influence of the beys had weakened. However, after
the disappearance of the great pashaliks, the old and once powerful
Muslim families tried to regain their power. When the Russo-Ottoman
war of 1829 came to an end, Sultan Mahmoud II resolved finally to
break the disobedience and independence of the Albanians. On 26
August 1830, the Porte's commander-in-chief, Mehmet Reshid Pasha,
invited all the southern Albanian beys to Monastir (Bitola), on the
pretext that they would be rewarded for their loyalty to the Porte. In
fact, five hundred of them were treacherously massacred that after-
noon. The following year, Mehmet Reshid Pasha besieged Mustapha
Bushati in the Rozafat castle at Shkoder. The Bushatis were finally
forced to surrender, thus ending the Pashalik of Shkoder.

In 1832 the Ottoman army destroyed the citadels of the other large
Albanian feudal estates which had developed. Nevertheless, the
massacre at Monastir did not end opposition to the Ottoman regime,

and throughout the 1830s the Porte once more tried to cripple the power of the beys by deporting a number of them to Asia Minor and destroying their fortresses. Loss of their autonomy, together with the heavy burden of compulsory military service, high taxes and debt repayments, often with extortionate rates of interest, helped intensify Albanian opposition and resistance to Ottoman rule. By now Ottoman fortunes were at their lowest ebb. Weighed down by foreign war and internal political problems, the Porte was increasingly unable to control its provincial officials and local Muslim notables. By then the timar system had broken down, but although the peasants had been freed from their feudal dependency upon the Sipahi they had instead become further dependent upon the Ottoman bureaucracy. The Ottoman government responded to the challenge of social change by initiating a series of reforms intended to strengthen the authority of central government. The primary aim of the *Tanzimat* reforms of 1839 was to create a strong modern apparatus with which to govern the empire, yet they were far from popular and as centralizing measures were difficult to apply.[25] A new system of taxes was to be levied, not as before by local Albanian beys, but by imperial Ottoman officials. In 1844 an uprising broke out in the towns of Uskub (Skopje), Tetova and Pristina, directed against the high taxation and increasingly centralized policy of the Ottoman regime. This was followed by another insurrection in Gjakova the following year. After yet another revolt in 1847, thousands of Albanians were imprisoned or deported to Asia Minor. Thousands more ruined peasants chose either to leave their villages to look for work in the few towns or to emigrate, especially to Turkey, Romania and Egypt.

The revolts themselves were spontaneous and without precise aims, nevertheless they served to pave the way for the tentative beginnings of an Albanian national movement. Despite the increased secularization of the laws and institutions of the Empire and its Christian millets resulting from the *Tanzimat* reforms, intolerance increased towards the Christian population. A new and harsh capital tax was levied on all non-Muslim subjects, whilst those who converted to Islam continued to receive grants of land and have their taxes lowered. It appears, however, from the notes of Edward Lear that even though the lowland Albanians adopted Islam, they no longer had the right to bear arms. Lear described the northern Ghegs as 'wild and savage … their long matted hair and brown visage giving them a ferocity which existed perhaps more in the outward than inner man; moreover, these

Ghegs were all armed whereas out of Ghegaria no Albanian is allowed to carry so much as a knife.'[26] Ottoman occupation had resulted in underdevelopment of the region and of the economy, and the population of the lowlands as a whole lived in generally wretched conditions. This phenomenon was noted by Lear, who on crossing south of the Shkumbi river noticed the distinction between the two halves of the country:

> I have now left Ghegheria and am in the land of the Toskides, a new tribe, the people seem a poorer and more squalid race, their dress is white even to their little skull caps, but dirt and squalor of the outer and timid wretchedness of the inner man seemed the characteristics of these pauper beings, who arose from the ground in their rags and saluted me with looks of terror – widely differing from the haughty gaze of the crimson-coated Gheghe.[27]

Following the crushing of the independent pashaliks, the Porte planned to create a substantial and compact group of Muslims in the Albanian-inhabited provinces of Monastir, Janina, Shkoder and Old Serbia – who, it was hoped, would be ideologically, politically and socially committed to the basic interests of the empire, and might also provide recruitment to secure peace on the empire's increasingly vulnerable frontiers. Therefore in 1865 the Albanian regions, which included large populations of other nationalities, were split into the three vilayets of Shkoder, Monastir and Janina; a fourth, Kosova, was added in 1878. Each had its own governor and garrison, in order, it was hoped, to render any alignment of the Albanians impossible for the foreseeable future. As the Albanians occupied such a strategic position in the Balkans, the Porte wished to avoid creating homogenous Albanian vilayets which would give a definite demarcation to what was still the vague geographic notion of 'Albania'.

Throughout the nineteenth century, the overriding concern of the Porte was to hold the Empire together under highly adverse circumstances. As a result of the Crimean War of 1853–6 the European Powers became increasingly interested in the Balkans. Russia's ambition of destroying the Ottoman Empire was vehemently opposed by England and France. The Porte had therefore to face the challenge not only of the Christian nationalities and the Albanians but also the interference of the Great Powers, who pressed to control, directly or indirectly, the decisions of the Ottoman state. The conditions that led to the establishment of a French–British–Russian protectorate in

Greece and a Russian protectorate in Serbia and the Danubian prin-
cipalities resulted in similar measures of domination in Istanbul at
various times by either Russia or Britain.[28]

The Advent of the Albanian Cultural Movement

Whilst many Albanians profited under Ottoman rule, their cultural
advancement was severely restricted. Nowhere was the Albanian
language taught, nor had a standard alphabet been devised. Books in
Albanian were virtually non-existent, and what few schools there were
taught only in Turkish, Greek or Italian. In contrast to the tolerance
shown to other nationalities, the Ottoman administration opposed the
use of the Albanian language in schools so as to delay the awakening
of an Albanian national consciousness. Education was exclusively religious, run by ecclesiastical institutions, and because of their Muslim
faith most Albanians were classified as Turks. In 1860, the Jesuits
opened the Albanian Papal Seminary in Shkoder, followed ten years
later by a Franciscan theological college under Austrian auspices.
Austria–Hungary had become increasingly aware that the Albanian-
inhabited areas of the Balkans would become an important factor in
the event of the collapse of the Ottoman Empire. Vienna, therefore,
had striven to establish a growing political influence over the Catholic
areas of northern Albania, having already developed strong commercial links with Shkoder. The Catholic priests were apparently unpopular because they involved themselves in commercial activities and
were able to undersell local tradesmen. They were also thought to be
the agents of Austria–Hungary, whose intentions towards Albania had
long been the subject of much suspicion among Albanians.[29]

One of the first advocates of teaching in the Albanian language was
Naum Veqilharxhi. Born in Korca in 1797, he left the area to study
law in Romania, where he participated in the abortive Romanian
rebellion against the Porte in 1821. In 1845, borrowing elements from
old alphabets, Veqilharxhi published two elementary schoolbooks
under the title *Evetor*. Then, in 1850, he set up an Albanian Cultural
Association in Bucharest, where he preached that a people without
education were like slaves, and that no nation could acquire knowledge
in any language other than its own. 'Culture', he wrote 'could be
gained only in the mother tongue.'[30] The question of a single alphabet
for the Albanian language had been the cause of much dispute. With
no alphabet, cultural advancement was severely curtailed. While

admitting the right of all peoples of the empire to be taught in their native language, in the case of the Albanians, divided as they were into three different religious groups, there was no chance that they could obtain their own schools. The writer Sami Frasheri summed up the situation: 'Albania cannot exist without Albanians, the Albanians cannot exist without the Albanian language and the latter cannot exist without its own alphabet and without schools.'[31] Although the pioneers of the Albanian national movement were few in number, Velqilharxhi was followed by other Albanians, mostly Orthodox and from the Korca district, the majority of whom settled in Bucharest where they were exposed to nationalist ideas. In 1877 an Albanian Committee was formed in Istanbul in order to revive the Albanian language amongst the large Albanian community, and build up some form of Albanian literature.

The Treaty of San Stefano and the Formation of the Prizren League

In the meantime, Austria–Hungary had increasingly turned her attentions towards the Balkans, where she continued to regard the survival of the Ottoman Empire as a vital interest. In the Reichstadt Agreement of 1876, Austria–Hungary had made it clear that she would oppose, at all costs, the formation of a Great Slavic State in the Balkans, hence the importance of developing some form of Albanian national consciousness as a counterpoise to Slavism. Around the same time, in order to counter Austrian influence, Italy began to found Italian-language schools, also in Shkoder. During the last quarter of the nineteenth century intensifying internal decay, as well as external pressure, had severely weakened the Porte. The first signs of a threat to the relatively privileged position of Albanians within the Ottoman Empire came with the crisis which erupted in Bosnia-Hercegovina in 1875. Here rebel Christian peasants backed by Russia, Serbia and Montenegro demanded autonomy from the Ottoman Empire. The following year Ottoman troops suppressed a rebellion in Bulgaria, killing between twelve and fifteen thousand Bulgarians. A shock-wave swept through Europe, although the large-scale killing of Muslims by Christians that was also part of the picture had virtually been ignored. This was especially the case in England, where the 'Bulgarian Massacres' were used by the Liberal opposition under Gladstone as a propaganda instrument against the Conservative government of

Disraeli (which was accused of being pro-Turkish and thus an accessory to the killings).[32]

In the hope of saving them from inevitable defeat, the Great Powers hastily signed a protocol obliging the Ottomans to form an autonomous province in Bosnia-Hercegovina. But the Porte ignored the protocol, thus giving Russia, later joined by Serbia and Montenegro, the excuse to declare war in April 1877. In January the following year Serbian troops invaded the region of northern Kosova, and the Montenegrins advanced towards Shkoder. In February the Greeks also took advantage of the situation by invading the vilayet of Janina. The Serbian army expelled those Albanians living in the region stretching from Leskovac to Nis, which they annexed to Serbia. The Albanian population was driven deeper into the Kosova region, where relations between Serbs and Albanians were already strained. Following the defeat of the Porte in March 1878 Russia imposed on the Ottoman administration the harsh Treaty of San Stefano. This was designed to curb Austro-Hungarian influence in the Balkans, to satisfy the Pan-Slavists who wished to see the liberation of all Slavs, and to strengthen Russia's position in the area. Albania was one of the principal victims of the treaty, which ceded substantial territories inhabited by Albanians to Serbia, Montenegro and a greatly enlarged Bulgaria. Serbia was allotted a large part of the sanjak of Pristina, Montenegro received the north Albanian regions including Peja (Pec), Ulqin, Hoti, Plava, Gucia and Podgorica. Bulgaria received a vast area of western Albania, including Korca, Dibra and Tetova. The Albanian reaction to San Stefano was swift and spontaneous: local committees of defence were hastily formed throughout the vilayets of Kosova, Shkoder and Monastir.

On 3 May, Herbert Green, the British consul in Shkoder, reported to his Foreign Office:

> In the districts of Gussinie, Plava, Berani, Granici and most of the eastern slopes of the North Albanian mountains, a league has been entered into between the Mohammedans binding themselves collectively and individually to resist until death all attempts coming either from abroad or from the Supreme Government to change the present state of their territory. Steps are being taken by these populations to place themselves in accord with the Albanians further south, near Prizrend, Pristina, Fandi, Dibra, Ohrid and even as far as Monastir.[33]

The vilayet of Kosova was compelled to put up the most resistance to territorial amputation, and therefore emerged as the centre of strongest Albanian resistance. The highland regions of Albania had always shown the most stubborn resistance to outside rule. The pre-Ottoman Albanians had fled up into the mountains, where they had become increasingly aware of their unique identity and grown accustomed to their virtually autonomous lifestyle. At the beginning of the century Hobhouse had noted that 'nationality is a passion at all times stronger in the mountaineers than in the inhabitants of the plains.'[34] Nevertheless, religious oppositions were still able to divide the northern Albanian tribes: in 1876 Muslims from Gjakova, Ljuma and the Mati region had given their support to the Ottoman forces which devastated the Catholic Mirdite region.

Organized protests continued against the assignment of Albanian territory to Slavic states by the San Stefano Treaty. On 10 June 1878, a meeting of Albanian nationalist leaders was held in the Kosova town of Prizren. It was attended by over three hundred delegates, mostly from Kosova and Western Macedonia, but a handful of delegates from southern Albania were also present: although no Albanian territory had been granted to Greece by the Treaty of San Stefano, several southerners felt it necessary to show solidarity with the north. The most important delegate to attend the meeting, Abdul Frasheri, came from the south. Frasheri, a Bektashi, was born near Korca in 1839; after studying at a Greek school in Janina he eventually became director of finance of the vilayet of Janina. The primary purpose of the League was to organize political and military opposition to the dismemberment of Albanian-inhabited territory, and to petition the Sultan to unite the four vilayets of Janina, Monastir, Shkoder and Kosova into one political and administrative unit. However, the boundaries of Albanian territory at that time were not easy to define. Using language as a criterion to define nationality instead of religion, a language boundary had been traced in a memorandum to the Austro-Hungarian government in 1877 by F. Lippich, its consul in Shkoder, who had good personal knowledge of north Albania. According to Lippich, the northern linguistic frontier from west to east began just below Antivari (Bar) and ran via Kolasin to Rozaj (south-west of Novi Pazar), then up to the Serbian frontier and along the course of the Morava river. It then crossed the Vardar Valley, through the sanjak of Monastir, running along the boundary with Dibra as far as the northern shore of Lake Ohrid.[35]

However, it was to be another forty years before Albania's frontiers were finally settled, and these were to bear little resemblance to the linguistic boundaries on Lippich's map. The aim of the League was not only to defend Albanian territories, but also, as soon as circumstances allowed, to fight for autonomy within the empire. The Porte initially encouraged the League, as it too was naturally opposed to the San Stefano Treaty. The majority of those who gathered at Prizren were Muslim conservatives, and through them the Porte hoped to exercise an influence in its own interests. One of the greatest obstacles to the cultural, national and political advancement of the Albanians was the Ottoman administration's continued refusal to recognize that Albanians were not Turks but a separate people with a distinct identity of their own. The conversion of so many Albanians to Islam, and the security provided by the Porte against the Slavs and the Greeks, had eventually led to a general identification with Ottoman Turkish, rather than specifically Albanian ideals and aims. Thus the very nature of Ottoman rule delayed the rise of an Albanian national consciousness and a subsequent national movement, and ensured that the Albanians became the last Balkan nation to achieve their independence from the Ottoman Empire.

2

Political and Cultural Moves to Consolidate the Albanian National Movement

As the meeting at Prizren drew to a close, the delegates dispersed to form regional committees in their local areas. Abdul Frasheri returned to his native village of Frasher, where he made contact with the Bektashi *tekke* there. He was aware that the majority of the Muslim Albanians of the south would support the Prizren League if he managed to win over the Bektashi Babas to the cause. Himself a Bektashi, Abdul visited various *tekkes*, and with the support of Baba Alush of Frasher persuaded the Bektashi order to help the Albanian movement and to exercise influence on Albanian notables.[1] Despite the fact that the Ottoman Empire seemed near to collapse, the Porte was determined not to surrender any of its possessions. The League therefore took the initial step of forging a semblance of unity between the northern and southern Albanians, enabling them to channel and focus their aims towards a common goal. This was rather ambitious, for although the League remained unified over the question of defending Albanian territorial integrity, its conservative and radical elements were deeply divided on the issue of autonomy.

The threatened disintegration of the Ottoman Empire caused alarm among the European Powers. Britain, France, Austria–Hungary, Germany and Italy assumed that the enlarged Bulgaria created at the Treaty of San Stefano would simply become an extension of Russia. They were concerned that whichever power it was that controlled the strategic region of Istanbul and the Straits would eventually dominate the Sultan's Christian subjects. The whole balance of forces in Central Europe and the Mediterranean was at stake, as well as the outcome of

European rivalries in Asia. In order, therefore, to find an acceptable solution to the 'Eastern Question', the Powers compelled Russia to submit to a new peace settlement at the Congress of Berlin, which was presided over by Bismarck, in June 1878. In the hope of diminishing Russian influence in the Balkans, the Congress pushed back the frontiers of Bulgaria. The new, drastically smaller, Bulgaria was confined to the area between the Danube and the Balkan mountains and was recognized as an autonomous principality under the nominal suzerainty of the Sultan; southern Bulgaria was made into a new and less autonomous province of the Ottoman Empire known as Eastern Rumelia. The Berlin Congress more or less stifled Russia's ambitions in the Balkans. She had henceforth to turn her attentions eastward, where before long she came into conflict with the newly emerging power of Japan. All the Albanian-inhabited areas were returned to the Porte's control. Serbia's claims on Albanian territory were curtailed, as she was refused the sanjak of Pristina and retained only the areas she had occupied before the war. The events of 1877–8 were a disaster for the empire. The loss of territory even after the Berlin Congress was enormous, including as it did Romania, Serbia, Montenegro, Bosnia-Hercegovina, Bulgaria, Thessalia, parts of Anatolia and Cyprus – all in all about a third of the empire's territory and over 20 per cent of its population.[2]

Throughout the month-long Berlin Congress, a flood of protests and petitions had poured in from the Albanians. The Albanians' principal desire was for the unification of the southern vilayets with those of Shkoder, Uskub and Kosova, and to make Ohrid the capital owing to its central position. One of the first acts of the Albanian League was to send a memorandum to Lord Beaconsfield, Britain's delegate to the Berlin Congress. It read – 'Just as we are not and do not want to be Turks, so we shall oppose with all our might anyone who would like to turn us into Slavs or Austrians or Greeks, we want to be Albanians.'[3] At this stage the Porte continued to support the League, in the hope that it might exert some pressure on the Powers to reconsider the entire 'Eastern Question' and the dangers resulting from further extension of the independent Balkan states, thereby helping to prop up weakened Ottoman rule in the region. The Porte, having never forgotten the lesson of Ali Pasha, had ever since made repeated attempts to interfere with local Albanian autonomy. Before long, however, the Albanians began replacing their political protest with acts of civil disobedience and armed force. The League decided to defy the authority of the Porte's officials by refusing to send military recruits. Thus, towards the end of 1878, even though they still possessed only a rudimentary national consciousness, the peoples of northern Albania began refusing to do military service or pay taxes to the Ottoman authorities. This coincided with anti-Ottoman demonstrations throughout all the Albanian-inhabited vilayets.

The Albanians now began to direct serious attention towards the question of autonomy. Before 1912, the majority of Albanians did not wish to see the Ottoman Empire dismembered; nor did they seek an independent state. Autonomy within the empire seemed the best guarantee of their local interests and national safety. As the northerners had long enjoyed certain local autonomy, they resented the centralistic policies of the Porte more than the southerners. There was less support for the League in central Albania. The big landowning families of central Albania did not feel the same pressure to defend either the northern or southern frontier regions. Instead, having relatives in high positions within the Ottoman administration, they felt the League's autonomy programme would harm their interests and privileges at the Porte. Nevertheless, the programme of the Albanian League, which was set before the Porte in January 1879, contained the following five demands: the unification of all the Albanian provinces into a single vilayet; the setting up of a national assembly to govern the vilayet; that all the officials of the vilayet should be able to speak Albanian; that teaching should be in the Albanian language; and that some of the income of the vilayet should be used for public spending in the vilayet itself.[4] The Ottoman authorities, however, chose for the time being to ignore the League's programme.

The Conflict with Montenegro

The League reacted to the territorial concessions to Montenegro by amassing, in a very short time, an army of thousands of Albanian volunteers on the Montenegrin frontier. The Montenegrin ruler, Prince Nicholas, countered the Albanian threat by ordering a general offensive, only to find his army quickly defeated by the Albanians. Although Bismarck had declared impatiently at the Berlin Congress that 'there is no Albanian nationality', the European Powers could no longer dismiss the Albanian question. After their stand against both Montenegro and the Porte, the Albanians had become an international problem. The Montenegrin failure forced the Powers to reconsider the decisions made at Berlin. In February 1879, the Powers insisted that the Porte give up the Albanian-claimed areas of Plava, Podgorica, Gucia and Ulcinj, and withdraw all Ottoman troops from the disputed zones. In January the following year, the Porte suggested to the Congress commissioners that, instead of giving to Montenegro the Albanian Muslim areas, it should surrender the Catholic Albanian regions of Hoti and Gruda while still allowing the persistent Montenegrin claim to Ulcinj. When rumours of this suggestion spread, both Catholic and Muslim Albanians declared that if such a scheme were implemented they would no longer consider themselves Ottoman subjects, but would defend their lands themselves with their own weapons.

In April the Powers, ignoring the Albanian pleas, finally agreed to the Corti Line which granted to Montenegro the Catholic Albanian regions of Hoti and Gruda, instead of the Muslim areas of Plava and Gusinj. Basically, the Powers' representatives at the Berlin Congress treated Albania as merely a geographical, rather than a national entity. This decision only served to stiffen the Albanians' resolve to defy any ruling which would further dismember their lands. In June, after renewed fighting, the Powers tried once more to settle matters by giving to Montenegro the town of Ulcinj instead of Hoti and Gruda. This was rather a dubious prize for Montenegro, as it was inhabited entirely by Albanian seamen who were controlled by more than six thousand pirates. On 22 April, when the Ottoman army withdrew from the Albanian areas to allow occupation by the Montenegrins, the forces of the League took possession of them. It was then that the Powers finally understood that the League was not just a puppet organization created for manipulation by the Porte. After much discussion, the Powers informed the Sultan that, in view of the actions of the Albanians, the Porte appeared to be in no position to suggest territorial concessions opposed by the Albanian League. By September, their patience wearing thin, the Powers ultimately advised the Porte that if it did not compel its subjects to yield, they would occupy the Turkish port of Smyrna. This finally prompted the Porte to act, and reinforcements were hurridly sent to oversee the surrender of Ulcinj.

The Albanians, however, steadfastly refused to relinquish their hold over the town and the forces of the League, assisted by Ulcinj's large Albanian population, engaged in fierce fighting with the imperial forces. Nevertheless, by the end of November 1880, the League's resistance was eventually broken and Ulcinj was handed over to

Montenegro. This was the start of a long series of bloody skirmishes before Albania's northern frontiers were finally settled. The English traveller and champion of the Albanian cause, Mary Edith Durham, later wrote of the impracticality of the Congress's decision to divide Albanian territory: 'The frontiers drawn by the Treaty of Berlin were so impossible that in many places they could not be defined, much less enforced. As the borderers themselves described it ... The frontier floated on blood.'[5] The inhabitants of Ulcinj protested vigorously against the cession of their town to Montenegro, as did the residents of Podgorica, which in 1880 had only around thirty Montenegrin inhabitants. So ended any cooperation between the League and the empire, as Albanians on the whole felt their loyalty to the Porte had been betrayed. During the last decade of the nineteenth century, the northern Albanians were in a state of perpetual armed conflict along the border with Montenegro, and also began an organized resistance to the Porte. To the rest of Europe though, Albania's frontier issue remained of little interest. Albania appeared not only as remote as the interior of Africa, but received probably fewer visitors.

However, one intrepid young Englishman, Edward Knight, spent the summer of 1879 exploring Montenegro and northern Albania with a companion, and later wrote a detailed account of general life and politics in the region. After arriving in Montenegro, Knight noted his apprehension upon leaving the relative safety of Centinje: 'The nearer we approached Albania, the worse was the reputation of its fierce inhabitants for murder and robbery; the more earnestly we were warned against travelling in such a cut-throat region.'[6] Knight noticed how Prince Nicholas had skilfully managed to court Europe's sympathies at the expense of Albania:

> Albania has an ill name among those who know her not. She is the scape-goat of the Adriatic, the cause of all the troubles here abouts it is said. Montenegro, on the other hand, enjoys a high reputation. Subsidized or bribed by the Powers that be, petted by the same, she plays a good game, and encourages the superstition that she is much more virtuous and civilized than the neighbour whose territory she lusts after. The unfortunate Albanian has no prince Nikita [Nicholas], is robbed by the so-called government of Turkey when it is strong enough to affect him in any way, has no friends, but is surrounded by cunning enemies, hungry for his lands.[7]

Having become more familiar with the country, Knight, like Durham, was also dismayed at the decisions made in Berlin: 'It was thought fit to give her [Montenegro] districts and villages inhabited by the most fiercely fanatical Mohamedans of Albania. That bloodshed and future troubles would result, anyone who knew the country could have forseen.'[8] Knight described the overall situation and how, by 1879, the Porte had virtually lost its hold on northern Albania:

> The government is very weak here, neither feared nor respected, merely tolerated. Albania is in a state of positive anarchy, the gendarmerie is on strike, the soldiers refusing to salute their officers, neither having received pay for months, while the natives hold seditious meetings publicly and unmolested in the mosques of the garrison towns, in which rebellion against the Porte is fearlessly advocated. Nowhere is the rotten condition and utter helplessness of the Porte more apparent than here.[9]

Following the Berlin Congress, the debatable lands on the border between Albania and Montenegro had become a desert region which no one dared to build or cultivate, never knowing when war would come again. The rich and fertile plains were left to the wolf and the lynx, as the people scratched out a living in the barren but more secure fastness of the mountains.

The Congress of Berlin and Epirus

As the northern branch of the League was resisting Montenegrin encroachments, the southern branch was occupied with petitioning the Great Powers against the loss of Albanian territory to Greece. In July 1880, the Albanian League held a meeting in the southern town of Girokaster, where claims for mere provincial autonomy within the Empire gave way to demands for an autonomous Albanian state with its own government and with only the governor-general appointed by the Porte. This meeting was effectively to substantiate the programme for autonomy agreed in Frasher in 1878. However, while the delegates were in general agreement over the ultimate goal of autonomy, they differed as to how to achieve it. Some argued for immediate action, before the Ottomans had time to move against them. But the more moderate delegates, mostly the feudal beys, preferred to wait. The radical element eventually won, and it was agreed to act as soon as possible. The province of Epirus then comprised the four sanjaks of Berat, Girokaster, Janina and Prevesa. What the Albanians called Chameria (or southern Albania), the Greeks called northern Epirus, despite the fact that it forms a single geographical unity, as Janina is

separated from Thessaly by the Pindus range. The region continued
to have a very blurred ethnicity. As one visitor noted: 'The whole of
the Tosk country has been strongly influenced by Greece, or rather it
would be difficult to say whether Epirus is Greek or North-Western
Greece Albanian. Though the southern dialect of Albanian is used for
conversation, Greek is universally understood.'[10]

The Congress of Berlin had invited the Greeks and Albanians to
come to some sort of agreement, based on the line formed by the
Kalamas and Salamavria rivers, which would allot the vilayet of Janina
to Greece. When the Albanian delegates from Janina petitioned the
Marquis of Salisbury they mentioned their affection for the Ottoman
Government, 'to which we are bound by our political existence of
four centuries'.[11] They believed that annexation to Greece would
eventually result in their annihilation, and declared that they were
prepared to fight rather than be handed over to Greece. Within a
Graeco-Albanian union, the Muslim Albanians stood to lose the
privileged position they were accustomed to holding in the Ottoman
Empire. The London *Times* correspondent in Athens reported on
what he believed to be the real motives behind the Greek bid to
annexe Janina:

> The object they have in view is the Hellenisation of Albania. The whole of
> the southern portion carries its commerce through Janina and the inhabit-
> ants regard this town as their capital. As yet their aspirations to form a
> distinct nationality are thought to be weak and ill-defined, so that the
> Greeks hope, with the possession of Janina, to amalgamate the two races
> and gain over to the cause of Hellenism the finest and most warlike race in
> southern Europe.[12]

Meanwhile, in December 1878, the Porte's representative, Moukhtar
Pasha, had arrived in Epirus, where he advised Abdul Frasheri and
other prominent Albanians to prepare resistance against any incorporation of Albanian territory by Greece. He said the Porte was prepared
to cede to Greece only that portion of Epirus south of the river Arta.[13]
The mission of the Porte's commissioner was to obstruct by all means
possible the realization of the decisions of the Congress of Berlin.
Almost certainly he was not aware that, on 10 November, Frasheri and
other southern leaders had already met to draw up a programme for
the administrative autonomy of the country with the approval of the
Albanian Istanbul Committee. The advent to power of the Liberal
government in England marked the arrival of a new and ardent phil-

hellenism in Britain, which had important repercussions for Albania. Indeed, in a petition to Lord Salisbury, the Albanian (Prizren) League accused the British of promoting their love of Hellenism to the extent of sacrificing the Albanian nation: 'If the Albanians are less educated than the Greeks, their work is not less sacred and worthy of the interest of civilized nations.' Appealing to the conscience of Europe, the writers of the petition dramatically pledged that they would leave to Greece 'nothing but a vast field of carnage, still smoking with the blood of our children, and we will not retire into our mountains until we are lighted on our way by the flames from our burning houses.'[14]

On a more practical level, the petition also mentioned that Albanians would go hungry if they lost the fertile southern portion of Epirus, and also that their commerce would cease if they were denied access to their only ports on the coast. This appeal, however, had little impact on the British, who were apparently as unconcerned by the Albanian pleas as they were by the Porte's manoeuvres, and felt that they were in a position to neutralize both. On 30 March 1879 Abdul Frasheri and Mehmet Ali Vrioni from Berat left Preveza to visit the principal European capitals, where they worked tirelessly to present the wishes of the south Albanian population. On 12 May they called on Lord Salisbury and explained to him, among other things, that of the 650,000 population of Epirus, only about 74,000 spoke Greek as well as Albanian, and these consisted chiefly of men, the women speaking almost exclusively Albanian. This contradicted the earlier observations of Hobhouse, who had noted, 'The Christians of Janina, though inhabiting part of Albania, and governed by Albanian masters, call themselves Greek. They neither wear the Albanian dress nor speak the Albanian language. They partake also in every particular of the manners and customs of the Greeks of the Morea and Rumelli etc.'[15] Hobhouse also mentioned that as he came within sight of Girokaster he noticed how the dress of the peasants changed from the loose woollen skirt of the Greeks to the cotton kilt of the Albanians. Nor did they any longer speak Greek. He was told that Albania proper, or 'at least the native country of the Albanians begins from the town of Delvinaki'.[16] The negotiations over the future of Epirus dragged on for almost two years. Greece and the Porte eventually reached an agreement in 1881, by which Greece was to receive Thessaly and Arta in Epirus, but not the Janina vilayet.

In the meantime, back in the north, not all Albanians were enthusiastic about the ideals of the Prizren League. In Shkoder the

Christians were highly sceptical. The anti-Christian tenor of the League worried non-Muslim Albanians, who wavered over joining it. During the 1880s Mr Kirby-Green was the British consul-general for North Albania. His was a particularly lonely job, and he was more than glad to receive Mr Knight and his companion. Monitoring the political situation, he too had observed the religious divisions that lay beneath the surface of the League. Upon hearing that the two Englishmen intended to go to Prizren, he warned them, 'Prizren, let me tell you, is the headquarters of the Albanian League, an organization of the most fanatical Mussulmen of the country ... these men are now worked up to a high pitch of religious zeal, and hatred of the Christians. Prizren is, with perhaps the exception of Mecca, the most dangerous spot for a Christian in all Mohammedan countries.'[17] Nevertheless, the majority of Catholics eventually joined the League, but only after it had become obvious that the waning power of the Porte threatened their absorption by an Orthodox Slavic state, either Serbia or Montenegro. The Catholic population were themselves polarized. Some, such as the Mirdites, were extremely poor and lived in a perpetual state of half-starvation because Ottoman troops were persistently making incursions into the heart of their valleys, driving off their flocks, burning their villages and compelling them to flee to the safety of the barren mountains. This was not the case with the wild and isolated Catholic tribes further west. The Hoti, Skreli, Kastrati, Nikaj and others were, as Christians, forbidden by law to carry arms in the towns. But these tribes were too strong and powerful to heed such government regulations, so they stalked proudly through the towns bristling with arms, and no one dared to interfere with them.

The forces of the League were daily swollen by refugees from Bosnia and deserters from the Ottoman army. The League's men, feeling their growing strength, extended their programme calling for autonomy in order to resist the advances of both Austria from the north and Greece from the south. The fact that Austria was ready to step in to quell the emerging Albanian national movement was noted by Knight: 'It is only too probable that the Dual Empire will be compelled to carry her arms into this province, for a lawless, fanatical, self-ruling Albania will be far too troublesome and dangerous a neighbour for her disaffected Bosnia. An occupation of Albania is confidently spoken of by all the Austrian officers I met in Dalmatia.'[18] The Sultan believed that Austria–Hungary was extending its influence over the League in order to use the resulting instability as a pretext for an invasion to restore peace. The Albanians themselves, however, had realistic fears that Montenegro would try to extend its frontiers to include Prizren and Shkoder. They were disgusted by what they perceived as the Porte's betrayal over the Albanian-inhabited areas ceded to Montenegro. In Shkoder a leader of the Albanian League told Knight that

> the government of Turkey did not find favour in the eyes of the Albanians: 'The Turks!' cried out the Chief angrily, 'what do they do for us? Tax us, rob us – that is all. These effeminate pashas, these farmers of customs, do nothing for us in return for what they steal. Can they defend us? Protect us? No! ... I tell you we will have the Turk no more. The Chiefs of the League have sworn it. Independence has been given to Montenegro, to Bulgaria, Albania shall have her independence and the Great Powers shall recognize us. If not, we care not. Leave us alone, that is enough for us.'[19]

The Crushing of the Prizren League

The Prizren League took it upon itself to unite the Albanian regions since the Porte was demonstrably unable to do so. Albanian resistance thus began in earnest in Kosova on 4 January 1881, when the Prizren contingent, under the command of Sulejman Vokshi, first occupied Uskub and from there moved north to Mitrovica and parts of the sanjak of Novi Pazar. By the end of the month, the forces of the League had taken control of Pristina. They eventually expelled the Ottoman administrators from the whole of Kosova and proclaimed themselves the provincial government. From Kosova they prepared to march south. The Porte began to fear the ability of the League to speak with a single voice on behalf of the majority of Albanians. This was the first time the Ottoman Empire had encountered nationalism among Muslims. The growing Albanian movement directly challenged Ottoman rule and created conditions that invited foreign intervention. As a consequence, the Sultan was advised to crush the League as soon as possible. Having reached an agreement with Greece over Thessaly, the Porte was now free to turn its attention to destroying the Albanian League. On 23 March, members of the League Committee of Istanbul were arrested and deported to the island of Rhodes. A month later, an Ottoman army of ten thousand men, commanded by Dervish Pasha, an advocate of centralization, marched into Kosova, and after stiff resistance, occupied Prizren. The League's headquarters were hastily transferred to Gjakova, where resistance to the empire

lasted but a few days. There were similar moves to destroy the southern branch of the League. Within weeks military tribunals had sat in
judgement on the League's leaders, who were mostly exiled to remote
parts of Anatolia. Abdul Frasheri fled but was captured at the end of
April. His death sentence was commuted to life imprisonment, and he
was released by the Sultan in 1885 following a general amnesty. He
died in 1894.

The League may have been crushed, but its ideals continued to
exercise a powerful influence on Albanian intellectuals for several
decades. The League had been the first barrier against the expansionist
policies of the neighbouring Balkan states, uniting the nationalist
movement in its demands for administrative and cultural autonomy
within the framework of the empire. The motivating force behind this
early expression of nationalism was self-preservation rather than a
wish to disturb the status quo. Although the Porte effectively
destroyed the League it could not destroy either the spirit of rebellion
it had awakened or the national awareness it had aroused, and these
continued to grow. The period following the dissolution of the
Albanian League saw a series of local revolts sparked off by Ottoman
administrators' attempts to collect old taxes and impose new ones. In
1885, the whole of Kosova rose in revolt, primarily in opposition to
higher taxes and the census. The Porte tried to placate the Kosovars
(Albanians from Kosova) by freeing some political prisoners. But the
regime of Sultan Abdul Hamid II (1876–1909) had begun a further
reign of terror throughout the Albanian regions: nationalists were
regularly arrested, and all local organizations linked to the League
were disbanded.

In January 1889, over four hundred delegates from all parts of
Kosova gathered in Peja (Pec), where the Prizren League was reformed
under the new name of the League of Peja, presided over by Haxhi
Mulla Zeka. It had essentially a Muslim character, showing little
regard for the demands for reform being made at that time by the
Macedonian, as well as Albanian, Christians. As with all previous
Albanian movements, there was a struggle between moderate and more
radical factions. The moderates argued for essentially cultural reforms,
whilst the radicals demanded political reform in the shape of genuine
autonomy. The main purpose of the meeting, however, was to protect
the Muslim religion. The conflicts of the northern Albanians at this
time, against both the Porte and the Slavs, gave Kosova a special
place in Albanian folklore, inspiring the great Albanian poet Gjergi

Fishta (1871–1940) to write his epic 'Lahuta e Malsise' ('Lute of the Mountains'). As yet, however, the northern tribes possessed only a very rudimentary national consciousness. The national idea still had to compete with tribal particularism. Christian Albanians were united primarily by their intense mistrust and dislike of Ottoman rule. The predominantly Muslim Kosovars were conservative by nature, and identified themselves religiously with the Ottomans. The southern Orthodox Christians, for their part, were heavily influenced by Greece, many of their notables desiring union with Greece.

Albanians were thus divided not only by religion but also by class and region. Europe was understandably confused by the actions of the Albanians: sometimes fighting against the Porte, at other times for it, but on no occasion fighting on the side of the Christian Greeks or Slavs. Those without an understanding of the Ottoman system of government could not hope to comprehend the disjunction between religion and nationality. Christian Orthodox Albanians were considered by the Ottomans to be either Greeks or Slavs, depending on whether they lived in the south or the north; and, as previously stated, Muslim Albanians were automatically classified as Turks. Whenever the Porte was involved in hostilities with the Greeks or Slavs, the Albanians were still ready to defend it. There were mutual interests: a defeat of the Ottoman Empire would result in amputations of Albanian territory. Therefore, both Tosks and Ghegs fought on the side of the Porte during the Graeco-Ottoman war of 1897, which followed an insurrection on Crete. It was Albanian battalions that pushed back the Greeks from Penepigadia in Epirus and penetrated into Thessaly. The Greeks, who had imagined that the Orthodox Albanians had been won over to Hellenism and wanted unification with Greece, were disappointed to see that not a single battalion of the 'bilingual' (Orthodox) Albanians came to the rescue of the Greek army.[20] Nevertheless, the Porte still regarded the Albanians with deep suspicion, and gave orders to Ottoman officials to watch the moves of the Albanians and to suppress forcibly any signs of renewed agitation. In May 1901 Albanian bands pillaged and partly burned Novi Pazar, Sjenica and Pristina, attacking the Slavs everywhere. The Serbian populations suffered most, because of their proximity to Albanians, who occupied Kolasin and massacred a considerable number of Serbs.[21]

During the 1880s the Great Powers began to reform their alliance groupings in the hope of establishing a new equilibrium among themselves. The French occupation of Tunisia in 1881 prompted Italy to join with Germany and Austria–Hungary in the Triple Alliance of 1882, which was designed to counter further Russian and French expansion, primarily in the Balkans. When the Triple Alliance was renewed in 1887, it was accompanied by a separate Austro–Italian Treaty, whereby the two parties pledged themselves to preserve the status quo in the Balkans, which they regarded as the best foundation for the maintenance of peace in the area. This did not dispel the mistrust between Italy and Austria–Hungary, both of whom recognized the strategic importance of Albania. In the event of the collapse of the Ottoman Empire, Austria–Hungary planned for an autonomous Albania under her protection, to prevent Albania falling under another Power's influence. This foreign influence was most likely to be Italy's, who likewise did not wish to see Albania in the hands of Austria–Hungary. Italy's interests appeared to depend on extending the sphere of Italian influence across the Adriatic to compensate for the failure of her other colonial ventures. Despite a turbulent domestic situation, the Porte's confidence grew slightly as it realized that the European Powers were determined to maintain, for as long as possible, the status quo in the Balkans and to help stifle any national movement that threatened to alter the political map of the region.

Albanian Cultural Developments

The Ottoman government had been alarmed at the Albanians' drive not only for political autonomy, but also for cultural autonomy. Before the Prizren League Albanian nationalism had been based, like all early Balkan nationalist movements, upon a literary revival or, in Albania's case, a literary beginning. With the obvious decline of the Ottoman Empire, emphasis switched to overcoming cultural and linguistic divisions rather than religious ones. In 1881, the Society of Istanbul organized a branch in Bucharest, which published a cultural periodical called *Drita*, or light. This became the title of the Istanbul Society when it was forced to move from Istanbul to Bucharest in 1885. The society printed and distributed books in Albanian and raised funds for Albanian schools. Nationalist leaders continued to regard teaching in the Albanian language, together with the diffusion of national literature, as the best policy for the continued awakening of Albanian national identity. In the 1890s the Albanian Society of Istanbul was reformed as the Albanian Committee, led by Sami Frasheri. Orthodox Albanians began to argue for the creation of an autocephalous

Albanian Orthodox Church, with Albanian priests and a liturgy different from that of the other Balkan Orthodox churches. Nevertheless, it was several years until this goal could be realized and even then it was in America, not Albania, that a self-styled Albanian church was founded.

The spirit of the Prizren League continued to live on through much cultural activity. Some thirty Albanian language newspapers and journals were established in the years leading up to 1908, both within the empire and abroad, and a number of Albanian-language schools were opened. Educationally, Islam had hindered rather than helped the majority of Albanians, as all religious communities within the empire had their own schools except the Albanians, who were taught as Turks. If the people were to be united, the new schools had to be non-denominational. During the 1890s, the Albanian Committee, still with Sami Frasheri as president, was reorganized in Istanbul in order to maintain the newly aroused spirit of nationalism and to consider ways of securing the inviolability of Albanian-inhabited lands. Sami Frasheri bitterly resented Greek attempts to Hellenize and separate the Albanian Orthodox Christians. His brother Naim, a poet, had also joined the society in 1882 and, like their older brother Abdul, became one of the most influential personalities in the Albanian national movement. At the same time, the society continued assisting the Albanian cultural society in Bucharest, also called *Drita*. The Bucharest society, in turn, assisted the founding of the first Albanian boys' school, for both Christians and Muslims, in Korca in 1885. Muslim girls did not yet go to school.

Before long, however, the Porte decided to curtail Albanian educational activities, and under Ottoman coercion the Muslim pupils were forced to leave the school. The Orthodox clergy also put pressure on parents to withdraw their children by threatening them with excommunication. The first Albanian school for girls was founded in 1891, again in Korca. As the education of girls was accorded a very low priority, the school was given financial assistance primarily by British and American religious missions. Other schools appeared but all were short-lived, most running out of funds before the Porte could close them. The Albanians responded by forming secret societies to promote the teaching of the Albanian language, which was suppressed not only by the Ottoman government but also by the Greek ecclesiastical authorities.

The creation of Albanian schools inevitably gave rise to the question

of an Albanian alphabet. A few years before the founding of the Prizren
League, several Albanian intellectuals had gathered to discuss the
pressing question of an Albanian orthography. However, differences of
opinion had arisen between those who favoured the Arabic script,
others who preferred the Greek and yet others advocating the Latin
alphabet. At this time a number of very different alphabets based on
the Latin, Greek or Arabic scripts were in use, adding yet further
division to the debate. This so exasperated Vasa Pasha Effendi, a
Catholic from Shkoder and an advocate of the Latin alphabet, that he
was moved to write in a poem: 'Albanians, you are killing your brothers,
you are divided into a hundred parties. Some say I am a Christian,
others, I am a Turk, another I am a Latin. Still others, I am a Greek,
a Slav and others. But you are brothers all of you. The priests and
Hodjas have confused you, unite in one faith; the faith of Albanians
is Albaniandom.'[22] The demand for a single Albanian alphabet continued to grow. Konstandin Kristofordhi (1830–95), who published trans-
lations of the Bible and other works into Albanian, wrote: 'If the
Albanian language is not written, in a short time there will be no
Albania on the surface of the earth nor will the name Albania appear
on the map of the world.'[23]

Another Albanian intellectual who wielded great influence was Faik
Konitza, a Muslim born in Konitza in 1876. He rediscovered and
popularized the exploits of Skanderbeg, especially promoting Skanderbeg's emblem, the black doubleheaded eagle on a red background,
which later became the national flag. In Brussels in 1897 he brought
out the periodical *Albania*, which dealt with a wide variety of topics
relating to the development of an Albanian national consciousness.
Konitza believed that the union of all Albanians was indispensable for
their progress and national development, but even as ardent a patriot
as he believed that Albania was still not ready for independence. He
therefore recommended autonomy under the continued suzerainty of
the Sultan. As the struggle for cultural affirmation gathered momentum, the Bektashi *tekkes* became important centres for the smuggling
and distribution of books within Albania, with Dervishes acting as
carriers.[24] From 1902, new laws made it a punishable offence to be in
possession of an Albanian book or even to use the Albanian language
in correspondence. This meant the closure of all the Albanian-language
schools.

Towards the turn of the century, Albanian national literature had
begun to appear in Italy amongst the Italo-Albanians, the Arbaresh,

who in 1794 had founded an Albanian-language school in Calabria. They actively strove to publicize, throughout Italy and Europe, the aims of the Albanian national movement through their journal *Fjamuri Arberit*, (Flag of Albania). The Italo-Albanians found a supporter in Elena Ghika. Under her pen name Dora d'Istria, this Romanian princess of Albanian descent published a study of the Albanian nationality on the basis of folk songs. She pointed out in this and other studies that 'the Albanians, although divided by religion, formed one nation and had the right to enjoy freedom and progress'.[25] The Italo-Albanians were, however, out of touch with political realities within the Ottoman Empire. They thought that by introducing Albanian as the official language of the five vilayets they could define Albania as a national territory, thus ignoring the non-Albanian elements of the vilayets. In June 1901 a delegate said before the Italian parliament: 'On the future of Albania will depend the rights and interests of Italy in the Adriatic. Whoever possesses the port of Vlore will be the absolute ruler over the Adriatic.'[26]

General Riccioti Garibaldi, the son of the Italian revolutionary hero, was like his father sympathetic to the Albanian cause. In 1904 he took control of the Albanian movement in Italy, becoming president of the Consiglio Albanese, the aim of which was to gain Italian support for Albanian national aspirations. However, Garibaldi's sincerity was questioned by many Albanians. Faik Konitza drew attention to the fact that during the Graeco-Ottoman war of 1897, Garibaldi had helped the Greeks to occupy southern Albania and, in 1902, had proclaimed to the world that he was ready to assist Macedonia, which meant that he would lend a helping hand to the Slavs in order to subjugate half of Albania.[27] Away from Italy, Albanian émigrés continued to found patriotic societies in Romania, Bulgaria, Egypt and the United States. The publication which had the most impact was first published in Sofia in November 1901, and was again called *Drita*. Numbering among its readers Albanian officers in the Ottoman army and high government officials,. *Drita* had an uplifting influence on Albanian official opinion through its pure nationalist programme, which laid stress on union.[28] The main Albanian societies in Romania united to form an influential new society, *Bashkimi* (the Union). By the beginning of the twentieth century, the Albanian colony in America had become the most influential Albanian settlement abroad. The immigrants were mostly Orthodox, from the district of Korca, and had settled primarily in Massachusetts, with Boston as their centre. The publication of a weekly journal, *Kombi*, from June 1906, laid the cornerstone of their national movement.[29]

The Continued Weakening of the Porte's Authority

As the nineteenth century drew to a close, it was becoming increasingly obvious that the Ottoman Empire had run its course. Both Russia and Austria–Hungary became even more concerned to consolidate their spheres of influence in the Balkans. Bulgaria's absorption of Eastern Rumelia in 1885 effectively did what the Russians had been prevented from doing at San Stefano. The movement for Albanian administrative autonomy continued to gather momentum, as it was generally realized that the Porte would be unlikely to grant administrative autonomy of its own accord. In 1903 thousands of Albanians rose in revolt in Kosova, impatient at the delay in establishing better conditions and angry at the despotic rule of Sultan Abdul Hamid. At the same time the citizens of the district of Berat began an insurrection calling for a reduction in taxes and the replacement of all government officials by Albanians. This weakening of Ottoman authority gave Russia and Austria–Hungary an excuse to interfere in the empire's affairs under the guise of protecting their co-religionists. This in turn encouraged Albania's Balkan neighbours in their quest for more territory. Meanwhile, tension in the Balkans had increased considerably as the powers intensified their pressure on the Porte to put reforms into effect in Macedonia. The region then known as Macedonia was bounded to the north and east by the Sar and Rhodope mountains, on the south by the Aegean sea and the Pindus mountains, and on the west by lakes Ohrid and Prespa. Its population of two million comprised virtually every ethnic group to be found in the Balkan peninsula – Bulgars, Turks, Serbs, Gypsies, Albanians, Vlachs, Jews, Greeks, and Macedonian Slavs. Macedonia also contained the most important and strategic port in the Balkans, Thessalonika.

Due to the immense strategic importance of Macedonia, the Balkan states – Bulgaria, Greece and Serbia – all wished to acquire a major portion of it, for whoever controlled Macedonia would be the strongest power in the peninsula. All three Balkan states claimed Macedonia as their own for historical reasons, the region having been a major part of their past empires. The Serbo-Bulgarian war of 1885 worsened relations between those two countries and rendered Macedonia even more of a tinderbox. Macedonia became the all-absorbing interest of the Bulgarians, who plotted for its annexation.[30] The Great Powers too recognized the strategic value of the region in relation to Istanbul and the Turkish Straits. It was for this reason that they had so vehemently opposed the creation of a greater Bulgaria at San Stefano. They had pressed the Porte to implement reforms to counter the growing dissatisfaction among the empire's Christian subjects. Initially the Sultan agreed, but anarchy prevailed throughout Macedonia as the Porte failed to implement the promised reforms. Finally, in January 1903, the Bashibazouks (irregular Ottoman troops), most of whom were Albanian, were sent in to Macedonia.

On 2 August 1903 around twenty–five thousand Macedonian Slavs staged an uprising precipitated by the Internal Macedonian Revolutionary Organization, IMRO, which aimed to seize the vilayet of Monastir and so liberate Macedonia from the Ottomans. Following the ruthless crushing of this uprising, the Powers hastily tried to put into effect a new series of reforms they had drawn up at Murtzeg, by which means they hoped to appease the Christian population and perhaps defuse the explosive situation. However, before the Porte could implement any reforms guerilla bands, acting under the direction of Greece, Bulgaria or Serbia, began to operate throughout Macedonia, spreading yet more terror. In the spring of 1903 Albanian highlanders, led by the Mirdite, had also begun an insurrection against the Porte, demanding the return of their exiled chief, Prenk Bib Doda. In March the predominantly Muslim Kosovars also revolted against one of the Murtzeg reforms, which proposed that the number of Christian police in the Porte's European provinces be increased in proportion to their number in the population. Discontent and violent unrest continued throughout the following years. In May 1905, when the people of Elbasan expelled their Ottoman governor and the chief of the gendarmerie, the Sultan had to send troops to return them to office.

During this period, the Bektashi monasteries became noted centres of patriotic activity. In 1905 the Bektashis of a village near Girokaster demonstrated against the Ottoman authorities protesting against the unfair detention in Janina of the Dervishes of the *tekke* of Baba Hajdar, whom they accused of nationalist activity.[31] By now the authority of the Porte was virtually non-existent, as the English journalist William Miller then wrote:

Albania is one of the riddles of the Eastern Question. It seems incredible that a fine country, with at least two harbours possible of development, and within a few hours steam of Italy, should be the most uncivilised land in the Balkan peninsula, and that for centuries no European power should have made any serious attempt to acquire it as a colony. Thus what might be one of the finest countries in Europe, is left in a condition such as nowadays disgraces few Central African tribes. The Ottoman government has merely nominal authority over the country, and I remember well, when a few years ago the Ottoman Minister in Montenegro desired to visit the Albanian town of Scutari, he could find no one who was willing to drive him, for fear of those bullets of which the Albanians always carry in such quantity. Here the real power is not vested in the Governors sent from Constantinople, but in the native chiefs whose word is practically the only law current in the country.[32]

The decay of the Ottoman Empire was evident in the crumbling fabric of Albania, and economic improvement was now the most pressing need of the country. Although Shkoder's port bore the grandiose name of San Giovani di Medua, it had little to deserve such a title. Not even one road of any sort had been built between the port and Shkoder – which was, after all, the major trading and commercial centre of north Albania. At the turn of the century San Giovani contained just a few dilapidated old cottages, one unsavoury *han* or inn, an Ottoman army barracks and one rather fine house belonging to the Austrian Lloyd's steamer agent. Although San Giovani had a naturally fine harbour, it was almost abandoned, and the Austrians were left with a virtual monopoly on Albanian coastal trade. Travellers told of the gruelling eight hours hard riding to reach Shkoder. According to one traveller,

> San Giovani di Medua is the landing place for Scutari in Albania, it figures on Lloyd's timetables, and is the terminus of a projected railway. On the other hand, there is little to distinguish it from the rest of the coast; a rotten pier, some sheds, an inn, and ten Turkish soldiers constitute its claims to be called a town.

He continued with the problem of how to leave San Giovani:

> You cannot drive, because firstly, there are no carriages, and secondly, there is no road. It is therefore necessary to hire some lean and sullen nags, and a native with a sense of direction, and plunge into the country hoping to sometime reach the town and lake of Scutari.[33]

Miller was equally dismayed by the neglect of Albania's coastal towns:

If Medua be one of the Turk's many lost opportunities, Durazzo, the next place on the coast, is a terrible example of fallen greatness. As one walks through the poor and ill-paved streets of this decayed town, followed by some Turkish spy, suspected by every ragged soldier that one passes, one can scarcely realise that this was once the flourishing Dyracchium, the starting point of the great Egnation road to Constantinople.[34]

He continued:

Trade, manufactures, agriculture, art and literature are alike neglected in Albania. There is a certain consumption of cheap Austrian goods ... but the ports consist, like Medua, of a few offices on a desolate shore, and are not connected to the interior by any servicable roads ... the country is bare and uncultivated, except for a few fields and gardens round each village.[35]

The years leading up to 1908 were filled with various Albanian revolts and uprisings, as the Ottoman Empire underwent a deep economic, political and social crisis. Unrest spread throughout Macedonia as Bulgarian, Greek, Serbian and Macedonian bands continued their fight to gain territory for themselves and to impose their nationality on the territory's inhabitants. Armed rebellions had become a chronic feature of life throughout Macedonia, but the severe Ottoman reprisals against them indicated that the chances of reforms being implemented were wearing pretty thin. This caused concern to the European Powers, whose attempts to push the Ottoman government into reform were fraught with danger. One of the reasons for the empire's survival through so many vicissitudes had been its inefficiency, which gave so many warring interests the illusion that they could achieve their own ends while retaining the structure of the regime. Corruption had played the role of delegation of power in encouraging private initiative, and a miserable stability prevailed in the provinces, where successive generations of officials had pragmatically established the limits at which extortion defeats its own ends.[36] As the situation in Macedonia deteriorated, the Committee for the Liberation of Albania was hastily formed in Monastir to inject some sense of direction into the Albanian political movement. At the beginning of 1906, a branch of the Committee was established in Gjakova, headed amongst others by the Kosovar Chieftain, Bajram Curri. Committees were also established in the other vilayets. Not long afterwards a guerilla movement began in Albania. At the time Macedonia was infested with guerilla bands, the majority of whom were as unfriendly to Albanians as they were to the Ottoman troops.

In order to defend themselves, the Albanians formed their own guerilla bands known as *cheta*.

During these years Albania had became the buffer between the interests of Austria–Hungary and those of the Slavs in the Balkans. Already in 1878 the Austrians had seen in the spirited Albanian protests to the Berlin Congress evidence of a potentially useful barrier against the complete Slavicization of the Balkans.[37] The Albanians in the northeast were surrounded by Slavs and felt their very existence was at stake. Despite their discontent, therefore, they preferred to wait until the Slav threat had abated before revolting once more against the Porte. With just and realistic reforms and an improved administration it might have been possible for the empire to induce the Albanian nationalist movement to defer demands for autonomy at a time of such difficulties for the Porte. A good deal of national cohesion could have been created, and the Porte might have succeeded in making Albania a loyal Ottoman barrier. As it was, after decades of ignored petitions and memoranda, the nationalists felt the time had come to resort to action.

3

Albanian Independence and the End of Ottoman Rule

The Turkish Empire is an old house, decayed and crumbling. It is propped within and without and will stand for who knows how long. But if anyone tries to repair it and moves but one prop – but one brick even – it will fall about his ears. It is too late to repair it.

Edith Durham, quoting an elderly Albanian man
in 1908, *High Albania*, p 273

Towards the end of the nineteenth century a new political factor had emerged within the Ottoman Empire, the roots of which went back to the 1860s. This was the Young Turk Movement, which formed a liberal opposition to the oppressive rule of Sultan Abdul Hamid. An emerging sense of 'Turkish' national identity had by now made its appearance. The Young Turks were a product of the earlier reforms and the better education provided in schools modelled on Western lines. New recourse to texts in the Koran supporting the concept of government by discussion, combined with a new literary movement based on French models, created an atmosphere of change and progress. Thus the foundations were being laid for an eventual Turkish national state distinct from the Ottoman Empire. In 1906 the Young Turks established their headquarters at Thessalonika, where they formed the Committee of Union and Progress. Before long branches sprang up in neighbouring towns, and many Albanian members of the Young Turk Committee were at the same time members of the local committee of the Prizren League.

The influence of the Young Turk movement gradually extended throughout the army, until a general and spontaneous uprising heralded a military coup which overthrew the Sultan and brought the Young Turks to power in July 1908. The revolution was greatly assisted by Albanians, especially Kosovars, as the Young Turks promised to relieve the Albanians of their heavy burden of taxation and to award them full constitutional rights together with their traditional privileges. The Young Turks also gave assurances that Albanians would remain in possession of their arms and be allowed schools which taught in their own language, and that provincial autonomy was to be granted to the various nationalities. Elections for the new parliament were followed by the adoption of a constitution which ended the absolutist regime. Throughout the empire there was a general expectation that change was under way.

To the Albanians the proclamation of the constitution marked the beginning of a new era of freedom and equality. The *chetas* came down from the hills, many political exiles returned, and Albanian newspapers appeared in the variety of alphabets used to write the Albanian language. In general the Albanians had little confidence in the durability of the new regime, but saw it as a means to an end. In the new Young Turk parliament there were 26 Albanian deputies, the majority of whom were prominent figures with strong regional followings such as Ismail Kemal, Hassan Pristina and Essad Pasha Toptani. These deputies all worked for decentralization of government, and thus for a brief time the Albanians enjoyed Ottoman benevolence. Edith Durham, a friend of the Albanian cause with an attitude towards her chosen people that though benevolent could not conceal a typically European sense of superiority, described the promulgation of the Young Turk Constitution as follows:

> The mysterious unknown something that had come upon the land: It was the 27th of July and Scutari was all astir with the news of the Constitution. What, Where, How, When, Why? – no one knew ... all that was known was 'Constitution' ... It was not till August 2nd that Scutari formally accepted the Constitution. The crowd was largely Moslem, a Turkish official on a platform read an inaudible proclamation in Turkish (a tongue understood by very few) ... Then a Catholic Albanian, a schoolmaster, leapt up and spoke in Albanian – an impromptu address – and the people found voice: 'we are free' ... The impossible had happened. The pent up emotions of centuries burst forth, and the child-people were whirled away in a torrent of joy and hope.[1]

Not unreasonably, the Albanians thought 'constitution' meant a new era of justice. For twelve days there was feasting, dancing and celebrating. Durham watched 1,500 chosen representatives of all the Christian tribes march triumphantly through the streets of Shkoder to hail the constitution which was to give equal rights to all nationalities, Christian and Muslim alike. However, the Muslim tribes felt tricked by the constitution: 'Such freedom as they had retained under the Old Turk, they did not mean to be swindled out of by the Young.'[2] A mood of impatience soon prevailed. In the village of Kthela, Durham's guide explained to her before an applauding audience that 'so far, Konstitutzioon was a dead failure - It promised to give us roads, and railways, and schools, and to keep order and justice. We have had it two whole months and it has done none of these things. We have given our *besa* til St. Dimitri (six weeks hence), and if it has not done them by then – good-bye Konstitutzioon.'[3] Durham tried to explain at length the cost and the time it took to organize such things as schools, railways and the gendarmerie and that they would have to pay taxes for them. She received the reply: 'If Konstitutzioon is not rich enough to do these things, it can go to the devil – the sooner the better.' Durham attempted to explain the incomprehension among Albanians of what was happening: 'of this intangible, invisible Konstitutzioon, they understood and, could understand, nothing ... It is hard to be hurled from somewhere about the fourth century, at latest, into the twentieth, without one breathing space. I asked myself doubtfully whether Konstititzioon understood them any better than they did it.'[4]

Nevertheless, the new spirit of freedom did lead to a demand for material in the Albanian language. A congress was therefore convened on 14 November 1908 at Monastir, to approve an Albanian alphabet. It was chaired by Midhat Frasheri, nephew of the Frasheri brothers, and was attended by delegates from all over Albania and the Albanian colonies abroad. As the demand for Albanian national development and autonomy grew, the adoption of the Latin alphabet was seen as a way of uniting Christian and Muslim, Gheg and Tosk, and making them more conscious of their common heritage. Two currents finally emerged, the first favouring the Latin alphabet; the other supporting the Istanbul (Arabic) alphabet. Eventually it was agreed to adopt both alphabets – hardly an ideal solution, but one which at least enabled material published in the north to be read in the south and vice versa. The Young Turks naturally gave their backing to the Istanbul alphabet, and organized demonstrations in support of it. The primary aim of the Young Turks was to use the congress as a demonstration to the

European and Ottoman public that the Albanians were for the Constitution, were ready to defend it, and did not have separatist tendencies.[5]

It was difficult, however, to raise adequate funding for Albanian schools. The Muslims of north Albania, especially in Shkoder and Kosova, were reluctant to adopt a script that was not that of the Koran. They were also disinclined to see Albanian taught in the schools, for they recognized only Turkish as the official state language, even though the majority could not understand it. In general the northern Muslims were pro-Ottoman and pro-Islamic, and time and again this allegiance to the old order proved an obstacle to national development. They were regarded by most observers as the most backward and fanatical of all Albanian religious groups. In 1908 the Austro-Hungarian consul in Prizren, Prohaska, reported a poor response to the nationalist propaganda spread by the southern Tosks. The people were heavily influenced by the old clans and their leaders, who had little interest in the national issue. He did, however, report the existence of certain nationalist activities among younger students. In some areas, like Prizren, nationalist ideas were condemned because of a strong Ottoman influence; there an individual's Islamic beliefs were considered to be of far greater importance than his feelings of Albanian nationalism.[6]

By the end of the year, northern Albania was alive with the brewing hostility. The situation in Macedonia had deteriorated as Bulgarian insurgents increased their activities. In June 1908, as the Powers decided to revive the programme of reforms for Macedonia, the Young Turks saw a renewed threat to the empire, as the reforms might lead to an autonomous Macedonia, which would include Albanian territory, or eventually to its loss. Durham sensed the coming conflict: 'As I write the rough draft of this, in Scutari, at the end of November 1908, with war clouds thick on all frontiers, and discontent already smouldering against the Young Turks, the mountain men are seeing blood in all the bones.'[7] The region had become a hotbed of intrigue, and Shkoder swarmed with foreign consuls. Prizren, like Shkoder, was also a centre of conspiracy, with spies from every consul reporting on the actions of fellow diplomats. Durham observed from Prizren:

Each nation that designs to pick up the pieces when Turkey in Europe bursts up, keeps a Consul on the spot. A Russian represents Slav interests, to claim the land as Old Servia. An acute Austrian is posted there to forward his country's plan of 'Advance, Austria', and Italy has had to plant a man to see what he is doing.[8]

Initially the Young Turks carried out the promises they made, and at the end of 1908 they not only enacted electoral laws but also allowed elections to be held. However, it was not long before deep divisions appeared between the Albanians and the Young Turks. The electoral law of September 1908 had stipulated that the candidates should present themselves as Ottomans and have a knowledge of the Turkish language. This ruled out the majority of Albanians, whether Muslim or Christian. Nevertheless, as much as the Albanians distrusted the Young Turks they also feared a return of the old absolutist regime. The Albanians continued to advocate a greater decentralization within the empire and autonomy for their national regions, whilst the Young Turks adopted a series of measures designed to reinforce central power. A clash was therefore inevitable, because the Young Turks were totally opposed to nationalism within the empire and believed in an enforced Turkification of all subjects as a means to keep the empire strong and intact.

Austro-Hungarian and Italian plans for extending their influence in Albania were thwarted by the Young Turk revolution. Austria's main fear was that Serbia, under Russian patronage, would assimilate Bosnia–Hercegovina, thereby creating a Greater Serbia. Vienna saw the control of Bosnia–Hercegovina as absolutely essential to provide security for her Dalmatian coast, and also to curb Serbian and, more importantly, Russian influence. And so, on 5 October 1908, Austria–Hungary announced her annexation of Bosnia-Hercegovina. The diplomatic crisis which followed galvanized Russia into organizing the Balkan states to oppose the Habsburg monarchy. In Albania the Bosnian annexation prompted Muslim anger against both the Catholics (who were nominally under Austrian protection) and the Porte for submitting to it. In a feeble reaction to the annexation the Ottoman government boycotted all Austro-Hungarian goods, but as the bulk of Shkoder's imports came from Trieste the town and the surrounding area suffered severely. To quell Albanian misgivings at foreign intervention, Austria reassured the northern Albanians that she had no intention of annexing Albanian-inhabited land, and that as she considered the sanjak of Novi Pazar to be Albanian territory she would not allow other states to seize it at the expense of the Albanians. The Austrian foreign minister, Count Goluchowski, firmly believed that if the Balkan status quo could no longer be preserved, Austria–Hungary must insist on the possession of Bosnia, Hercegovina, and the sanjak of Novi Pazar (for Serbia and Montenegro must at all costs be kept

apart); a large Albanian state must be created; and Russia and Austria–
Hungary must later come to some agreement to ensure that no Balkan
state grew so big as to upset the Balkan balance.[9] Bulgaria had meanwhile taken the opportunity to declare her full independence from the
Ottomans.

All this diplomatic activity coincided with increased Greek guerilla
activity in Epirus, until it became obvious to all that the Porte now
had but a very dubious hold over its rebellious subjects. As the war
clouds grew ever thicker, the few Serbs still living in Kosova were
terrified of attacks by Albanians and were desperately trying to assert
their presence in the province. By then the Serbs were, but for small
pockets, to be found living only along the Serbian and Montenegrin
frontiers, consolidated in towns like Peja (Pec), Mitrovica and Beraria.
Whilst travelling in Kosova, Durham wrote of the Serb plight in the
district of Prizren:

> The school, a fine building, recently enlarged and repaired, holds a hundred
> students. Many come from Montenegro even. I went over it sadly. It seemed
> sheer folly to make a large and costly Serb theological school in a Moslem
> Albanian town, and to import masters and students, when funds are so
> urgently needed to develop free Serb lands ... The white castle of Tsar
> Lazar was but a dream in the night of the past. Around us in the daylight
> was the Albanian population, waiting under arms, to defend the land that
> had been theirs in the beginning of time...
>
> I felt that so far as Prizren and its neighbourhood were concerned, the
> cause was lost, dead and gone – as lost as is Calais to England and the
> English claim to Normandy ... And for I do not know how the manyeth
> time I cursed the Berlin Treaty, which did not award to this people the
> truly Serb lands of Bosnia and Hercegovina, where they could have
> gathered their scattered forces and developed, but gave them to be crushed
> under Austria.[10]

In Kosova the Serbs and Montenegrins remained in a distinct and
recognizably inferior position; even their houses were not permitted
to be more conspicuous or to overlook those of their Muslim neighbours. This fact was noted by Leon Trotsky, who was posted to the
Balkans in 1912 as war correspondent for *Pravda*. He wrote:

> The Albanian villages are much better, much richer than the Serbian ones.
> The Serbs, even the rich ones, don't build fine houses in villages where
> there are Albanians. If a Serb has a two-storey house he refrains from
> painting it so that it shan't look better than the Albanian houses.[11]

Durham summed up the Serbs' tenuous presence in Kosova and the Albanians' determination to rid the province of its remaining Slav element:

> The Albanians are almost solely Albanophone, whereas the scattered Serbs usually speak both languages and when addressed in Serb often replied at first in Albanian. Were it not for the support and instruction that has long been supplied from without, it is probable that the Serb element would have been almost, if not quite, absorbed or suppressed by this time ... Ineradicably fixed in the breast of the Albanian ... is the belief that the land has been his rightly for all time. The Serb conquered him, held him for a few passing centuries, was swept out and shall never return again. He has but done to the Serb as he was done by.[12]

Growing Opposition to the Young Turks

By the beginning of 1909 disenchantment with the Constitution had become widespread, as the new regime began to show its true nature. After consolidating their power, the Young Turks soon reneged on their promises to the Albanians and the empire's other subject peoples. The regime now planned to enforce a uniform Turkification of the various Ottoman dependencies. It became increasingly difficult to publicize non-Ottoman national ideas, or to discuss political affairs of any kind in the newly formed Albanian cultural clubs and societies. A notable exception was the British and Foreign Bible Society, which was begrudgingly permitted by the Sultan to translate and sell Bibles and Christian literature in Albania. The Society thus provided the only source of reading material in the Albanian language at the time of the Ottoman ban on all other printed material in the Albanian language. Durham describes the methods used by the Porte to silence nationalists: 'When Dervish Hima, a well known Albanian literary man, returned from Scutari after a long absence in Europe, he was arrested for speaking of the hopes of Albania and thrown into prison. There was no Albanian nation said the new government; all were Ottomans.'[13]

The general sense of disillusionment eventually led to open revolt, particularly in the north. Throughout the summer of 1909, the Kosova Muslim clans, led by Isa Boletini, rose in rebellion against the Young Turks for threatening to withdraw from them the very privileges the Sultan had recognized. They objected especially to the payment of new and higher taxes. The Porte had to send over troops of fifty thousand men to quell the uprisings. From then on the Kosovars became the most ardent opponents of the Young Turk regime. Initially the Young Turks, who regarded the Albanians as natural allies and supporters, did not realize the extent to which Albanian national sentiment had grown since the formation of the Prizren League, and were not aware of the appearance of a new, intelligentsia-inspired Albanian national consciousness which resented the Young Turks' notion of a centralized Empire. Albanian intellectual leaders such as Faik Konitza travelled throughout the country stressing the importance of union between Christians and Muslims. As a result, Albanians had gradually begun to see themselves not just as Muslim members of a Muslim empire, but also as members of an Albanian nation.

In September, another congress in Elbasan addressed further questions relating to issues of education and culture in Albania. It was attended by 35 delegates, all from central and southern Albania. The congress officially endorsed the Monastir decision to use the Latin alphabet rather than the Arabic script for written Albanian. Latin letters were considered more suitable than either Arabic or Greek characters, and were more readily learned. The Latin alphabet also corresponded to the sounds and consonants of the Albanian language more easily than the other scripts. Moreover, Albanian intellectuals were anxious to avail themselves of every opportunity to establish the individuality of their nation, to disassociate themselves from the perceived backwardness of the Ottoman Empire, and to bring themselves into closer contact with the West.[14] It was also decided to open a training college for teachers in Elbasan. This college, the first of its kind, opened on 1 December 1909. Albanians may have been 'free' to open as many schools as they wanted, but they were seriously hindered by lack of funds, by the several alphabets in use in Albania and by opposition from conservative Muslims. In Shkoder, Monastir and Elbasan, hodjas and mullahs condemned the use of the Latin alphabet as being against the interests of Islam. The divisions between Albanian patriots and the Young Turks widened as the Ottoman government did everything in its power to prevent the adoption of the Latin alphabet. The Young Turks could not remain indifferent to the prospect of new Albanian schools, and responded by closing down all Albanian newspapers, national clubs and schools in a determined effort to suppress Albanian nationalism.

The Greeks too sought to curtail the spread of nationalism amongst the southern Orthodox Albanians, not only in Albania but also in the

Albanian colonies in America. The Orthodox Albanians in the United States were very active in promoting national consciousness among Albanian-Americans, and in 1906 an Orthodox Albanian had founded the National Movement in America with the first publication of the newspaper *Kombi* (Nation) in Boston. These nationalist activities, however, ran contrary to the wishes of the Greek Patriarch in Istanbul, who threatened to excommunicate those Albanians who used their own language. In 1908 an Orthodox League was formed in Korca to resist the policy of Hellenization and interference in Albanian affairs pursued by the Patriarchate.[15] It was in the United States that the first Albanian Orthodox Church was founded, and on 22 March 1908, in the Knights of Honour Hall in Boston, the first liturgy in Albanian was celebrated, expedited by Greek obstruction. The previous year, a young Albanian had died in Hudson, Massachusetts, and the local Greek priest had refused to officiate at the funeral service, on the grounds that the young man was an Albanian nationalist and as such 'automatically excommunicated'. No other Orthodox priest being available in the neighbourhood, the deceased was buried without any religious service. The incident provoked indignation among the Albanians of Massachusetts, who held a meeting which decided to have an Albanian priest ordained. They invited Fan S. Noli to undertake the mission, and he hastened to accept it. Platon, the Russian archbishop of New York, ordained him priest on 8 March 1908, at the age of 26.[16] This young man was destined to play a leading role in Albania's interwar history.

Another major obstacle to the diffusion of Albanian national ideas and education was the sheer difficulty of physical communication. 'Balkan' is a Persian word meaning mountain, and much of Albania, like neighbouring Montenegro, was isolated from the rest of the empire in its mountain fastness. Travel was extremely difficult and often dangerous. As late as 1912 there were only around one hundred and fifty kilometres of paved roads, and these were mostly in the south of the country. The losses of Bosnia-Hercegovina and Bulgaria were a severe blow to the morale of the Young Turks, who after all had come to power to save the empire. Therefore, in April 1909, the empire's conservative old guard staged a brief counterrevolution which overthrew the Young Turks and restored the former absolutist regime. The organizers of the uprising believed they would find ready support among the northern Albanians, who resented the loss of their privileges under the Young Turks. Nevertheless, conservative as they were, these Albanians did not favour the return of Abdul Hamid, whom they claimed would hinder Albanian national and cultural development. The rising, which gained little support outside Istanbul, was soon crushed by Young Turk troops. Sultan Abdul Hamid was in turn deposed, and his younger brother Mahmoud, a tool of the Young Turks, was placed on the throne.

The Policy of Ottomanization

The Young Turks now hastened to propagate the idea of the unity of the peoples of the empire, under the name of 'Ottomanization'. In Thessalonika, the Committee of Union and Progress rushed through a series of measures, most of which severely curtailed the internal autonomy of the non-Muslim communities. The first step towards forcible Ottomanization of the Albanians was to deny their existence as such. But when, in the Ottoman Assembly, the minister of the interior declared that there was no Albanian nationality, he was fiercely contradicted by cries of 'Var, Efendim, Var!' ('There is, Efendi, there is') from the Albanian deputies present.[17] Extensive reorganization was planned for the armed forces, together with a uniform system of education throughout the empire. From now on Turkish was to be the main language of instruction in the higher schools for all nationalities. There was to be compulsory military service for all nationalities, plus a considerable increase in taxation to pay for all these expensive reforms. In May 1909, the Young Turks sent a military expedition to Kosova to suppress the resistance to census registration, which the Albanians saw as a prelude to compulsory military service and tax collection. However, the primary object of this expedition was the capture of the redoubtable Isa Boletini, who possessed supreme authority among the Albanians of the Kosova vilayet and was leading the resistance. Although the Ottomans razed Boletini's village to the ground, the chieftain himself had managed to escape. Of a meeting with this great leader at Mitrovitsa in August 1912, the British colonel Aubrey Herbert, who later involved himself in campaigning on behalf of Albania, wrote:

> We walked quickly through the streets outside the town to a *han* where Isa had come to meet me. He was surrounded by numbers of his wild Albanian mountaineers covered with weapons. I went into a fair-size room, where I found Isa Boletini, a very tall lithe, well-made Albanian, aquiline, with restless eyes and a handsome fierce face, in the Gheg dress.[18]

A number of new laws were now passed, designed to strengthen central authority, curb individual and collective freedoms, and crush any resistance movements. In November, the 'law on guerilla bands' was passed in Istanbul, making it punishable by death to belong to a *cheta*. The new law on associations declared that national societies could only exist if they refrained from any discussion of politics and engaged solely in cultural–literary pursuits. Thus the Young Turks strove to weaken the Albanian national movement. Amongst Albanians there was considerable opposition to the government's efforts to halt brigandage by disarming the northern tribesmen. Another major cause of the deteriorating relationship was the continuing conflict that arose over the Albanian alphabet. The Young Turks still insisted on the use of the traditional Arabic script, but in the spring of 1910, in the north as well as the south of Albania, there were huge popular gatherings in favour of the much simpler Latin alphabet. Albanians in general were by now utterly disillusioned, and throughout 1909 until the outbreak of the First Balkan War in October 1912, Albanian history is largely a chronicle of revolts and their suppression.

One of the most serious Albanian uprisings broke out in Pristina in March 1910, after the people refused to pay new and severe taxes levied from Istanbul on imported goods. The revolt soon spread to the whole of Kosova. The Porte replied by sending twenty thousand men, led by General Shefket Turgut, to Kosova to stamp out the rebellion and disarm the people. The severity with which the rising was suppressed – whole villages were burnt and Albanian leaders were flogged in public – only ensured the continuation of unrest.[19] After five months the Ottoman forces regained control of the vilayet, but many of the insurgents found refuge in Montenegro, and a considerable number of refugees followed them, putting Montenegro at risk of a conflict with the Porte. Although the Kosovars had been among the earliest supporters of the Young Turk revolution, they were soon compelled to defend their national integrity against it.

The Young Turks now instituted a reign of terror throughout Albania, prompting Russia to warn the Ottoman government not to extend hostilities against Montenegro. In March 1911 the Catholic tribes, together with the thousands of refugees from Kosova who had fled to Montenegro, staged a general insurrection. It began in the mountains north of Shkoder, and the Porte again sent an army commanded by General Turgut to crush the insurgents. The fighting raged along the Albanian–Montenegrin border, and Podgorica became the headquarters of the insurgents, due to the support the Albanians received from King Nicholas of Montenegro (he had assumed the title of King in 1910), who ensured they got the weapons they needed to continue the struggle. The situation suited the King, for apart from being bound by it to Montenegro, the Albanians would naturally be weakened by the continued fighting and thus be more willing to collaborate with Montenegro in its inevitable conflict with the Porte. Eventually Austria–Hungary, feeling her prestige at stake as protector of the Catholic Albanians, let the Porte know that she could no longer ignore the savage repression of the Catholic tribes and would have to take action if this continued. This was enough to halt the Porte. Fearful of Austrian intervention, it announced on 12 June 1911 that the Sultan himself was to visit Kosova, where he would grant a general amnesty to the Albanian insurgents. In the hope of containing the revolt and appeasing the population, Sultan Mehmet V signed a decree of amnesty and permitted the opening of Albanian-language schools. Having no more need to offer sanctuary to the insurgents, King Nicholas advised the Albanians to accept the Sultan's peace overtures and return to their burnt and pillaged homes.

Fearing that the events in Kosova could be repeated elsewhere, the Ottoman authorities turned their attention to central Albania. Here the population was forcibly disarmed, military tribunals were set up and heavy sentences were imposed on the hundreds of Albanians arrested for nationalist activities. The Albanian resistance movement was still for the most part dictated by local particularisms: as yet there existed no universally recognized Albanian authority to coordinate and direct the nationalist cause; and the tribes continued to act independently, at their own discretion and in defence of their own particular interests.[20] By the summer of 1911, living conditions in the north were grim, following the devastations of war which had displaced thousands of families. Edith Durham, with her own money, did her best to supply basic food and clothing to the destitute, some of whom were the same people who had offered her such warm hospitality on the 1908 journey on which she had acquired the name Kraljica e Malesorevit (The Queen of the Highlands). She wrote of the grinding misery of the sick, but also mentions how the traditional customs of the people themselves helped to cause unnecessary deaths:

> Infant mortality in north Albania is cruelly high. The child, tightly swaddled, lies always in a wooden cradle, over which is bound, with cords, a

thick and heavy woolen cover ... as thick as an ordinary hearthrug and shuts out almost all air. If the child be a healthy one it is taken out of doors and ... has plenty of fresh air, but if sickly it is released only from its prison by death. It is always indoors, the unhappy mother takes the most jealous care that not for a single moment shall it be uncovered. She even gives it suck by taking the whole cradle on her knee and lifting only the tiniest corner of the fatal cover. To touch it with water she thinks would be fatal. Filthy, blanched by want of light, and poisoned by vitiated air, the child fades and dies in spite of the amulets hung round its head and neck to ward off the Shtriga and Evil Eye.[21]

The First Balkan War and the
Establishment of the Albanian State

The dismemberment of the Ottoman Empire really began in earnest with Italy's declaration of war on the Porte in September 1911, in the hope of capturing Tripolitania (modern Libya). There Ottoman forces were easily defeated, since the province was largely undefended. The Porte could not send an expeditionary force, due to Italian control of the seas. Italian troops therefore had little difficulty in occupying the coastal area. Desperately in need of support, the Porte was obliged to enter into political negotiations with the Albanians. Sensing he had perhaps reached a point of no return, the Sultan retreated behind the high walls of his palace overlooking the Bosphorus in order to plot his survival amidst the atmosphere of revolutionary nationalism sweeping his disintegrating empire. The other Balkan states saw in the Porte's weakness a chance to realize their territorial designs on Ottoman territory. By the autumn of 1911, Albanian *cheta* composed of both Christians and Muslims were operating throughout the Albanian regions. The Serbian and Montenegrin governments worked actively to support these Albanian guerilla bands. In order to prevent a peace between the Albanians and the Porte which might result in the creation of an autonomous Albania, the Balkan states fomented revolts between Ottomans and Albanians. In fact, the newly formed Serbian secret organization, Ujedinjenje ili Smrt (Union or Death), popularly known as the Black Hand, offered Albanian leaders like Isa Boletini arms and money to encourage them to revolt. The Porte tried to appease the Albanians once again by promising financial support for Albanian cultural activities. But by now the repressive measures of the Young Turks and their broken promises had only increased the hold of nationalist and separatist ideas on the Albanians.

In March 1912 the Balkan states, seeing their best chance to realize their national ambitions, formed an alliance, agreeing to divide the European Ottoman possessions between themselves. The first accord, between Serbia and Bulgaria, agreed upon Serbia's annexation of Kosova and northern Albania but left much of Macedonia unassigned. This was followed in May by a treaty between Bulgaria and Greece against the Porte: yet another treaty was signed in October by Montenegro with both Serbia and Bulgaria.[22] So was formed the Balkan League, whose principal objective was the ejection of the Ottomans from Europe. Serbia's main concern was securing herself an exit to the Adriatic sea and protecting herself from the further expansion of Austria–Hungary into the Balkan peninsula. Through diplomatic manoeuvres Serbia was hoping to gain permission to construct an Adriatic railway from the Romanian border to the Albanian port of San Giovani de Medua. Another motivating factor in the formation of the Balkan League was the rise of Albanian national identity. The Balkan states feared the formation of an autonomous Albania which, in the event of the defeat of the Porte, would be far harder to carve up between themselves than it would be if it remained merely an Ottoman province. Their anticipation of the imminent defeat of the Porte was justified as it was at war with a major power, its army was unprepared, the government was torn by political strife and leaders were divided over numerous issues.

In the summer of 1912 Serbia and Montenegro sent messengers to invite the Albanian leaders to discuss the role Albania might play in the coming war against the Porte. Milan Milojevic, the Serbian consul in Pristina during the 1912 uprising, considered it a great error to treat the Albanian movement as an insignificant phenomenon in the context of the developing Balkan crisis. He saw that the Albanians had begun to establish an increasingly explicit notion of themselves as a separate people, and emphasized that this must be taken seriously.[23] The Kosovar leaders, Hassan Pristina, Isa Boletini, Bajram Curri and Bajram Daklani, needed little encouragement to call on the people to rebel. By then the north and much of central and southern Albania was already up in arms. Albanian soldiers began to desert in ever increasing numbers from the Ottoman army. The occupation of Skopje (Uskub) by nearly 30,000 rebels led by Isa Boletini caused alarm in Istanbul, as the Porte struggled to appease the Albanians in the face of imminent attack by the Balkan allies. By September all of Kosova as well as central and southern Albania were in the hands of the rebels.

As a result of the Albanian successes, the Ottoman administration was completely paralysed. The government in Istanbul was forced to resign in favour of Mouktar Pasha and his followers, who opposed the radical Turkification policies of the Committee of Union and Progress. The new Ottoman administration induced many Albanians to abandon their rebellion through promises of further reforms and free elections, though others with rather longer memories refused to moderate their demands. At the same time, however, Albanians feared the likely occupation of their lands by the Balkan states, should they prove victorious, and thus chose to stall for time whilst they built up their own arms. Consequently, they agreed to the Porte's offer to grant the non-Turkish populations the right to be governed by administrators who spoke their language. The leading Albanian intellectual Ismail Kemal, formerly a prominent official in the Ottoman administration, was aware that the preservation of Albanian territory depended upon the rivalry of the Great Powers. He believed that Austria–Hungary was the only potential defender of Albania. However, at that time Austria-Hungary was striving to maintain the status quo, and therefore advised the Albanians that their security was best assured by remaining within the Ottoman Empire. Austria, in particular, feared that the weakening of the Kosovars would strengthen Pan-Slavism, for Kosova stood as a buffer to Serbian expansion southward.

Meanwhile, to the complete surprise of both the Porte and the European Powers, on 8 October 1912 Montenegro suddenly opened hostilities with the Porte by attacking Albania. Serbia, Bulgaria and Greece then also declared war on the Porte. The Albanians hoped to follow a course of neutrality and non-engagement, but found this impossible as the Ottoman army collapsed faster than had been anticipated, and the Balkan allies marched deep into Albanian territory. Following the old dogma, 'Better the devil you know', the Albanians fought with the empire against the Balkan armies. The Porte, however, after the first reverses, attempted to use the Albanian detachments in order to protect its retreating armies – a strategy which helped to precipitate Albanian desertion from the front.[24] The outbreak of the First Balkan War saw the western flank of the Ottoman Empire relatively undefended, with the bulk of the Ottoman army deployed along the coastline of Asia Minor and Syria. Reluctantly the Powers had to acknowledge that the empire was on the point of collapse, and the status quo could no longer be maintained. Austria's concern intensified as she became aware of the extent of the crisis on her southern border. In the event of an Ottoman defeat, Austria contemplated occupying Kosova herself, as she had done Bosnia-Hercegovina, thereby preventing the union of Serbia and Montenegro.

As the Sultan desperately sought the mediation of the Great Powers, the Albanians finally came to terms with the fact that the Ottoman Empire was about to be ejected from Europe. Ismail Kemal travelled to Vienna and Budapest in search of diplomatic support from Austria–Hungary, and to plead for the national rights of the Albanian people and their country. Kemal knew the time had come to make a bid for independence before the Balkan allies took complete control of Albanian territory. In his memoirs he wrote: 'When the Balkan Allies declared war on Turkey and the Bulgarian armies were in occupation of Kirk-Kilise, while the Serbs had seized Uskub, I realized that the time had arrived for us Albanians to take vigorous measures for our own salvation.'[25] He returned to Albania, and after staying a few days in Durres arrived in Vlore on 26 November.

Austria–Hungary's principal concern was that Greece and Serbia would partition Albania at the Shkumbi river. Foreign Minister Berchtold stressed that in no circumstances must Serbia be allowed to expand to the Adriatic. Basically, this principle reflected the fear that a Serbian port might some day become a Russian port (or as Archduke Franz Ferdinand feared, an Italian port); the well-founded apprehensions of Vienna as to the effect on the southern Slavs of too great an increase in Serbia's prestige; and the desire to restrict Serbia's economic independence by forcing her to channel her drive to the sea through Austro-Hungarian territory.[26] Austria realized that only the creation of an independent Albania could now secure the Habsburg interests in the area. So with the diplomatic support of Vienna 83 delegates, both Christian and Muslim, from all over Albania gathered at the Congress of Vlore on 28 November 1912. Here, under very precarious circumstances, Skanderbeg's black-eagled emblem was raised, and the independent state of Albania was proclaimed.

At the same time, further up the coast, the Serbian armies were approaching the port of Durres and with it the realization of their ultimate goal of gaining an exit to the sea. The atrocities committed by the Serbs as they marched towards the Adriatic were recorded by numerous writers and journalists. The Serbian socialist writer, Dimitri Tucovic, wrote: 'The bourgeois press clamoured for a merciless extermination and the army executed the orders. The Albanian villages, from which the people had made a timely flight, were burnt down;

there were at the same time barbaric cremations in which hundreds of Albanian women and children were burnt alive.'[27] Leon Trotsky was given the following account by a Serbian army officer:

> The horrors actually began as soon as we crossed into Kosova, entire Albanian villages had been turned into pillars of fire, dwellings, possessions accumulated by fathers and grandfathers were going up in flames, the picture was repeated the whole way to Skopje. There the Serbs broke into Turkish and Albanian houses and performed the same task in every case: plundering and killing. For two days before my arrival in Skopje the inhabitants had woken up to the sight of heaps of Albanian corpses with severed heads. Among the mass of soldiers you see Serb peasants who have come from every part of Serbia on the pretext of looking for their sons and brothers. They cross the plain of Kosova and start plundering, from the area around Vranje the population has crossed over en masse into the Albanian villages to pick up whatever may catch the eye. Peasant women carry away even the doors and windows of Albanian houses.[28]

The Vlore government's position became ever more precarious as the Balkan Allies penetrated deeper into Albanian territory. As the Serbian army was approaching the Albanian coast, Austria–Hungary warned Serbia that she would not be permitted to occupy any Adriatic seaport. When the Greek navy attacked the Albanian port of Vlore on 3 December, both Austria and Italy told Greece that she would not be allowed to capture the town. Ever since the Berlin Conference of 1878, Albania had become the crucial southern meeting place of Austro-Italian collaboration and rivalry. Back in December 1900 the two countries had signed a special agreement on Albania, where both were busily developing their strategic, commercial and cultural interests. From 1911, Italy placed the real focus of her diplomacy in the Adriatic. Albania was of particular importance, as the Italians regarded Sazan island, which lay off the port of Vlore, as the 'Gibraltar of the Adriatic'. At the beginning of December 1912, Serbia and Montenegro agreed to an armistice with the Porte. Greece, however, refused, and her troops pressed on deeper into Albania. The collapse of political order in Albania raised the possibility of one of the Great Powers intervening and establishing itself in the area.

The Conference of Ambassadors

The future of Albania was discussed at the hastily convened Conference of Ambassadors held in London in December 1912. The

Conference, which was presided over by the British foreign secretary, Sir Edward Grey, debated three main issues: the international status of Albania; the organization of the new Albanian state; and the establishment of internationally acceptable frontiers. Although it was agreed in principle to support the establishment of Albania as a new political entity, the Conference nevertheless awarded the Balkan allies large areas of Albanian-claimed territory, regardless of its ethnic composition. A major part of northern and western Albania went to Serbia and Montenegro, while Greece received the large southern region of Chameria, leaving the Albanian state reduced to the central regions together with the town of Shkoder and its surrounding territory. Over half the Albanian population was thus left outside the borders of the new Albanian state. The fairness or otherwise of the frontiers can be judged by a speech made by Grey to the House of Commons on 12 August 1913, in which he openly stated that the basic objective of the agreement on the borders was to satisfy the Great Powers, but that many criticisms could be raised by anyone who really knew Albania and viewed the issue from the standpoint of that country.

The Conference decided to make Albania autonomous under Ottoman suzerainty, thus appeasing Austria–Hungary, which was determined to prevent a hostile power from replacing the Porte in Albania. An independent Albania, firmly under Austria's influence, could provide another counter to Serbia in the Balkans. Austria had already tried and failed to cripple Serbia's economy in the 'Pig War' of 1906–11, following Serbia's signature of a customs union with Bulgaria. Attempting to force Serbia to renounce the agreement, the Habsburgs closed their border to all Serbian livestock exports, most of which were pigs. The annexation of Bosnia-Hercegovina in 1908 had blocked Serbia's expansion northward, and the creation of an Albanian state in 1912–13 was to do the same with the path to the west, so that for Serbia the only real alternative was to move into Old Serbia and Macedonia, where Serbian claims would inevitably conflict with those of its new allies.[29] After 1908, Austria–Hungary's economic and political pressure on Serbia intensified, and the danger of further encirclement grew. Thus Serbia's foreign-policy goals were, first, to make a division of the Balkans between Russia and Austria–Hungary impossible; and, second, to prevent the emergence of an autonomous Macedonia which could then fall to Bulgaria. Albanian claims to lands as far east as Skopje and the Vardar valley therefore seriously endangered both Serbia's and Bulgaria's plans.

The Ambassadors' Conference found the fate of Shkoder particularly difficult to determine, as it was still under siege by Montenegrin
troops, who were backed diplomatically by Russia. On the one hand,
both Britain and Germany were convinced of the utter worthlessness
of the northern Albanian regions. Sir Arthur Nicolson, Permanent
Undersecretary of State for Foreign Affairs, wrote to the British
ambassador in St Petersburg:

> I quite agree with you that the question of Scutari [Shkoder] will be a
> troublesome one. Strictly speaking it should logically no doubt belong to
> Albania, but Russia makes so strong a point of it being ceded to Monte-
> negro we intend to support her for that purpose. To my mind it is a matter,
> selfishly speaking, of perfect indifference to us as to who should be the
> possessor of Scutari, but it is of great importance that we should adopt no
> line which would in any way weaken or impair our understanding with
> Russia.[30]

Austria, however, argued vehemently that Shkoder's inclusion in the
new state was essential to Albania's economy. In response to German
pressure not to jeopardize the Conference Austria made a series of
concessions, until Russia finally agreed to the inclusion of Shkoder in
Albania. Russia, moreover, was adamant that the purely Albanian town
of Gjakova was to remain in Serbia, as public opinion in Russia was
deeply anti-Austrian, and had rallied to the support of their fellow
Orthodox Slavs. For weeks the peace of Europe hung upon the fate of
Gjakova, a small Kosovar market town, which Austria claimed for
Albania and Russia for Serbia.[31] The town itself appeared to be of
dubious benefit to Serbia, being described by one visitor as 'the most
primitive, not to say primeval, town in the least civilized of European
countries, but the Serbs insisted that it was an integral and important
part of old Serbia'.[32]

The Siege of Shkoder

The Powers were now faced with the problem of how to dislodge the
Montenegrins from Shkoder, as by virtue of a treaty concluded with
Essad Pasha Toptani, Montenegro had gained control of the town.
Essad Pasha was a member of an influential Muslim family who owned
extensive property around Tirana. His reputation as an opportunist
with a voracious appetite for power was acknowledged throughout
Albania, and even among his allies the Serbs. Before 1912, Essad had
been an officer in the Ottoman army. He was a deputy to Hussein

Riza Pasha, the Commander of Shkoder, whom Essad murdered in an ambush whilst the Ottoman army was surrounding the town in 1912. He thus got command of Shkoder, securing his position by signing the treaty with Montenegro. According to Edith Durham, who was in Shkoder at the time,

> After Hussein Riza had supped with Essad, he was shot dead a few yards away from the house by two men disguised as women. Osman Bali and Mehmed Kavaja, both servants of Essad, boasted afterwards they had done the deed. The town crier proclaimed that nothing was to be said about the murder, and Essad now took command and soon entered into communications with the Montenegrins.

Durham went on to describe the terms of the agreement made between Essad and the Montenegrins over the control of Shkoder:

> Provided he [Essad] evacuated the town in time for Montenegro to occupy it before the Powers could stop it, he was to leave with all honours and a large supply of arms and food. He was also to aid the Serbs to reach Durazzo [Durres] later, and as a reward was to be recognized as ruler in his own district of Tirana.[33]

Another English observer who knew Essad described him as

> one of the most unscrupulous adventurers who has ever achieved political notoriety. While in command of the Ottoman gendarmerie at Janina, he won an unenviable reputation by taking advantage of his position to enrich himself, and advance his personal ends, at the expense of his fellow countrymen. After the revolution of 1908 he was sent to Shkoder in the same capacity, and while there professed ardent nationalism; but he was universally disliked and distrusted even by his own tenants around Tirana.[34]

The situation in northern Albania became increasingly unstable, as Serbian troops entrenched themselves in the Mirdite region and Shkoder continued to be held by the Montenegrins. Conditions in the city and the surrounding area were quite desperate.[35] In 1913 an international committee including three Nobel prizewinners reported from northern Albania on the 'burning down of houses and villages, murders of disarmed and innocent people, unheard of violence, plundering and brutality of all sorts. These are the means used by the Serbo-Montenegrin troops in order to completely change the ethnic character of regions exclusively inhabited by Albanians.'[36] On 5 May, Essad Pasha announced through Cetinje that in order to assist the Balkan Alliance he would proclaim himself Prince of Albania, on condition that he receive political and financial backing for his plans, and that he would fortify Albania's borders. The Serbian prime minister, Nikola Pasic, accepted this initiative, yet he opposed Essad Pasha's mention of borders since he felt that this would create difficulties and lead to intervention by the Great Powers. Essad then held a meeting in Durres with a Serbian emissary, Zivojin Balugdzic, at which he expressed his interest in reaching an agreement with Serbia. Essad failed to realize his plans, yet holding on to his power in central Albania he demonstrated his continued support for the Balkan allies and for Serbia in particular.[37]

Austria–Hungary, meanwhile, was making tremendous efforts to bring Essad Pasha closer to the Vlore government, thereby hoping to avoid a territorial division of Albania. As the diplomatic manoeuvres intensified, martial law was proclaimed in Bosnia-Hercegovina. Austria–Hungary, adamant that Montenegro should evacuate Shkoder, prepared to march south towards the city. The Powers eventually decided that a combined naval blockade at Antivari (Bar) was now necessary to force the Montenegrins to stop the massacres of Albanian civilians in Shkoder and vacate the city. On 26 April 1913, the Conference of Ambassadors notified King Nicholas that his forces had to leave Shkoder. Four days later came indications that, in return for adequate compensation, the Montenegrins would relinquish the city. Both the probability of compensation and fear of Austrian action forced the King to acquiesce in placing Shkoder in the hands of the powers. On 15 May the city passed to the British Royal Navy. With the surrender of Shkoder the Montenegrins' participation in the First Balkan War came to an end. During the summer the Powers arranged a loan of 6 million francs as a reward for the King, who had rightly feared their intervention. Thousands of Montenegrins had already died in the fighting, his people were weary, they longed for peace, and the fields of their tiny country had to be harvested.

As the crisis subsided, Austria was exasperated, having had her prey snatched from her at the last moment. The international fleet, however, remained anchored off the Montenegrin coast. On 26 May, a visit was made to Admiral Burney, commander of the international fleet, by 130 of the principal men of the Malissori tribes – the Hoti, Gruda, Klementi, Skreli and Kastrati. Their object was to petition Burney to use his influence to prevent the Hoti and Gruda tribes from being severed from their 'Five-Banner Group' and incorporated in Montenegro. They warned that unless the five tribes were allowed to remain entirely Albanian, blood would continue to flow. Burney replied that their petition would be laid before the Ambassadorial Conference in London.[38] At the end of May 1913, after seven months of constant warring, the Powers finally compelled the Balkan states to stop fighting and to accept the terms of the Treaty of London, under which the Porte would renounce all its European territories west of a line drawn between Enos on the Aegean and Midia on the Black Sea. One result of this was that Thessalonika and the island of Crete went to Greece.

The Second Balkan War

The importance of the Ottoman losses in the First Balkan War cannot be overstated. It was a disaster in human, economic and cultural terms. As in 1878, Istanbul was deluged with Muslim refugees who had lost everything. But the significance went even deeper: the areas lost (Macedonia, Albania, Thrace) had been core areas of the empire for over five hundred years. They were the richest and most developed provinces, and a disproportionate part of the Ottoman ruling elite originated from them. Thessalonika, after all, had been the cradle of the Committee of Union and Progress.[39] Thus Ottoman Europe was reduced to Istanbul and the surrounding territory.

The Balkan League was doomed to break up once the empire had been defeated. Rival claims prevented Bulgaria from agreeing a territorial settlement with Greece over Thrace, Thessalonika and southern Macedonia. In addition, Bulgaria saw Serbia as the chief obstacle to the realization of her aspirations in the rest of Macedonia, as both countries' claims collided in the region. The proposed division of Ottoman territory had allocated to Serbia the land north of the Sar mountains, while Bulgaria was to receive all regions east of the Struma river and the Rhodope mountains. This left the majority of Macedonian territory unassigned.

Negotiations at the Ambassadors' Conference were continually frustrated by the Serbs and Greeks, who had obvious interests in preventing a definite peace with the Porte, thus ensuring that large numbers of Bulgarian troops would be tied down covering the Ottoman army and so could not be used in Macedonia. Both Serbia and Greece were frustrated by the creation of Albania, which they had hoped to partition between themselves. They therefore sought compensation in Macedonia, leading in turn to a confrontation with

Bulgaria. The Serbian prime minister, Nikola Pasic, suggested that because of Serbia's loss of northern Albania, the original zonal divisions of Macedonia be redefined, but Bulgaria demanded strict adherence to the territorial division agreed upon in 1912. If Bulgaria were allowed to retain central Macedonia, she would adjoin Albania, leaving Greece at the mercy of a Bulgarian–Albanian alliance to the north, whilst the Serbs would now have two frontiers between them and the Aegean. Only if Bulgaria waved her claim to central Macedonia could Serbia be compensated. This the Bulgarians would not do, well knowing that the master of the Vardar valley is the master of the Balkan peninsula.[40]

The uncertain outcome of the First Balkan War, therefore, made a Second Balkan War a virtual certainty. Fearing Bulgaria as their chief competitor, Serbia and Greece secretly agreed on the division of Macedonia between themselves. Bulgaria, wary of Russia's pro-Serbian stance over Macedonia, concluded that another war was inevitable and that it was better to fight now rather than later. Bulgaria, however, hopelessly misjudged the situation, and was convinced she could win a swift military victory by attacking Greece and Serbia. At dawn on 30 June 1913, with no formal declaration of war, Bulgarian troops attacked the Serbian and Greek armies in Macedonia. This was a disastrous mistake, as Romanian, Montenegrin and Ottoman troops also quickly entered the war against the Bulgarians. Following a fierce battle with Serbian troops at Bregalnica, Bulgaria was forced to capitulate. The Bulgarians thus had sacrificed nearly all their gains made in the first war. In the peace treaty made with the Balkan allies in May 1913, the Porte renounced all rights to Albania, and in June the last Ottoman troops left Albanian soil after five hundred years of occupation.

The conclusion of the Second Balkan War still left fundamental issues to be resolved. Macedonia remained a continual source of discord among the Balkan states; the new Albanian state failed to encompass all the areas predominantly inhabited by Albanians; and Serbia remained cut off from the Adriatic. Serbia was now acutely anxious about her economic survival, and thus rail links with the port of Thessalonika became her most pressing concern. It was therefore essential that the rail connection to Thessalonika, via Skopje, be under Serbian control. Although a new Balkan bloc was needed to keep Austria in check, once the Ottoman Empire had been defeated there was nothing left to hold the League together. The Treaty of Bucharest, concluded on 10 August 1913, provisionally settled the contest over the division of the Albanian and Macedonian territories. The terms were, as could be expected, extremely damaging to Bulgaria. Adrianople and most of eastern Thrace reverted to Ottoman control, Romania took southern Dobrudja, Greece extended her border to about fifty miles north of Thessalonika and eastward beyond the port of Kavalla. In the west, Greece annexed Epirus including Janina. Serbia almost doubled in size, with the acquisition of the major portion of Slavic Macedonia.[41] The Second Balkan War so embittered relations among the former allies that conditions became even more explosive than in preceding years. The Ottoman Empire and Bulgaria hungered for revenge, making them easy prey for alliance with Austria and Germany. For the Albanians, the actions of the Young Turks had propelled and accelerated their national movement, which otherwise might have taken another fifty years to mature. For the first time, rather than fight for just local privileges, Albanians were compelled to join in a united struggle on a national level against the territorial aspirations of their Balkan neighbours.

4

The Reign of Prince Wied
and the First World War

Those Balkan peoples ... unfortunately make more history than
they can consume locally.

Saki (H.H. Munro)

Now that the Balkan wars were over, serious discussion had to begin
over the future of the new Albanian state. In the spring of 1913 the
London Ambassadors' Conference finally concluded its plans for the
country. Albania was to be neutralized; it was to remain under
Ottoman suzerainty at first and, after some years, to be granted full
independence. Before long, however, it became obvious that the Porte
would eventually lose all of Macedonia and therefore its territorial
connection with Albania. It was thus deemed necessary to grant
Albania full independence under a constitutional monarchy which
would be guaranteed by the Powers. The Treaty of London of 30
May 1913 formally recognized an independent Albania, but the final
settlement of the frontiers of the new state was postponed. The Powers
found themselves faced with the impossible task of reconciling the
competing claims of the victorious Serbs, Greeks and Montenegrins,
with those of the Albanian population.[1] In August, an International
Commission of Control was announced. Its primary duty was to draw
up a constitution and fundamental laws, following an investigation of
local conditions. A gendarmerie, under officers selected from one of
the smaller neutral powers (Holland), and a foreign prince, were to be
chosen by the Great Powers.[2] Ismail Kemal, who headed Albania's
provisional government at Vlore, argued that Elbasan should be the
new Albanian capital, owing to its central location and to its dialect,

77

which shared the characteristics of both Gheg and Tosk. However the Powers refused to recognize Kemal's government until Albania's borders had been formally recognized. Instead, the International Control Commission secured control of Shkoder for Albania.

The Allocation of Albania's Frontiers

The Albanian frontier issue was particularly complex, because the Balkan allied troops were still in possession of the regions in dispute. A Northern Albanian Frontier Commission was appointed by the Ambassadors to survey the region and to make recommendations regarding the Albanian–Serbian–Montenegrin frontiers. An Albanian delegation representing the provisional Albanian government claimed from the Frontier Commissioners much more territory than they could possibly have expected to get. They proposed for the new frontier a line following the then existing Montenegrin frontier to its easternmost point, and thence onwards so as to include the towns of Peja (Pec), Mitrovitsa, Pristina, Uskub (Skopje) and Monastir with their hinterlands. The line then extended to a point south of Lake Prespa, from which it turned almost due south, leaving Kastoria on the east to Greece, and reaching the Greek frontier a little east of Metzovo. For the rest, the line followed the then existing Greek frontier down to the Gulf of Arta.[3] The frontier proposed by Austria followed the Albanian claim very closely. The Powers, however, not wanting to anger Russia, who supported the Serb and Greek claims, did not feel it prudent to adopt the Albanian claim. Instead, they compromised with a delimitation halfway between the Austrian proposal and that of the Balkan allies. The Powers' boundary allotted Peja, Gjakova, Prizren, and Diber (Debar) to Serbia, despite the knowledge that apart from Shkoder these were the only market towns for the north Albanian population. Although Greece was awarded the town of Janina, she still coveted the towns of Sarande, Girokaster and Korca, where several thousand ethnic Greeks continued to live.

In the autumn of 1913, Serbia was hoping to present the Powers with a *fait accompli* by her reoccupation of more Albanian territory, thus forcing a rectification of the proposed frontier. As the Serbs marched further into the Albanian regions, there was a general uprising of the local population against the atrocities committed by the advancing Serbian soldiers. In a letter to a friend, a bewildered young Serbian soldier wrote of his horror at what was happening:

> I may say that Ljuma [an Albanian region along the river of the same name] no longer exists. There is nothing but corpses, dust and ashes. There are villages of a hundred and fifty, two hundred houses, where there is no longer a single man, literally *not one*. We collect them in bodies of forty to fifty, and then we pierce them with our bayonets to the last man. Pillage is going on everywhere. The officers tell the soldiers to go to Prizren and sell the things they have stolen.[4]

As reports reached the powers of the renewed Serbian advances, Austria–Hungary concluded that an ultimatum should be presented to Serbia, ordering her withdrawal. A note to this effect was dispatched to Belgrade. Following the Romanian government's notification to Belgrade that it could not support Serbia in a conflict with Austria, Serbian troops eventually withdrew from Albania on 25 October 1913.

Neither economic, cultural nor ethnographic arguments were to determine the fate of southern Albania. Although Austria was determined to halt Greek claims to the Korca region, Britain had no real interest in the area. Vansittart, a Foreign Office clerk, minuted that his government did not have 'much feeling about southern Albania one way or another', adding that 'Albania will not last long anyhow and it's not worth fighting about'.[5] Greece had emerged from the Balkan wars with a heightened sense of achievement, and a determination to try to secure southern Albania for Greece. The national programme in Greece was expressed by the Megali Idea, or Great Idea, a plan of expansion which would include all Greeks within a single Greek state, as well as entailing the revival of the Byzantine Empire, together with the acquisition of Constantinople as the capital rather than Athens. Although the lands to be joined in this empire were not closely defined, they usually included Epirus, Thessaly, Macedonia, Thrace, the Aegean islands, Crete, Cyprus, the west coast of Asia Minor, and the territory between the Balkan and Rhodope mountains. The emphasis was not on territory that was ethnically strictly Greek, but rather on the lands in which Hellenic civilization was believed to be predominant.[6]

In October the Epirote insurrection broke out, as Greek volunteers and Cretan irregulars raided southern Albania, terrorizing its inhabitants by burning their villages. The Greek objective was to set up an autonomous Vorio Epirus (Northern Epirus, Chameria to the

Albanians), in an attempt to sabotage the international discussions being held in Florence on the future status of the region. Eventually, as in the north, an International Frontier Commission was set up to decide the Greek–Albanian border. This was hampered by over-enthusiastic Greek propagandists, trying to prove a case for Greek occupation of Albanian-inhabited regions. An apparently typical Greek ploy was described by a Captain Leveson Gower who travelled in Albania in 1913. He noted:

> The Boundary Commission come by night to a certain village, they are accosted by a man speaking Greek and they hear the ringing of an apparently Orthodox bell. Surely they must believe such irrefutable evidence? Unluckily one of the *kavasses* [armed guard] of the party comes from this village and he assures the Commission that not only are there no Greeks in the village, but there is not even a church there. It is discovered that the Greeks have rigged up an impromptu belfry in a tree top and are ringing lustily to hood wink the representatives of Europe.[7]

The desperate protestations by the Greeks only served to heighten the impatience of the Powers over the unsettled frontier issue. Finally, in December 1913, the Powers agreed on the terms of the Protocol of Florence, whereby, in return for Serbia's retreat from Albanian territory, Austria reluctantly agreed that the districts including the towns of Peja, Prizren, Gjakova and Diber should be formally ceded to Serbia. Greece received the large southern region of Chameria (Epirus). The Florence Line that decided the frontiers of the new Albanian state satisfied neither the Albanians nor their Balkan neighbours. Serbia was deprived of an Albanian port, Montenegro lost the town of Shkoder, and Greece had to relinquish southern Albania including the towns of Korca, Girokaster and Saranda. Following the establishment of the Florence Line, some Greek troops began to withdraw from Chameria. Greek guerilla bands, however, remained as active as ever. The Albanian school at Korca was still closed, by order of the Greeks who occupied the town.[8] On 2 March 1914, a short-lived provisional government of Vorio Epirus, extending its influence over Chameria, Sarande, Delvina and Girokaster, was set up and presided over by the former Greek foreign minister, Christaki Zographos. Nevertheless, Prime Minister Venizelos believed the region was irretrievably lost to Greece, and therefore told the Greek assembly to ignore the activities of Zographos. Venizelos realized his country's vulnerable situation, threatened as it was by the Ottomans and Bulgaria. He therefore ordered all Greek troops to return to Greece, and on 18 June, Sazan island and northern Epirus were formally ceded to Albania. Edith Durham went to great lengths, however, to inform the British Foreign Office that the Greeks had not totally evacuated the occupied districts. She later wrote:

> The army departed from Koritza [Korca], but left a so-called hospital of wounded 'not fit to be moved', and joined it to the Greek frontier by telephone. Much of the army, however, remained in out-of-the-way spots, removing and concealing their insignia, so that the Greek government might be able to deny that they were soldiers ... Had the Powers meant honestly by Albania they would have sent a force to clear the land of the lurking Greek bands of soldiery. But in spite of several questions asked in the House of Commons, Cretan and Greek *komitadjis* [guerilla bands] continued to land at Saranda, the Greek government persistently denying all knowledge.[9]

For a long while after the Powers had agreed upon the northern boundary of Albania, Serbian troops had remained on Albanian soil, ignoring the various ultimatums to withdraw. The northern Albanian tribes rose once more in revolt against Albanian-inhabited land being transferred to Serbia and Montenegro. They protested at their exclusion from age-old market centres in Serbia, which were reached by an ancient trade route that ran from Shkoder to Gjakova and on to Prizren. The continuous violation of the frontier by the Albanians was caused by the fact that when the Serbs withdrew from Albania on orders from the Powers, they took with them livestock belonging to the Albanians, who then pursued their animals over the border. It was in Serbia's interest that unrest should continue to prevail in northern Albania, thereby preventing the new state from becoming a viable entity. The Serbs strove to obtain a pro-Serbian government in Albania, and actively encouraged Essad Pasha to become ruler of Albania. Essad, however, was in a dilemma as to which of the three interested governments would help keep him in power: the Porte, Italy or Serbia? It must be remembered that at the time Essad, like many others, was not at all sure if, or for how long, Albania could remain an independent state. He gathered round him a group of discontented Muslim priests disgruntled by Ismail Kemal's reforms that threatened their privileges, and proclaimed himself the saviour of Albania and the champion of Islam. He then announced his intention to overthrow the provisional government, declaring that central Albania desired a Muslim sovereign. Between Durres and Tirana, notably at Bazar Shjak, there were large settlements of Muslim

Bosniaks who, during the two preceding centuries, had for various reasons fled from Bosnia and sought refuge in this region.[10]

According to the Russian consul in Belgrade, Serbia had come to an understanding with Essad. He described the Serbian plan as follows:

> The impecunious Essad Pasha will be sent money, the military plan calls for the complete annihilation and dispersion of Ismail Kemal, Isa Boletin and their friends, whereupon Essad Pasha will be set up as governor-general at Vlore. The latter, with whom the Serbian government has been in touch for some time, is prepared to recognize the suzerainty of the Sultan as is shown by his flag with the Eagle and half-moon. He is also willing to undertake a boundary rectification, in accordance with Serbia's wishes, up to the Black Drin. At the request of Essad this surrendered territory will be occupied, supposedly temporarily, by Serbian troops in order to maintain order. After establishing his power Essad will have himself proclaimed Prince of Albania.[11]

The isolated Kemal government would not have been able to rely for support upon the majority of the northern, predominantly Catholic tribes, who felt they had been neglected by the Vlore government in favour of the influential central and southern landowners and towndwellers. The loosely knit highland tribes remained jealous of their independence, and were as unwilling to surrender to a national government as they had been to do so to the Porte. The Young Turks, for their part, still had hopes of restoring Ottoman suzerainty over Albania. They therefore sent agents to encourage an insurrection among those who were disaffected with the provisional government. Before any disaffected Albanians could be enticed to revolt, however, the Young Turk plot was discovered by Ismail Kemal's agents; one of the Porte's chief representatives, Major Beqir Grebnaly, was subsequently executed. The Powers were angered by this display of independence by Kemal's government, which they deemed provocative and damaging to the delicate diplomacy in which they were engaged. As a result, the International Commission forced Kemal to step aside. Kemal subsequently left Albania and later died in Perugia, Italy, on 26 January 1919.

The Reign of Prince Wied

When deciding on the choice of a prince for Albania, the Powers followed the pattern they had set in Greece, Bulgaria and Romania, by selecting a German. In November 1913, Prince William of Wied –

third son of William Prince of Wied, and Mary, Princess of Holland
– was nominated as their candidate for the throne of the new Albanian
principality. To many Albanians, the appointment of Wied was tangible
evidence of the European Powers' recognition of and support for the
new Albanian state. The 35-year-old prince, however, was completely
unaware of the danger of his new position. According to Edith
Durham, who observed the affair in detail,

> The true reason for his [Wied's] unanimous selection was probably that
> the Powers, who had planned Albania's destruction, knew him to be a man
> of little ability, and therefore the more easily to be got rid of. France and
> Russia were combined to overthrow him, even while agreeing to his elec-
> tion. When Greece and Bulgaria were respectively liberated and put under
> a foreign Prince, he was given in each case, sufficient military force to
> maintain order until a native army could be organized. In the case of
> Albania it was arranged that he should be provided with no armed force –
> otherwise he would be difficult to evict.[12]

Wied's naivety concerning Balkan affairs and diplomacy was quickly
appreciated by the many who conspired against him. On 21 February
1914 Essad Pasha headed a deputation of Albanian notables to
Neuwied, to offer Wied the crown. The same month the Powers guaranteed a loan of £3 million to give the new state a start, of which
£500,000 was advanced by Austria and Italy to the prince, and a small
international force under an English officer was stationed at Shkoder.
There matters ended. No constitution ever saw the light, and Prince
Wied himself, though he began by forming a cabinet, never governed
outside Durres.[13] Almost immediately fighting broke out between supporters of Kemal and Essad, as opportunists from both camps schemed
to take advantage of the prince's weakness. It was not only Albanians
that Wied had to be wary of: the Italians, who regarded the Prince as
too pro-Austrian, also openly intrigued against him and found ready
collaborators among ambitious Albanians who themselves aspired to
the throne. By establishing himself at Durres instead of Shkoder,
Wied was virtually at the mercy of Essad Pasha. During his hapless
reign he barely ventured outside the town of Durres, and remained
there as a virtual prisoner. Wied's first cabinet was composed of men
who had not been prominent in the national movement. Much to the
dismay of many Albanians, one of his first acts was to appoint Essad
to the key post of minister of national defence, which was the
collective title for the heads of the Ministry of the Interior and the
Ministry of War, thus giving him control over armaments.

It was now widely believed that Essad Pasha was seriously conspiring with the Serbs. One foreign observer wrote:

> Henceforth, there were calls from the Powers and nationalist Albanians for action to be taken against Essad, who was now quickly trying to raise an army of supporters. He found ready recruits amongst the Bosnian Muslims of Bazar Shjak, who believed that Prince Wied intended to deport them to Turkey because of their fanaticism. Those who had worked to provoke an upheaval now proclaimed that the universal *besa* given to, and by the Prince had been broken, an unpardonable crime, and central Albania rose in revolt with the intention of evicting those responsible for it.[14]

In mid-May, as the insurgents advanced on Durres, Essad was arrested in the port by the Austrians. They believed him to be implicated in a revolt which would ultimately have dethroned Wied. Convinced that Essad was a traitor, the prince, with Austrian backing, had him deported to Italy – the government of which had, he believed, been subsidizing Essad's activities to strengthen their influence in central Albania. The removal of Essad brought to the fore the rivalry between Italy and Austria–Hungary for influence in Albania. The Italian government denied any involvement with either the peasant disturbances in Tirana or Essad's supposed plans to topple Wied. Italy had managed, in a modest but subtly influential manner, firmly to establish her cultural policy in Albania. Italian was widely spoken in the central and southern coastal regions, and by the spring of 1914 the Italian school in Durres had four hundred and fifty pupils. However, due to the unstable political situation in Italy itself, the Italian authorities had no wish at this time to cause or abet any disturbances in Albania, for which they would have to send troops better needed to quell possible domestic unrest.

To counter Italian influence in Albania, the Austrian government established a strongly anti-Italian 'Albanian Committee' in Vienna. This organization strove to promote Austrian interests in Albania by cultivating ties with the Catholic tribes and creating an Austrophile atmosphere in Durres. Essad's anti-Austrian sympathies were well-known. But whereas Italy had no immediate reason for wishing to dispense with Essad, Austria–Hungary desired to get rid of him because of his connections with Serbia and the desire of Vienna to establish a stronger presence in Durres, with a view to possible military intervention should Wied's regime collapse. The artillery that had pounded Essad's house the night of his arrest had been operated by Austrian officers, and the Austrians had been very reluctant to hand over Essad from their ship, the *Szigetvar*, to an Italian ship.

The political chaos and unabated rebellions did not, however, subside with the departure of Essad. In fact the situation deteriorated, as Ottoman agents further convinced the peasants of Shjak that Wied was anti-Muslim. In order to contain the trouble the Dutch-controlled gendarmerie hastened towards Tirana, where they fired on a crowd of peasants whom they believed to be demonstrators, killing several. This attack incensed the population of Shjak and Tirana, who, after managing to disarm the gendarmerie, began to march towards Durres. As the angry crowd neared the capital, Austrian officers bombarded them. News of the Austrian assault caused the remainder of central Albania to rise up in arms, convinced more than ever of Wied's 'treachery' to Albania. According to the Austrian government, these Austrian 'officers' were in fact volunteers recruited by the 'Albanian Committee' in Vienna, but employed by the Albanian government. The chaotic situation eventually exhausted Prince Wied's finances, patience and stamina. This naïve young man was totally lacking in administrative experience, and the difficulties in governing Albania, of which he knew nothing, proved insurmountable. On 3 September 1914, just six months after his arrival, Prince William of Wied left Albania, never to return.

Once installed, Wied had been all but abandoned by the Powers, despite numerous appeals for help. His shortcomings had been apparent from the first. Yet though he was universally blamed for his incompetency, only a man of unusual force of character and intimate knowledge of Albania could have made any progress against all the forces combined against him. Barely a week after Wied's departure yet another violent revolt, this time led by supporters of the Young Turks, laid siege to Durres. The rebels raised the Ottoman flag, imprisoned Wied's supporters and called for, among other things, a Muslim prince. Having achieved this much, the insurgents set up a Senate for Central Albania. They then sent a delegate to Istanbul to offer the Sultan the crown of Albania. There were still those who supported the idea of the reunion of Albania with the Ottoman Empire. Central Albanian peasants remained Muslims; as such they were, in many instances, easy prey for the Ottoman propaganda that proclaimed the government was but a tool of the Christian powers. Nevertheless, the vast majority of northern and southern Albanians disassociated themselves from the actions of the Senate. It could not yet be said that they wished to assert their 'national' identity in a European context, for such a notion was still embryonic. The Albanian population in general was simply weary of the incessant uprisings and general instability that had become the main feature of their lives, and which they associated with the domination of the Ottoman Empire.

The First World War

Before Albania's borders could be formally agreed, the Austrian Archduke Franz Ferdinand and his wife were assassinated by a Serb student in Sarajevo on 28 June 1914. There followed Austria's declaration of war on Serbia a month later, which in turn led to the outbreak of the First World War. The period between the end of the Balkan Wars and the beginning of the First World War had seen Albania's frontiers fixed in theory but not in practice. The outbreak of war gave the neighbouring countries an opportunity to seize what land they could, amidst the confusion of rapidly mobilizing armies throughout the region. The Southern Boundary Commission had managed to submit its report in December 1913, but the Northern Commission did not finish its work until June 1914. The news that Austria–Hungary had declared war on Serbia was received with satisfaction throughout Albania. This was especially true in the north, where the population had persistently petitioned Austria–Hungary for support against Serbian and Montenegrin territorial aspirations. The Albanians had been prepared to fight for the Entente – providing their independence was guaranteed and the 1913 frontier was revised to restore Kosova to Albania. This, however, was considered too high a price to pay by Serbia, who was backed by her protectors Russia and France. The Serbs continued to regard Albania as an abortive creation which deprived them of territory, and they had a similarly low regard for the Albanian people – whom, because of their predominantly Muslim faith, they associated with the Ottoman Empire. Kosova therefore witnessed vicious fighting between Serbs and Albanians, and atrocities were committed on both sides as they waged relentless guerilla warfare.

After Wied had gone, Albania reverted to its prewar state of political dissension and chaos. There was no united opposition to foreign interventions. Northern Albania continued to rely on local self-government, with each clan uniting under its own chief; whilst southern Albania continued to suffer raids from Greek 'Epirot' bands. Throughout the duration of the war Albania found herself in a condition of political anarchy, as supporters of the various rebel groups fought among themselves for political influence. Essad Pasha now saw an opportunity to reassert his claim to power. In October 1914 Essad returned to Albania, where he managed – with Italian and Serbian financial backing and a force raised in Diber – to march into the interior of Albania to take Durres. He encountered little opposition as most government troops were in the south fighting the Greeks, who had reoccupied southern Albania. Essad took the opportunity of the void left by Wied to set himself up in Durres, where he proclaimed himself leader of the government. Like Wied, however, he exercised little control outside Durres, being dependent on the Serbs who invaded Albania the following spring. Essad managed to remain in command of parts of central Albania, despite violent protests against him, solely as a result of Serb backing and complete Serb control over the areas he administered.

Albanian protests were ignored, as the dismemberment of Albania was recognized by the Western allies on 26 April 1915, in the secret Pact of London. To encourage Italy to enter the war on the side of the Entente, the Pact, which was later made public by the Bolsheviks in 1917, agreed to divide up Albania between Greece and Italy, leaving a small autonomous state in the central regions. According to the terms of the treaty, Italy was granted possession of Sazan (Saseno) island and the port of Vlore, and was awarded a mandate over central Albania. In addition, it was agreed that if Italy acquired Trentino, Istria and Dalmatia, as stipulated in the pact, then Greece would take southern Albania, and Serbia and Montenegro could partition northern Albania. Greece and Serbia were also to establish a common frontier west of Lake Ohrid through the annexation of Albanian territory. The central portion was to be set up as an autonomous, not independent, state, which would be represented in foreign affairs by Italy.[15] And so the Powers, who rushed to war over the violation of the Belgian Treaty, disregarded without hesitation their treaty with Albania. They failed to take the necessary measures to protect the country and looked on passively as Serb, Montenegrin and Greek troops infringed Albania's fragile frontiers. In June, using border incidents as pretexts, the Montenegrins entered Shkoder, whilst the Serbs, whose principal aim was to acquire the port of Durres, occupied central Albania. Thus came the gradual encroachment of the war onto Albanian soil. On entering Shkoder, the Montenegrins had found the inhabitants all but exhausted. Many died of starvation. A British

officer described the scene: 'A temporary hospital in the zone of bom-
bardment was choked with unburied corpses; Essad Pasha had not
dared for days to appear in the streets, as he was followed by hungry
crowds crying for bread or a capitulation.'[16]

Eventually Albania became everybody's battleground. In July,
having consolidated her position in the Shkoder region, Montenegro
gave assurance to the Albanians that she desired no further territory.
Following the truce, however, tensions remained between the Montenegrins and the thousands of Albanians who remained on the Montenegrin side of the border. Isa Boletini and his family went to Podgorica
to negotiate with King Nicholas. It appears that a fight broke out in
the town between Albanians and Montenegrins, the result of which
left Boletini, his family and three friends dead. By the beginning of
October, as the result of Bulgaria's entry into the war, Serbia's military
position had become untenable even though she had defeated three
major Austro–Hungarian offensives. Faced with a combined Austro-
Bulgarian offensive, the Serbian army had no alternative but to make
its epic and tragic retreat across the snow-bound mountain passes of
northern Albania. With the army went the sick King Peter I of Serbia,
carried on a stretcher, and a mass of the Serbian civilian population
fleeing the bloody massacres perpetrated by Austro-Hungarian troops.
The Serbs had hoped to win through to Shkoder where the Allies
promised to await them with food and supplies.

The route of the Serbian army passed through central Albania, via
Elbasan. At the same time, the Bulgarians were pushing into Albania
from the East. On 9 December 1914, an Austrian fleet sailed into the
harbours of Durres and San Giovani di Medua. It sank all the
shipping in both ports, thus seriously impeding the British Adriatic
Mission's (BAM) task of supplying food, clothing and equipment for
the Serbian army at Shkoder. The BAM was unable to provide enough
food for the starving Serbs, who died in their thousands in the freezing
conditions. Their journey was described by one observer:

> The roads southward from Scutari lay through a country that was at any
> rate nominally friendly. Here the influence of Essad Pasha, the one central
> authority left in Albania whose name commands any widespread respect,
> was exercised on behalf of the Allies. But this did not prevent the in-
> habitants of the plain from following the example of the Albanians of the
> mountains in regard to the extortion of money. At the ferries they
> demanded gold, and those who could not pay might remain where they
> were and die. Those who went through that whole retreat say that the last

stages through the marshes and mud of central Albania were the worst of all ... When at last Vlore was reached, thousands still died neglected, before they could be taken off by the French and British ships.... From Vlore the army of 150,000 strong finally left Albania and crossed over to Corfu.[17]

On the whole, the Albanians refrained from physically attacking the pitiful columns of Serbs. An estimated hundred thousand Serbs died on their gruelling trek through Albania. The majority lay unburied, covered by either snow or mud, so that only their bones were to be found the following spring.

Whilst the northern Albanians were fighting the Serbs and Montenegrins, the central and southern Albanians had to defend themselves against the Greeks. As the Italians seized the island of Sazan and took control of the port of Vlore, Greek troops again occupied southern Albania in October 1914, even though Greece remained officially neutral until 1917. The chance to incorporate more Greeks within Greece had come during the Balkan Wars, when among her other gains Greece annexed Epirus and the town of Janina. The allies consented to this, in the hope of winning Greece over to their side, but only on condition that Greece withdrew whenever the Powers requested her to do so. Not surprisingly, Greece paid scant attention to the conditions stipulated by the allies. Indeed, Venizelos had now decided that Vorio Epirus was not after all 'irreversibly lost' to Greece. In August 1915 he declared to the Greek Chamber that 'only colossal faults' could separate 'northern Epirus' from Greece, so confident was he that the temporary occupation would become permanent.[18] The Greeks occupied the whole of southern Albania including Korca and Berat, setting fire to the wheatfields and all 46 Muslim villages in the region. As a result of the large-scale massacres perpetrated by the Greek troops thousands of refugees fled to the olive groves of Vlore, where many of them died from starvation and disease.

One of the few written accounts of the Greek occupation of Korca has been left to us by Edith Durham. Many years later, in a letter to a friend, she wrote of her efforts to save the town for Albania:

> The pro-Greek gang at King's College started a story that I had had to fly for my life from Korca because they all wanted to be Greek and I had tried to stir up Albanian trouble. The truth being that I and Nevison, who was there as a correspondent, made a forced march of three days and two nights sleeping on the bare ground, across the mountains to Berat at the urgent request of the Albanians. Berat being the nearest station from which a telegram could be sent, uncontrolled by the Greeks. Nevison drafted the

telegram to the Council of Ambassadors in London begging that no attention be paid to the Greek account of a meeting asking for Greek rule. This
meeting having been a forced one, held with Greek bayonets. This telegram saved Korca. The Greek governor made everyone paint their shops
blue and white. And after the hideous cruelty of the Greeks when they
raided south Albania in 1914, I have no use whatever for Greeks. I can
never forget the crowds of refugee women and children dying and starving
under the olive trees around Vlore. The matter was never bothered about.[19]

There followed a rapid series of events throughout 1916 which
contributed to the total fragmentation of Albania. Essad Pasha had
made various attempts to extend his influence, but found himself
somewhat adrift without his Serbian backers. His position became so
uncertain that he too followed the Serbs out of Albania and went
into exile in Paris. There, with French support, he appointed himself
head of a government-in-exile. During the spring Austro-Hungarian
troops, who had been pursuing the retreating Serbian army, took
over most of central and northern Albania. They turned Durres into
a naval base that they held until the end of the war. The Bulgarians
handed over Elbasan to the Austrians as they moved further south.
In the south, Greek troops seized Albanian territory and used it as a
line of communication with the Austrian army until the Italians
moved down from Vlore to displace them. The French advanced from
Thessalonika to Korca, where they negotiated with the defending
Albanians on the status of the region. As a result, on 10 December
1916, Korca and its surrounding area was granted the status of an
autonomous province, to be governed by an Albanian administration
under the protection of French military authorities. Albanian became
the official language, and Albanian schools replaced Greek ones.
However, although Korca's autonomous state may have suited the
French military standpoint at the time, the French government did
not realize the serious international repercussions. Austria–Hungary
immediately proclaimed autonomy for the part of northern Albania
it occupied, and Girokaster was suddenly declared 'independent' but
under Italian protection. Congratulatory messages poured in to the
new 'Republic of Korca' from Albanian colonies abroad, much to the
embarrassment of the French government. The 'Korca Republic' was
seen as a hasty diplomatic blunder and was soon rectified by the
repeal of autonomous status, so that Korca became a mere 'area'
under French military control.

In the meantime, the Greeks had continued their guerilla activities in southern Albania, and had even allowed Greek-speaking deputies from that region to sit in the Greek chamber. The population of the south were said to be starving, due to the wholesale exportation of livestock and agricultural produce to Greece. At this point the allies decided, with the use of Italian troops, to force Greece out of southern Albania. By the summer the strength of the Italian expeditionary force had reached one hundred thousand men, and by October the Italians had pushed the Greeks back into Thessaly and set up their military headquarters in Girokaster. From June 1917 until the end of 1918 the Italians assumed in Albania the attitude of a benevolent although somewhat autocratic guardian, and the autonomy enjoyed by the people was very limited.[20]

The Paris Peace Conference

At the close of the First World War Albania was therefore in an extremely vulnerable and fragmented position, still threatened with partition by Serbia, Montenegro and Greece, so that the postwar period looked likely to be as menacing and traumatic as the war had been. Soon after peace was signed, at the beginning of November 1918, the Committee for the Defence of Kosova, which had existed in a much looser form since May 1915, was set up illegally in Shkoder. The Committee, led by Hoxha Kadriu from Pristina, consisted mainly of political exiles from Kosova, of whom two of the most prominent members were Hassan Pristina and Baijram Curri. The primary objectives of the Committee were to campaign against the borders of the London Conference, and for the liberation of Kosova and the unification of all Albanian-inhabited lands. The Committee for the Defence of Kosova became the leading coordinator of the *cheta*, or *katchak*, movement, establishing branches in every town of Kosova and Uskub.[21]

At the Paris Peace Conference, Venizelos and his colleagues energetically negotiated Greek claims, whilst Italy tried to obstruct almost all Greek demands on southern Albania by organizing and financing *cheta* (armed bands) and spreading anti-Greek propaganda in Greece itself. Italian policy in Albania was clearly aimed at the establishment of a central administration which would eventually lead to an Italian protectorate over the whole country. The Powers, having at last decided that the Albanian frontier should be drawn up on the basis of ethnicity, were again hindered by the continued Greek insistence that

southern Albania was ethnically Greek, containing a population of
115,000 Greeks but only 110,000 Muslims. The Greek argument was
further reinforced by the large number of Greek schools in southern
Albania, which sustained the Greek language and culture. Whereas
the Powers decided to use the language spoken in the family as the
criterion of nationality, Greece demanded that national feeling should
decide nationality, and that the Graeco-Albanian frontier should bring
together districts of Greek civilization. Venizelos – who, as a Cretan,
had experienced the feeling of being an 'unredeemed Greek' – argued
that since neither race nor language could determine nationality,
national consciousness alone should be considered. Bluffing, Venizelos
had even suggested holding a referendum in Epirus. This, however,
was only a diplomatic move aimed at reinforcing the sense that a
Greek majority existed.

In reality, the Greek authorities in Epirus had warned Athens that
the Greeks would have no chance of gaining a majority in the countryside, and it might even prove difficult in the towns. As one observer
emphasized:

> It must never be forgotten when dealing with the Balkan boundary question,
> that Greek, Bulgarian and Serbian meant the adherents of the Orthodox
> church, not necessarily men of those nationalities. Here the Albanians had
> the disadvantage of being known as Turks. Thus, in southern Albania
> statistics show that so many thousand inhabitants are Turks and so many
> thousand are Greeks, whereas really these people are Moslem or Orthodox
> Albanians. Occasionally race and religion tally but very rarely.[22]

Greek nationalistic claims could not mask the more important
strategic and economic arguments that raged. The Greeks argued
that if Italy were given Korca she would acquire a bridgehead into
Macedonia, and so dominate Balkan politics. For their part, the
Italians claimed that Greece wanted the coast from Vlore to Corfu for
purely military reasons: between Corfu and the Epirus coast was a
potential naval base which could only be controlled by the possession
of both. If Greece were given the Epirus coastline she would effectively control the entrance to the Adriatic, a situation which Italy
could not tolerate.

The Florence Line had deprived Greece of the Sarande district –
which, she argued, was predominantly Greek and was the natural
outlet to the sea for the Greek region north of Janina. Greece had
also asked for a frontier line passing north of Premiti, as the commerce

of this area was directly connected with Saranda and Janina. However, Venizelos was always eager to reach an agreement with Italy, and so Italy and Greece concluded a secret pact, the Tittoni–Venizelos agreement of July 1919, to back each other's claims at the Paris Conference. Italy was to recognize Greece's rights over Korca and Girokaster, in return for Greek acquiescence to Italy's sovereignty over Vlore and its mandate over the rest of the country.[23] Italy offered to support Greek claims to the Dodecanese and Smyrna on condition that Greece accept the loss of northern Epirus – except for Korca, which Greece would retain. Venizelos now had to decide where Greek priorities lay – in Albania or in Asia Minor. The annexation of northern Epirus was just one of several Greek aims at the Paris Conference. Greek public opinion had a growing territorial appetite; the war had ended too soon for Greece, who had hoped to inflict more damage on the Ottomans and thus be able to ask for greater concessions at the peace table. As it happened, Venizelos remained convinced that Greek claims to Smyrna took precedence over their claims to northern Epirus, and even over the recovery of Constantinople. Greece had no particular aversion to the idea of an Albanian state, provided it was located in central Albania and remained independent, which she correctly assumed was not possible.

During the war years, a considerable number of Albanians had emigrated to the United States, many fleeing the Greek atrocities in the southern region. Those Albanian emigrants living in America, together with others in Europe, had sent representatives to the Paris Conference to argue for the restoration and unification of their nation. In England, Edith Durham and other friends of Albania repeatedly lectured and wrote on behalf of the Albanian cause. Between 1918 and 1921 the Albanians of Montenegro and Serbia, who had been included in those states in 1913, also made repeated fruitless appeals to the Conference for union with Albania. All these pleas were wholly disregarded. The new Kingdom of Serbs, Croats and Slovenes which was proclaimed at the Declaration of Corfu in July 1917 contained almost half a million Albanians within its population of 12 million. The kingdom, known as Yugoslavia after 1929, regarded Albania as an unnecessary entity that deprived her of territory, and also felt threatened by Italy, which it was assumed was creating a buffer state in Albania. The new kingdom's desire for northern Albanian territory was therefore based primarily on strategic considerations aimed at preventing Albania from becoming a rival.

The Congress of Lushnja

Meanwhile in Albania an emergency government led by the prominent bey Turhan Pasha, had been established in Durres, the primary concern of which was to save the country from partition. It was under similar conditions that Ismail Kemal had so hastily proclaimed the birth of the Albanian state; now, seven years later, an independent Albanian state was no nearer to international acceptance. Throughout 1919 the Durres government remained in theory in control of Albania. In practice, however, it was little more than a puppet regime, reduced to a mere outpost of Italian colonial administration. The situation within the country was highly volatile and inflammatory, making the position of the Durres government even more precarious. The imminent threat to their lands led a group of influential Albanians to convene a National Congress in Lushnja in January 1920, under the presidency of the rather weak Suliman Delvina, whose supporters considered themselves 'Liberals' – a term much used in the fashionable cafés of Paris and Bucharest but which had little relevance to Albanian society at that time. In fact, the Congress could only meet after the proclamation of a *besa,* which was to last for several weeks, suspending the vendetta obligations of the still heavily clan-based social structure. A 'National Legislative Assembly' followed, together with the establishment of a regency and the setting up of a national army. Until a ruler was chosen, his functions were to be fulfilled by the High Council of State, composed of four regents. Two of these were Muslims, one each from the Bektashi and Sunni sects; the other two were Orthodox and Catholic. To assist the regency the Congress appointed a cabinet responsible not to the regency but to a 37-man senate, which was given principal power in the state.[24] Tirana, which at this time was still only a provincial city with a population of 17,000, was henceforth made the capital of the country. The town was seen as a neutral area half-way between Ghegs and Tosks, and it was also in close proximity to the port of Durres.

The Lushnja Congress may have appeared democratic, but in fact power was left in the hands of the few leaders who had organized the system. Their main opposition came from the traditional and more conservative elements within Albania's small ruling class, led by Shefqet Verlaci, one of the richest property owners in Albania at that time, and Ahmed Zogu, a nephew of Essad Pasha. Ahmed Zogu, born in 1895, was the son of a chief of the Muslim tribe of Mati, the largest and most influential tribe in Albania, who in 1921 comprised some 23,000 persons living in the mountains and basin surrounding the river Mat in central Albania. Zogu's grandmother was a Toptani, and he came from a line of hereditary chieftains who governed a virtually independent principality, for Mati was never more than nominally a part of the Ottoman Empire.[25] Zogu had earned a reputation as an intelligent and confident leader of his Mati tribesmen during the First World War. Although Zogu's main support came from his Mati followers, ex-Ottoman officials also supported him in the hope of retaining and enhancing their traditional privileges. In 1916, during the Austrian occupation of Durres, Zogu had at first commanded the Albanian forces cooperating with the Austro-Hungarians, but it was subsequently discovered that he was conspiring with the Bulgarians for the reestablishment of Albanian administrative independence. He was accordingly induced to travel to Vienna, where he was detained as a 'guest' of the Austrian government until 1919, when he was permitted to return to Albania. Zogu went to the Lushnja Congress as a delegate from Mati; within a short time he had established his reputation, and in February 1920 he was appointed Minister of the Interior in Delvina's cabinet.

The immediate problem facing Delvina's new government was to force the Italians to leave the country. The Assembly rejected any plans for a mandate or protectorate for Albania, and on 3 June 1920 the Italian high command was sent an ultimatum demanding that it hand over the towns of Vlore, Tepelena and Himara to the new Albanian government. The disdainful Italians totally ignored the ultimatum. Around three thousand peasants were therefore encouraged to attack the Italian troops, who were by then severely weakened with malaria. The Italians were eventually forced to sign an agreement with the Albanian government which led to their final withdrawal from all Albanian territory except the island of Sazan on 3 September. In the meantime, Yugoslav units had advanced to a strategic line inside the 1913 frontier, pending the decision of the Conference of Ambassadors which had by then reconvened. Unable to dislodge the Yugoslavs through military means, Zogu used his personal connections in Belgrade to assure the Yugoslavs that he would personally work against Kosovar irredentism in exchange for a secession of hostilities.[26] The ever hopeful and incredibly persistent Essad Pasha had, meanwhile, presented himself at the Peace Conference as the only legal representative of Albania. He had little chance, however, to make any impact as he was assassinated in front of the Hotel Continental in Paris by Avni Rustemi on 13 June. Rustemi, a student, was the founder of the *Bashkimi* (Unity) association, a small but radical youth wing of the liberal democratic movement, whose activities extended throughout Albania and among the émigré communities in Europe. As the Powers in Paris ponderously deliberated over Albania's future, the situation within the country reflected the years of war, upheaval and displacement. The International Red Cross of Geneva estimated that in 1920 no less than ten thousand Albanian refugees had died of exposure, sickness or starvation.[27]

Yugoslavia is Awarded Kosova

After prolonged debate over the Yugoslav-Italian border, Italy, Britain and France finally agreed that Italy should be given control of Istria, Rijeka and Zadar, and have a mandate over central Albania. In return, Yugoslavia would be given much of northern Albania, including Kosova and the Drin valley, whilst Greece gained parts of southern Albania. Following this, the allied occupation of Shkoder ended and the Albanian army took control of the city. A sense of fear, anger and betrayal pervaded the Albanian villages of Kosova. In July 1921 a petition was submitted to the League of Nations by the Kosovars, begging for reunion with Albania. The petition covered 72 pages, all describing atrocities committed by the Serbs, with the names and addresses of each victim. It stated that since 1918, throughout the vilayet of Kosova, 12,371 people had been killed and 22,000 imprisoned.[28]

The Albanian pleas were persistently ignored for two main reasons. First, the part played by Serbia in the Great War had prejudiced the Entente Powers to support Serbia's claim over Kosova. Indeed, during the war Serbia had become the darling of both the English and the French peoples. In 1916 a nationwide tribute to Serbia had been arranged in Britain to celebrate the anniversary of the Battle of Kosova: information about Serbia was widely disseminated; a shop opened in London to sell literature about Serbia, which British publishing houses printed in tens of thousands of copies; posters created from a *Punch* cartoon of 'Heroic Serbia' were displayed throughout the country; cinemas showed films about Serbia, and the Serbian national anthem was even played in some theatres.[29] Second, the Serbs argued successfully that they needed Kosova to reestablish their cultural identity after the horrendous casualties and trauma their nation had suffered during the war. The historical significance of the area for Serbs cannot be underestimated: Kosova held the most important treasures of Serbian religious art in the churches of Peja (Pec), Gracanica, and Decani; while Prizren was also the capital of Stefan Dushan's medieval Serbian Empire. The defeat, in 1389, of the Serbian Prince Lazar and the Balkan army by the Ottomans at the Battle of Kosovo Polje, had marked the end of the independent Serbian state and the beginning of more than four centuries of Ottoman rule.

Considering this had been a disastrous defeat for the Serbs, they nevertheless shrouded and enveloped the event in an elaborate web of heroic folklore, myth and legend. The difficult conditions of Ottoman occupation contributed to the development of the Kosovo myth, and the conflict between Christianity and Islam became the main theme of Serbian folk poetry. From then on the Kosovo legend became infused with the powerful ideology of rebellion against foreign rule and helped keep alive for centuries the ember of Serbian national consciousness. This eventually sparked the revolt of Karadjordie in 1804, which ultimately led to the founding of the independent Serbian Kingdom. The retention of Kosova was regarded as a central aspect of the Serbian historical identity despite the fact that the Serb population of the region was very small.

The future of the Albanian population of southeastern Europe was sealed by statesmen representing the European Powers, many of whom were wholly ignorant of Balkan affairs. While Yugoslav, Italian and Greek propaganda exercised a powerful influence on the outcome, Albanian arguments concerning the future of their nation received little attention. The whole Albanian question was barely understood by those who had been assigned the responsibility of determining Albania's fate. The fact that Albania emerged at all as an independent state in 1920 was indeed remarkable.

5

Political Instability and the June Revolution

In the Balkans, he who talks, can only be talking politics.
J. Swire, *King Zog's Albania*, London, 1937, p 22

By 1921 Albania was devastated and bankrupt, having been continuously at war since 1910. The political situation remained confused, and the country essentially reverted back to how it had been before the war, with rampant brigandage and lawlessness. Much of the south had never recovered from the ravages of the Greek bands in 1914, and areas such as the Drin valley remained desolate after the Serbs laid them to waste in 1920. International recognition of Albania's frontiers and membership of the League of Nations had not brought the Yugoslav occupation to a complete end. One-sixth of the country was still occupied, and the Greeks were still entrenched in several villages to the south of Korca. There was overwhelming poverty, with thousands of destitute refugees wholly dependent upon a few foreign philanthropists for their survival. In southern Albania tensions between Albanians and the Greek minority were exacerbated by what Greeks termed a 'persecution campaign', apparently orchestrated by the Albanian government. Following the enforced closure of several Greek schools, a serious incident occured at Korca on 28 April 1921, when Albanians seized a Greek church and killed some eleven Greeks.[1] However, the Greek government wished to avoid being drawn into forming another active front in northern Epirus. Greek attention was now turned towards the escalating conflict with Turkey, a struggle which required all her resources. Greece therefore limited its action to protests by the Ministry of Foreign Affairs to the League of Nations.

Throughout 1921, skirmishing continued along the frontier regions of northern Albania. Bands of insurgents, equipped and financed by Belgrade, hoped to convince the Ambassadors' Conference, which had reconvened in Paris at the beginning of November, that support for Yugoslav rule was widespread. In a report submitted to the League of Nations in August 1921 by a government representative, Midhat Frasheri, it was stated that Yugoslav troops had in June the previous year ravaged the Diber district, indiscriminately killing, looting and destroying 157 villages. This was later confirmed by a despatch from the British consul, Harry Eyres, in Durres, who visited the spot:

> When we reached the top of the range [Chafa Rounes] overlooking the Drin valley, a magnificent panorama was spread out before us, and we could see from beyond the town of Dibra to Ljuma in the north, some 600 square miles of one of the [formerly] most prosperous and fertile valleys in Albania. With the naked eye, and with the aid of glasses, we perceived nothing but burnt and ruined villages on all this vast expanse; lands untilled and the valley depopulated, with the exception of one village – Suhodol – which, for some unexplained reason, the Serb had spared.... I have no longer any doubt whatever that the number of destroyed villages given by the Albanian Commission of Inquiry – namely 157 – is correct. I should have supposed it to be under the mark. That evening we stayed at the village of Muhri on the Drin, where some 25 houses were more or less undamaged out of a total of 300. The next day we rode to Aras, which was entirely destroyed, and during six hours travelling every village and house we came across was burnt. Not til we reached Luria did we find a village intact.... There are many further details of this character which only deepen the general impression of the very serious character attaching to the Serb invasion.[2]

Following the Serbian action in the Drin valley, a deputation of Albanians from the region visited the British consul to beg his help. In his official report, Eyres wrote:

> The deputation declared that if nothing could be done for them they would return to their ruined homes and if prevented would fight, for it was better to die fighting than to die by inches as they were then doing. I warned them that no good would come to them from the course proposed, and that patience was their only resource, but I could not help feeling that I was only giving them cold comfort.[3]

The League of Nations had meanwhile proved unable to force the withdrawal of Yugoslav troops from the northern regions, despite repeated pleas from Albania's representative, Bishop Fan Noli. In

October, Yugoslav troops launched yet another attack on northern Albania. They quickly dispersed the ill-prepared Albanian troops and advanced upon Orosh, San Giovani di Medua and Lezhe. They marched within thirty miles of Tirana, where they hoped to present the Powers with a *fait accompli* by having secured their occupation of northern Albania.

The Yugoslavs paid no heed to the indignant outcry from the League of Nations representatives, who had acknowledged that the maintenance of peace in Europe was inextricably linked with the preservation of Albania's territorial integrity. Eventually the British Foreign Office, advised by such close observers of Albanian issues as Edith Durham and Aubrey Herbert, an honorary attaché at the British Embassy in Istanbul and frequent visitor to Albania, lost its patience with Belgrade. The British urged a quick decision from the Conference of Ambassadors regarding Albania's frontiers. Thus, on 9 November 1921, the Ambassadors finally reached a decision agreeing Albania's international borders. This involved only a slight revision of the 1913 frontier. Greece was forced to hand back 15 villages, which she reluctantly agreed to do. The new frontier awarded the town of Lin to Albania, but deprived her of the main part of the road which linked Lin with Diber and Struga, and hence her communication between the northeast and southeast. The decisions by the Conference of Ambassadors once again satisfied none of the states concerned. Both Greece and Yugoslavia protested vigorously against the revision of the frontier. Eventually, however, they had no alternative but to bow reluctantly to the Ambassadors' final decision.

Embryonic Political Developments

Although Albania had escaped partition, the country was placed under Italian tutelage in recognition of Italy's 'special interest' in the country. The Powers recognized that any threat to the Adriatic coastline constituted a threat to the security of Italy. So began Italy's gradual penetration into the economic and political life of Albania. By now the legislation agreed upon at the Congress of Lushnja had begun to show its limitations, leaving the government increasingly impotent. It was not long, therefore, before Suliman Delvina's weakly constructed government collapsed, and the first elections were subsequently held in April 1921. From then until 1924, the country underwent frequent changes of government. Albania barely possessed an intelligentsia,

there was no press, and a sizeable proportion of the population remained illiterate. Elections were, therefore, ultimately the prerogative
of a small number of influential people. In May 1921 the new government, supported primarily by prominent landowning beys, was
appointed with Iljas Bey Vrioni as prime minister. In the opinion of
Harry Eyres, Vrioni lacked intelligence but was honest and patriotic.
Eyres observed Vrioni battling against a wealth of opposing forces
and remarked, 'It is at times pathetic to watch his struggles against
the difficulties which surround him. He is not a very strong man and
has the defect of want of decision.'[4] The Vrioni administration was
adamantly opposed to any changes in the social or economic structure
of the country, in particular failing to institute agrarian reform. Instead it stood for the maintenance of the prewar social structure and
traditional privileges.

The first postwar years were characterized by incessant political
intrigue. Among the various political factions to emerge following the
1921 elections was the Democratic, or Popular, Party led by Bishop
Fan Noli and Luigj Gurakuqi, a leader of the northern Catholics.
Other prominent members included Hassan Pristina and Bajram
Curri. Ahmed Zogu was also a member of this group for a time, until
gradually he became restless with his less than powerful position
within the Popular Party. Followers of the Popular Party saw themselves as essentially liberal and western–oriented. For some that meant
little more than sitting in fashionable cafés discussing Voltaire; others,
however, were genuinely opposed to the stagnant policies of Shefqet
Verlaci's strongly conservative Progressive Party. This was often called
the Beys' Party, as it represented the interests of the landowners, who
opposed the much-needed land reform. More than half the arable
land still belonged to the great estates. Both the Popular Party and
the Progressive Party emerged from the elections with an almost equal
number of seats in the new parliament. There followed a bitter struggle between the two, causing an endless succession of governmental
crises. The resulting instability lasted until the formation of a national
coalition government in the autumn of 1921.

Despite its newfound political independence, Albania during this
period appears to have maintained the fatalism of its Islamic tradition
and the entrenched conservatism rooted in its isolated position and
peasant culture. The country was still acutely weakened by the
regional divisions which had so hindered Albania's unity before the
war. The government was seen not as an Albanian but rather as a

Tirana government, increasingly under the influence of the Muslim landowners. The beys frequently attempted to take advantage of the undeveloped character of the legislation to extend their ownership of land by oppressive or arbitrary measures, claiming property which had hitherto been held in common by communities. In many areas, especially those of central Albania, the sense of nationalism was weak, and patriotism was overshadowed by narrow self-interest. Above all, they feared the partition of their estates or other measures of agrarian reform.[5]

The Catholic population of the north, living in isolated communities in remote and roadless mountains, was largely neglected and ignored by the Tirana administration. Many of the northern leaders wanted Shkoder, not Tirana, to be the country's capital, not only because of its obvious commercial importance, but also due to its Catholic as well as Muslim traditions. So far the government had not felt itself strong enough to tax the northern Catholic tribes, who continued their timeless way of life, ignored by all but a few curious travellers. In 1921 an American, Rose Wilder Lane, embarked upon an extensive journey to the north Albanian highlands, which later inspired her to write *The Peaks of Shala*. This was a personal narrative which followed closely in the footsteps of Edith Durham. Lane confirms Durham's descriptions of the northern clans, and gives plenty of evidence that little had changed in the intervening ten years. She echoes Durham's experiences of Albanian hospitality offered to weary travellers:

> Preparations for feasts prepared in their honour only started upon their arrival which was always late at night when they were already cold, wet and tired. The hospitality was hard to enjoy as the travellers were expected to sit in their wet clothing and sociably discuss current events and await the meal which usually took several hours to prepare, often served at one or two in the morning by which time these weary foreign visitors were too tired to get pleasure from it. Furthermore many journeys started at around 3.30 or 4 am.[6]

The Mirdite Revolt

The largest of the Catholic tribes was the Mirdite, which was actually composed of three smaller clans. A legend explains the origin of the name Mirdite. Once there lived three brothers whose father left nothing when he died but a saddle and a winnowing sieve. The eldest son took the saddle (*shale*, in Albanian), the next the sieve (*shoshe*) and the youngest went his way emptyhanded, wishing his brothers good day (*mir dite*). This legend gives the three clans Shala, Shoshi and Mirdite, a common ancestor.[7]

The Mirdite remained deeply suspicious of the Tirana administration. This was evident to Rose Wilder Lane, who asked her guide to explain to her their mistrust of the government; he replied:

> These tribes do not understand that the new government in Tirana is an all-Albanian government. They don't think as a nation; they think as tribes. They think the government is a Tirana government, trying to destroy their liberty as the Romans and the Turks and the Austrians and the Italians and the Serbs and the Greeks and the Peace Council tried to do.[8]

In 1920 the hereditary chieftain of the Mirdite, Prenk Bib Doda, was killed in an ambush resulting from a blood feud. Prenk left no son or heir, his cousin Gjon Marka Gjoni expected therefore to succeed him, but found that Prenk had disinherited him owing to his unpopularity – Gjoni had apparently deserted the front in 1914. Prenk instead bequeathed his property to all the Mirdite. The Tirana regime, never penetrating the northern highlands, was unaware of the internal intrigues within the Mirdite. In an attempt, therefore, to secure the Mirdite's loyalty, Gjon Marka Gjoni was encouraged to participate in the new administration. This gives a striking example of how out of touch the Tirana government was with the northern clans, just as it was with the mountainous and remote regions of the south like Himara and the Greek-inhabited villages around Delvina. Gjoni, however, considered his status within the Mirdite to be more important than any post offered him by the government in Tirana. Therefore he refused the official post offered to him by the Tirana administration in April 1921, and hurriedly left Mirdite for Prizren to seek Yugoslav aid for his claim to be chief of the Mirdite. By helping Gjon Marka Gjoni, the Yugoslavs hoped to weaken and discredit the Tirana regime, and thereby to extend their influence throughout the northern regions.

Furnished with Yugoslav money, Gjoni returned to Mirdite to stir the clansmen against the Vrioni administration. This was not difficult, as the government had by now threatened to tax the whole country equally and the Mirdite had never paid taxes. Gjoni managed only to win over the Bajrak of Orosh, but the Yugoslavs from Prizren proclaimed a Mirdite Republic in Marka Gjoni's name and supplied

him with arms.[9] 'It was no difficult task', reported the League of
Nations Commission, 'to stir up the imagination of this extraordinarily
uneducated and ignorant population, living in a district absolutely
isolated and cut off from all communication.'[10] Gjon Marka Gjoni
accused the Tirana government of being Muslim, with 'Young Turk'
tendencies, and of intending to interfere with the religious liberty of
the Catholic Mirdites. Knowing he had the support of the Yugoslavs,
who had put funds, training and mountain guns at his disposal, Gjoni
attacked the government troops. His force comprised some two thousand men, only a few of whom were actually from Mirdite, the rest
being either Serb or Albanian irregulars, together with some ex-
supporters of Essad Pasha. The rebellion was shortlived, as the
majority of the Mirdites ignored his call to revolt. Within days,
government troops had captured the Mirdite capital, Orosh, and with
fifty of his men Gjon Marka Gjoni was forced to flee back to Prizren.
He died in 1925 and his son Djon, born in 1886, succeeded him as
Kapidan of the Mirdite. Djon, who was far less ambitious than his
father, withdrew into obscurity and the 'Republic of Mirdite' lived on
only in Prizren, Yugoslavia.

Political Divisions Intensify

Ahmed Zogu, meanwhile, was consolidating his grip on the central
government. At this time a point of serious contention arose, which
eventually split the Popular Party. The problem was Kosova. Zogu
and many of the southern leaders believed that Albania should first
establish itself as a viable state before pursuing irredentism, and many
of the Orthodox southern leaders also feared the massive influx of
Muslims. The Kosovars within this group, Bajram Curri and Hassan
Pristina, naturally took exception to this position.[11] Before long, the
central and southern beys, together with the Orthodox leaders, had
alienated the influential Kosova Committee group within the Popular
Party. This put extreme pressure on the Vrioni administration, which
eventually collapsed. The fall of the Vrioni government led to a cabinet
being formed by three generally accepted arbitrators: Avni Rustemi,
Bajram Curri, and Kazim Bey Koutzouli, the prefect of Tirana. These
three sought to appease the opposing factions by granting ministerial
posts to supporters of each group. Needless to say, this arrangement
failed to bring any unanimity to Albanian politics, and the situation
remained just as chaotic. During December 1921 no less than five

ministries were formed, the last being installed by a coup d'état, led by the Regent, Aqif Pasha, and Hassan Pristina. Pristina, Bajram Curri and other Kosovars had by now distanced themselves from Zogu, who had been appointed minister of war in the new cabinet. When Pristina was appointed prime minister by Aqif Pasha, he immediately replaced Zogu with Bajram Curri as war minister. Hassan Pristina, then aged 55, had been educated in Turkey and at one time was a member of the Ottoman parliament. He later quarrelled with the Young Turks, and was one of the promoters of the revolution in Kosova in 1912 in which 35,000 Albanians had marched upon and occupied Skopje. A British Foreign Office official described him as 'a born revolutionary, with a strong and fearless character, an inveterate opponent of Zogu, and a deadly enemy of the Serbs'.[12]

Away from the north, there was widespread opposition to what by now had become an entirely Gheg-dominated government. Apart from protests in the southern towns, the central beys were angered by such northern dominance. Within days of Hassan Pristina being appointed prime minister, Zogu, together with his Mati followers, marched on Tirana, and Pristina was forced to flee north with his supporters. The new year began with yet another government being formed under the landowner Xhafer Bey Ypi, with Zogu once again controlling matters as minister of the interior. Ypi's role remained that of a mere figurehead, whilst Zogu worked to extend his influence beyond his powerful ministerial position. One of Zogu's first tasks was to secure the support of the Catholics. Before the First World War, many of the Catholic tribes had been accustomed to living on the bribes paid to them by the Ottoman government to keep them in good humour. Now, however, with their former source of revenue cut off, some were beginning to look back nostalgically to the relative financial security they had previously enjoyed. A government official confided to Harry Eyres: 'They [the Catholic tribes] still consider that it is the business of the government to support them.' Another official admitted to Eyres that the government 'were compelled, for reasons of expediency, to submit to a certain extent to their demand, but payments are of necessity on a much reduced scale'.[13] The leaders of the major northern tribes were therefore paid 'peace money' and given the rank of colonel in the army. Each month large groups of heavily armed highlanders would descend on Tirana to collect their gold from the war department. Technically, they were paid to provide the army with irregular reserve troops, but in reality they were paid to refrain from staging uprisings against the government. In addition, the chiefs took an oath to Zogu personally, rather than to the country (a concept which was basically still foreign to them). Zogu was recognized as an over-chieftain and they subsequently looked to him personally for their 'peace money'.[14]

In January 1922, Britain and Albania finally established diplomatic relations. Consequently Harry Eyres was upgraded from the position of consul to British ambassador to Albania. Two months later, Mehmed Bey Konitza came to London to represent Albania. Almost immediately Eyres found his diplomatic skills in great demand. In the spring, a crisis erupted as Bajram Curri began an uprising against Zogu, in Puka. He was joined by other Kosovar leaders, until eventually the insurgents seized Durres and proceeded to march upon Tirana. Most of the government promptly fled to Elbasan, leaving Zogu and a few of his supporters to defend the capital. The remaining government troops fought with the rebels in the suburbs of Tirana. Eyres, at the behest of Zogu, managed to persuade the rebel leader Elez Jusuf (Bajram Curri having retired back to the north) to surrender on the promise of a safe pardon, which was duly respected. From this point onwards, Zogu began to confide in Eyres, who became so influential that, until 1926, he in effect controlled Albania's internal and foreign policy. Zogu was quickly able to reestablish order after a military court sentenced nine insurgent leaders to death. Bajram Curri was sentenced to death in his absence, and for a very brief period Albania experienced relative peace and tranquility.

The continuation of peaceful stability, however, in part depended upon the stimulation of commercial activity. This in turn relied upon the receipt of a financial loan from the League of Nations. A request by the Albanians for a loan had not been granted because the conditions set by the League included reform of the internal administration, and of the economy. This was an unrealistic demand on the part of the League, whose representatives were well aware of the desperate state of the country. The majority of Albanians were virtually self-sufficient and lived in varying degrees of poverty. The few roads that did exist, both north and south, became impassable during the winter months, with many places completely cut off. Thus commerce was restricted to a few isolated and stagnant communities. Apart from oil exploration, few surveys of Albania's potential natural reserves had been carried out. During the war the Austrians and Italians had discovered coal, silver, copper and oil, but exploration had ceased as soon as their troops left. In the meantime, the country remained seriously disunified. In the north of the country there was growing resentment of Prime Minister Ypi's centralist government, with its abundance of inadequate and incapable ministers. On 16 December 1922, to forestall a crisis, Zogu replaced Ypi as prime minister. However, a new and unpopular law was now introduced: throughout central and southern Albania it became illegal to carry arms. This law, it was hoped, would help diminish brigandage and at the same time reduce the threat to Zogu. It was impossible, however, to enforce this law among the northern tribes, who carried arms as a birthright and who needed their weapons to counter the continuous skirmishing with the Yugoslavs along the border.

The urban population remained caught up in the continual political debate, as their government precariously tried to appease all those with a vested interest in halting attempts to reform and modernize the country. An American working in the Red Cross school in Tirana described very effectively the mood of the country:

> The cafes, blue with the smoke of burning cigarettes and pungent with the odor of Turkish coffee, buzz with the conversations of the patrons who sit at the tables and for hours discuss and argue, plan and plot, destroy and defend, conspire and construct. Cabinets come and go, Parliament convenes and adjourns. One day a man is an 'Excellency' and has a soldier following him at fifteen paces as a personal bodyguard and the next day he is back at the table as a 'Zotni' [Mr]. There is much to talk about: relations with neighboring states, border warfare aggression, the boundary to be delimited by the 'Mother of this Child', the League of Nations, a Constituent Assembly to be summoned and a Constitution to be drawn up (updating that of 1914). These and many others furnish topic for hours of discussion, and in this these men excel. But there is also much to be done in the country. Roads and bridges must be repaired and rebuilt, the peasant idea that Allah made them so and will change them if he desires must be uprooted and cast off. A National Bank and Currency must be installed and a railroad to link the interior with the coastal ports. Then high up in the mountains, where the snow rests the year round, there are tribes of fearless but uneducated men who wonder what this is all about, this Government business and police and army and taxes and elections, and now and then they too make sorties to the capital for the purpose of discussing, but they 'discuss' in the only way they know how, with the eye squinted down the long blue steel rifle barrel.[15]

By the summer of 1923 signs of rebellion were becoming increasingly visible as the gap between landed and landless, northerner and southerner, liberal and conservative grew ever wider. One of the principal causes of discontent amongst the Orthodox Christians was their resentment of the Muslim landowners, and the precedence given to former Ottoman officials, who frequently took advantage of their position for personal ends. The Orthodox Albanians had expected, somewhat unreasonably in view of their inexperience, to obtain influence in the country.[16] Harry Eyres found the majority of Muslims to be imbued with feelings of superiority towards the Christians. He informed the Foreign Office that:

> the mental attitude of the Muslim to the Christian is unchanged, and some-times, I fear, unchangeable. The meaning of the word equality has not penetrated the recesses of the Muslim mind. They cannot bring them-selves to admit that a Christian can be anything but an inferior, and all their acts reflect this sentiment. I have conversed with the Ministers on this subject, and they protest that they make no difference between the two parties, and that they are most anxious to prove this by their acts. But they say – 'we Mussulmans are in a majority, and we therefore naturally keep the upper hand'. The Christians, on the other hand, are timorous, and have not been able to free themselves from the chains which their long-standing position of inferiority has riveted on them. But they are dissatis-fied, especially in the south. They say they might be willing to submit to a majority government but not to a majority domination. They fear that if they do not assert themselves they will fall under a domination of the old Turkish type. Here I may observe that there is a considerable Christian emigration from Central and Southern Albania, and a certain amount of Muslim immigration from surrounding countries, the combination of which is a disquieting feature.[17]

The Albanian Orthodox community in the south had believed they would automatically enjoy equal rights with the Muslims now that Albania had gained its independence. They knew their region was the most prosperous and developed in the country, and therefore paid the most into the state budget. Yet, with the arrival of the Muslim Zogu's government, most of their taxes went on funding the administration in Tirana, and little found its way back to southern Albania. Hence, the country was divided at every turn. Meanwhile, there was a rash of political assassinations, and the country slid further into political chaos. In August 1923, sensing the growing public dissatisfaction, Zogu announced that elections would be held for a Constituent Assembly before the National Council. During the same month, Albania's Muslims gathered at a congress in Tirana to discuss various reforms – which even the most conservative amongst them now reluctantly

agreed were necessary if Albanian society was to prosper. They therefore decided to sever their ties with traditional practices, to detach
themselves from the Caliphate and to abolish the title 'bey', together
with the practice of polygyny and the compulsory veiling of women.
Although polygyny existed in principle, most Albanian Muslims had
only one wife, and in general these changes had little effect on daily
life or in transforming society. Effectively though, the beys now felt
undermined, their influence on the wane, and uncertain of their status
and role in Albanian society.

The elections for the Constituent Assembly eventually took place;
the resulting division of parliamentary seats gave no party a clear
majority. The election results only served to weaken Zogu's position
further, as the government won only 40 of the 95 seats in the Constituent Assembly. Zogu's cabinet retained office by a slim margin, but
within two weeks he resigned, to be replaced by Shefqet Verlaci. Verlaci
was no more acceptable to the opposition than Ahmet Zogu.[18] Although
he was no longer premier, and although there was growing dissatisfaction with his policies, Zogu still controlled the government. Verlaci
only reluctantly accepted the post of prime minister, and the new
government shakily tried to forestall its collapse by falling back on the
old standbys of plotting and intrigue. At this time conditions throughout most of the country were continually degenerating. Rural areas
faced famine, and the opposition was effectively able to undermine the
government by calling for desperately needed agrarian reform.

In March 1924 one of Albania's most astute observers, Joseph
Swire, first visited the country. He found Tirana's streets unchanged
since Edward Lear had painted them. They were, he noted,

> mere alleys, cobbled and muddy, winding between single-story open-fronted
> shops, darkened by the wide eaves. Besides Stirling and the Legation
> people, there were no British in the country, nor were there any non-Balkan
> people there of any sort except the Italian, French and American diplomatic
> representatives. The Stirlings lived in the only baked brick house in
> Tirana.[19]

At the same time conditions in northern Albania had continued to
deteriorate, following the Yugoslav closure of the border to trade
between the two countries. As a result, there was an increased threat
of famine in the Albanian mountain regions. The destitute northern
tribes were now no longer able to buy the imported maize which had
always been their staple diet. On 13 March, a representative for

Albania at the League of Nations, M. Blinishti, made an emotional appeal to the League for relief for the distressed population of northern Albania. He mentioned that while every other Balkan state had enjoyed financial assistance during the initial stages of its development, Albania had received none. As a result of this plea, the League agreed to donate 50,000 Swiss francs for immediate relief work in the impoverished northern regions.

The June Revolution

Shortly after Joseph Swire's arrival in Albania, the sleepy atmosphere of Tirana was stirred into activity by a series of events that were eventually to bring about the June Revolution later that year. On 6 April 1924 two American tourists, G.B. de Long and R.L. Coleman, were shot dead as they drove on the road from Tirana to Shkoder. It was never fully determined who actually carried out the attack and why: one theory suggested that they had been mistaken for supporters of Fan Noli; another that the victims were mistakenly shot in a blood feud vendetta. A more plausible theory suggested that the crime was committed in order to discredit the government in the eyes of foreign observers. At that time there were continuing border disputes with both Greece and Yugoslavia. The murder of the two Americans caused great consternation throughout Albania, and deep anxiety for the government. Not long after the death of the Americans, on 5 May, Avni Rustemi, by then a prominent member of the Democratic Party, was also murdered. He was shot outside the Parliament House in Tirana either by a former follower of Essad Pasha, or by one of Zogu's retainers. The opposition accused the government of incompetence and withdrew 44 deputies from the Assembly, which was consequently reduced to constitutional impotence, being deprived of the quorum necessary for the purpose of passing legislation.[20] The murder of Rustemi was but one symbol of the mounting discontent with the government's policies. To the despair of Zogu, the opposition gathered in force in Vlore, where the young Rustemi was given a martyr's funeral and a large monument was erected in his honour.

Following Rustemi's funeral, the opposition sent an ultimatum from Vlore to the Supreme Council in Tirana. They demanded the dismissal of the Verlaci government and, in view of the recent spate of murders, accused the government of being unable to ensure the safety of either Albanian or foreign citizens. The country's desperate economic plight, the general poverty of the people, and the irredentist aspirations of the Kosova Committee contributed to the impatience and antagonism felt throughout the country towards the government. At the instigation of Eyres, in a last-ditch attempt to contain the revolt, a new government under Vrioni was installed. By this time, however, the tide of discontent had gathered momentum, with even some military garrisons siding with the rebels. The gravity of the situation increased as the top-ranking officials of the Vrioni administration fled to Italy. Army units then went over to the opposition. Sensing this mood, the opposition felt the time was now ripe to make their move against the government. Thus began what later became known as the June Revolution. In the far north, at Kukes, Bajram Curri led the rising with a call to arms. The old Kosovar had been biding his time in preparation for this revolt ever since he fled north following the rebellion of March 1922. In Vlore, Fan Noli presided over the revolutionary movement's operations. The revolt spread rapidly, and by June Zogu's position was hopeless. He therefore withdrew into Yugoslavia with his remaining forces, and settled in Belgrade to plot his return.

On 16 June 1924 Fan Noli became prime minister in a new Democratic government which had, as its principal aims, an ambitious programme of radical agricultural, legal and administrative reforms. Born in 1882 in Thrace, Noli had come into contact with Albanian nationalists whilst teaching in a Greek school in Egypt. Having gone to America to teach the ideas of Albanian nationalism to the large Albanian community there, he later obtained a degree from Harvard and in 1908 became bishop of the Albanian Orthodox Church. In 1920 the Albanian Americans chose him as their representative to the National Assembly at Lushnja. He thus came to Albania with little direct experience of political life in the country.[21] A measure of the faith many Albanians had in the new independent Albania can be judged by the fact that Noli and Mehmet Konitza were among twenty to thirty thousand Albanian émigrés to journey back from the United States between 1919 and 1925.[22] Noli was socially and politically very much out of touch when he arrived in Albania to take up the post of Orthodox Bishop of Durres. Whilst in America he had become deeply influenced by democratic ideas which were wholly impractical for, and incompatible with, the political realities of life in Albania. This was borne out after his hastily inaugurated scheme for the rapid modernization of the country was destroyed by the opposition of the landowners, who found renewed unity of purpose in fighting Noli's radical land-reform policies, which involved the transfer of land to the peasants. However, there was little doubt that agrarian reform was urgently needed. An official British survey conducted that year concluded that:

> central Albania is characterised by remnants of the feudal system repre-
> sented by large landowners, often descendents of Ottoman officials, who
> acquired land by tyranny or in default of taxes. They are powerful but
> unprogressive and unpopular. Some at least are influenced by Pan-Islamic
> ideas. Many of the Beys are absentees. The peasants working in extreme
> poverty on the Beys' estates have to surrender one-third of their own
> produce to the Bey and one tenth to the state.[23]

The country's educational system was severely limited during the 1920s. An observer sent by the Carnegie Foundation cites figures: there were 9 elementary schools of seven-year programmes; 51 others offered three to five years' instruction; 472 schools instructed only the first two primary grades. At a more advanced level only two institutions existed: the French Lycée at Korca, and a secondary school in Elbasan. He noted that the scarcity of teaching materials seriously handicapped little-trained instructors, but remarked an almost universal desire for education wherever he travelled about the country.[24] This avid desire for education was also witnessed by Rose Wilder Lane, who visited a small school which had recently opened in the village of Thethi, close to the Yugoslav border. A Catholic priest, Padre Marjan, was paid a hundred kronen a month by the government to teach. He told Lane that 'On the first day there were 43 pupils, on the second day 62, on the third day 97. All the tribe was sending its children to live with relatives in Thethi and go to school.' Lane described the bleak conditions within the schoolhouse:

> There were no benches or desks, of course; the children stood packed
> tightly in the cold room, and he taught them by writing with a piece of
> chalk on the walls. Already a boy could read and write words of one syllable,
> and merited a cake of soap. Padre Marjan, at his own expense, had sent two
> hundred miles to Tirana for fifty cakes of soap, to be used as prizes. There
> was, of course, no other soap in the tribe; a more magnificent gift could not
> have been imagined.[25]

Meanwhile, the position regarding the 20,000 or so Muslim Albanians, known as Chams, living in Chameria in Greece was being hotly debated at a special session of the Council of the League of Nations.

Chameria is the area of Epirus extended between Butrint and the mouth of the Acheron river, and eastward to the Pindus mountains. The convention that made possible the exchange of Greek and Turkish populations had been signed at the Lausanne Conference on 30 January 1923. The Albanian government had then insisted, via telegrams and delegations to the League, that the Greek authorities were forcing the Chams to leave their homes and move to Turkey, and that their lands were being settled by Greek immigrants from Asia Minor. The Albanians further claimed that the property of Muslim Albanians was being confiscated, their harvests being requisitioned, and that they were prohibited from sowing their corn or from selling or letting their property to forestall its expropriation. The Greeks countered these accusations by arguing that the term 'Albanian' could only be applied to those who were born in Albania, thereby excluding from consideration the Greek-born Albanian Muslims, who were equated with Turks. The League responded to the Albanian allegations by establishing a Mixed Commission to examine the question in detail.

In March 1924, the Mixed Commission decided that Greek subjects who were Muslims and of Albanian origin, and more specifically those residing in Epirus, had to be excluded from the compulsory exchange of populations between Greece and Turkey. Indeed, in accordance with the above-mentioned decision, a special delegation headed by the Swede Eric Einer Ekstrand visited Epirus (and Macedonia) to collect information on people of Albanian origin. However, the members of this delegation concluded that the great majority of Muslims who were Greek subjects thought of Turkey as their country of origin and were willing to be included in the exchange of populations.[26] As the great majority of Muslims living in Greece were ethnically Turks, the findings of Ekstrand's delegation came as no surprise. For the Albanian Chams, however, the issue centred around their claims to belong to the Albanian nation. The Council of the League discussed this matter during its thirtieth session (29 August–3 October): the Albanian position maintained that the Greek authorities were encouraging the 'Albanians of Epirus' to consider mass migration by calling them 'Greeks of Turkish origin' and convincing them to adopt the second identity in their public pronouncements. The Council finally decided to appoint the neutral members of the Mixed Commission as its 'mandatories' charged with the responsibility of protecting the 'Muslim minority of Albanian origin' residing in Greece.[27] The Cham issue became further embroiled in discussions over the treatment of minorities in Greece until new developments occured the following summer.

The Return of Ahmed Zogu

By acting in an autocratic and unconstitutional manner, the new government was discredited from the start. One of the first acts of the Noli administration was to set up a political court which sentenced several leaders of the previous government to death, in their absence, and ordered their properties to be confiscated. Noli also ordered several of his political opponents to be paraded continuously around Tirana's central square, whilst being force-fed cod-liver oil, until they defecated in front of the crowd. Initially, Noli had refused to legitimize his revolution through a general election. However, by November the Noli government was preparing for elections to the Constituent Assembly, in response to international pressure to give his revolutionary regime some legal status. Nevertheless, before elections could be called, discontented army officers felt the time was now right to move quickly against the government. Zogu himself had also decided that the moment had come to overthrow Noli.

On 13 December 1924, having recruited a mercenary force, which included Russian members of General Wrangle's refugee army, Zogu and around five hundred of his Mati tribesmen crossed from Yugoslavia into Albania and marched to Tirana. They had been adequately supplied with aid from the Yugoslav government. Ever since the Mirdite and other northern tribes had been effectively bought off by Zogu's payments, the Yugoslavs had been looking for another chance to exert their influence over Albanian affairs. To hide the involvement of the Yugoslavs, their troops were dressed in Albanian costume. Publicly, Belgrade claimed that she could not control the activities of the Albanians along her border. Bajram Curri led a band from Prizren over the border and a similar but smaller force of irregulars crossed the southern frontier from Greece. On 24 December, Zogu triumphantly reentered Tirana. Noli, with around five hundred of his fellow idealists, fled into exile. In 1930 Noli retired from active political life to concentrate once more on his academic and religious duties in America. And so ended Albania's brief experiment with 'democracy'.

Noli's administration had lasted just six months – long enough to demonstrate his political incompetence and naivety. He had con-

ABOVE RIGHT Abdul Frasheri (1839-92), one of the founders of the Albanian League, with fellow League activist, Mehmet Ali Vrioni, in spring 1879. (K. Frasheri, *Lidhja Shqiptare e Prizrenit*, Tirana 1979.)

RIGHT Ismail Kemal (1844-1919) headed the newly independent Albanian state's provisional government at Vlore, in December 1912. (K Naska, *Ismail Qemali ne Levizjen Kombetare Shqiptare*, Tirana 1987.)

ABOVE Hasan Pristina (1873-1933), Kosovar leader, active in the Committee for the Defence of Kosova. (Photograph in author's possession.)

RIGHT Prince Wilhelm of Wied, appointed by the Powers to administer Albania in 1913.

RIGHT Essad Pasha (left) in Durres in 1914. (J. Swire, *Albania: The Rise of a Kingdom*, London 1929.)

ABOVE A group of Mirdites, including Gjon Marka Gjoni, at the turn of the century.
(A. Degrand, *Souvenirs de la Haute-Albanie*, Paris 1901.) BELOW Three armed Ghegs,
members of the Hoti and Gruda tribes, photographed at the turn of the century
(K. Frasheri, *Lidhja Shqiptare,* ibid).

ABOVE LEFT Bajram Curri (1862-1925) activist of the Albanian League and the League of Peja. (*Fjalori Enciklopedik Shqiptare*, Tirana 1985.) BELOW Ahmed Zogu (later King Zog) entering Tirana after the Lushnja Congress in 1920 (C. Dako, *Zogu the First: King of the Albanians*, Tirana 1937.) ABOVE RIGHT Bishop Fan Stilian Noli (1882-1965), the founding head of the Albanian Orthodox Church in 1908 in Boston, who headed a six-month administration in Tirana in 1924. (*Fjalori Enciklopedik Shqiptare*, ibid.)

ABOVE King Zog and Queen Geraldine on their wedding day in Tirana in 1938. (Photograph in author's possession.)

RIGHT A Tosk wearing the traditional fustanella, Girokaster 1938. (Vandeleur Robinson, *Albania's Road to Freedom*, London 1941.)

ABOVE The construction of the Viale dell'Impero (Tirana's main street) by the Italians in 1941. (Gesandten E. von Luckwald, *Albanien: Land Zwishen Gestern und Morgen*, Munich 1942.)

RIGHT Enver Hoxha with Tito's emissary Miladin Popovic who, together with Dusan Mugosa, laid the foundations for a unified Albanian Communist Party; pictured here in 1943. (Pero Zlater, *Gospodar Zemplje Orlova*, Zagreb 1984.)

ABOVE A division of the National Liberation Army, Tirana 1944; the woman pictured is most probably Liri Belishova. (K. Frasheri, *Lidhja Shqiptare*, ibid.) BELOW Enver Hoxha and Mehmet Shehu at the victory celebrations in November 1944. (*Enver Hoxha, 1908-1985*, Tirana 1986.)

ABOVE Enver Hoxha with Stalin and Molotov in Moscow, July 1947. (*Enver Hoxha* ibid.)
RIGHT Enver Hoxha with his successor, Ramiz Alia, in 1983. (*Enver Hoxha*, ibid.)

demned his exiled opponents to death and confiscated their property when perhaps it would have been wiser and more diplomatic to proclaim an amnesty. His regime had from the start lacked unity. Many of his supporters had joined his revolution merely to oppose Zogu and not because they agreed with Noli's policies. Once the common goal of ejecting Zogu had been achieved, the coalition fragmented and the revolution was overtaken by disagreement, confusion and indecision. As well as lacking domestic support, Noli's administration had also failed to attract financial backing, and this failure to secure a foreign loan together with virtual diplomatic isolation sealed Noli's fate. The Powers had been suspicious of the way in which Noli's administration had tried to follow an independent foreign policy, beginning with the rejection of Mussolini's planned Treaty of Alliance, which aimed to reorganize Albania's military under Italian guidance. No government, either of the Great Powers or of the Balkan states, recognized Noli's regime. However, in June, Mussolini had taken an initiative with a view to recognition, for he believed the new government might be a useful tool for Italy. But he came up against vigorous resistance from Yugoslavia and also from Britain, who saw this as damaging to the interests of its oil companies.

During the war, the Austrians and the Italians had undertaken some fruitful oil explorations in Albania, which caused Britain no longer to consider Albania a 'worthless bit of territory'. Britain suddenly developed an 'Albania policy', which focused on the possibility of the Anglo-Persian Oil Company being granted rights to exploit Albania's oil reserves, and included backing for Albania's bid to join the League of Nations. The British, fearing for their oil concessions, had encouraged Sir Harry Eyres to openly oppose Noli in favour of Zogu. Thus the Anglo-Persian Oil Company agreed to give Zogu 50 million dinars, half of which was to be paid immediately, the other half once Zogu had regained power. Zogu used the money to pay off chiefs in the Diber region and Prizren.[28] Another notable deficiency of Noli's administration was the failure to build any military defence for his regime. When his government rejected the Italian–Albanian commercial agreement and plan of military alliance, Rome quickly abandoned the initiative. The Powers' anti-Albanian campaign reached its height when the agreement between the Albanian government and the Soviet Union on the establishment of diplomatic relations came to light. Certain Western newspapers, helped by propaganda from the Balkan states, made a great furore over 'the new hearth of bolshevism in the Balkans', and Noli himself was nicknamed 'the red bishop'.[29] Noli's greatest mistake, however, was his failure to push ahead with his promised agrarian reforms. Having announced a sweeping reform programme, he could then do little to implement it. Domestic opposition forced him to capitulate over this most important issue of all. He recognized this failure, and later told Joseph Swire: 'By insisting on the agrarian reforms I aroused the wrath of the landed aristocracy; by failing to carry them out I lost the support of the peasant masses.'[30]

6

The Consolidation of Zogu's Regime and the Italian Ascendancy

True, there are no brigands in Albania, because all of them have gone to Tirana, where they rob with authority from behind desks.
Popular saying in Albania in the 1930s

On 31 January 1925 the four-member Regency was abolished, Ahmed Zogu was elected president of a newly declared Albanian republic, and Tirana was endorsed officially as the country's permanent capital. The constitution which followed was designed to enhance Zogu's power to appoint or dismiss ministers at will. Zogu immediately set about consolidating his power and liquidating or exiling the more formidable of his former opponents. Luigj Gurakuqi was assassinated in a Bari café; his assassin was speedily acquitted. Bajram Curri was hunted down and his body found in a cave near Dragobi. Although it was generally accepted in Tirana that Curri died at the hands of Zogu's agents, local people insisted that he had committed suicide. Many other Kosova leaders – such as Zia Dibra, who was shot while attempting to escape police arrest – met with an untimely end. Zogu then instigated moves to curtail the activities of the Kosova Committee, which constituted a danger to the maintenance of his good relations with Yugoslavia. Troops that were loyal to Noli were disarmed and disbanded. This left the way clear for Zogu to set up his dictatorship – which, it could be argued, was better suited to the political realities of Albania than had been the alien concept of democracy. The country remained under martial law pending the restoration of a constitutional government. Henceforth, to enable him to cope with the intricate complexity of Albanian politics, Zogu gave himself unrestricted power of veto over any laws passed in the new government.

It was an authoritarian and conservative regime, the primary aim of which was the maintenance of stability and order. It was thus supported by the clan leaders and landowners, all of whom had a vested interest in preserving the status quo. Nevertheless, the new government did at least bring an end to the perennial regional rebellions that had been the country's fate during the first half of the 1920s. Under the new administration, the northern tribes were for the first time brought within the control of the central government, though they were allowed to retain their traditional organizations, as in the past. Although the new civil and criminal codes introduced by Zogu were in theory applied everywhere, the unwritten Kanun of Lek still prevailed in many parts. Although the northern districts were much neglected during Zogu's rule, he retained the loyalty of the northern tribes – partly by his own standing as a tribal chieftain, and partly by appointing other chieftains to posts in the army. Nevertheless, the Catholic tribes remained less well disposed towards him than were the Muslims.[1] Loyalty to the regime was fostered by a system of 'pensions' and 'salaries' connected with the granting of military titles. The usual procedure was that the beneficiaries were required to present themselves in Tirana once or twice a year to pledge their *besa*. They were received by Zogu, after which they returned home with their commissions and money.

Although the Yugoslavs had backed his return to Albania, they were not in a position to grant Zogu the financial assistance he had hoped for and needed to fund his new regime. He was therefore forced to adopt a policy of cooperation with Italy. A pact had been signed between Italy and Albania on 20 January 1925, whereby Italy gained a monopoly on shipping and trade concessions. This effectively barred other nations from competing against Italian interests. In the same month a National Bank of Albania had been set up by Italian financiers, which issued a paper currency for Albania. Until then there had been no Albanian currency nor any credit organization. Albania had relied on the ten- and twenty-franc gold pieces, worth at that time around US$4.00, and the silver krown, valued at an intrinsic bullion worth which fluctuated according to the state of the silver market.[2] Zogu's regime was also subsidized by an Italian loan of 50 million gold francs issued through the specially created Society for the Economic Development of Albania (SVEA), which granted low-interest loans for development programmes. In this way Italy gradually increased her economic and political interests in the country. The League of Nations would still not risk a loan to Albania until internal stability could be guaranteed, and so, due to the appalling financial condition of the country, Zogu had little choice but to turn to Italy. Italy was the only country solid enough, and with the strategic interest in Albania, to be willing to underwrite and support the chaotic Albanian economy.[3]

In February, the agreement between the National Assembly and Anglo-Persian Oil Company concluded in 1922 was ratified, whereby the Albanian government was to receive increased royalties and the area allowed for prospecting was also to be increased. By granting the concession, Zogu was assured of continued British diplomatic support. Several other oil companies also received concessions to drill for oil. Among them were Ferrovia Dello Stato Italiano, Syndicat France–Albanie and the Sinclair and Standard oil companies. However, the money paid for these concessions rarely turned up inside the state treasury.

At the same time the Albanians discouraged other foreign investment by demanding unreasonable, if not impossible, terms. Another event of importance was the establishment, in March 1922, of an air passenger and mail service between Tirana, Shkoder, Korca and Vlore by the Adria Aero Lloyd, a German company, which obtained a monopoly of air routes in Albania.[4] In an effort to add an appearance of legitimacy to Zogu's regime, a rather pointless general election took place at the end of April. The result, an overwhelming victory for the government, was a foregone conclusion, since most of the opposition leaders were in exile. This was followed by the signing of a military agreement with Italy, whereby Italy pledged to come to Albania's assistance in the event of an attack on her territory. And so the Italian ascendency in Albania gathered momentum. Zogu was only too aware that the slightest sign of internal unrest could serve as a pretext for Italian military intervention. In an effort to secure his own power-base, he therefore arranged for a British Inspectorate of Gendarmerie to be established. In comparison with other police forces, the British police were thought to be relatively honest, reliable and loyal. The Gendarmerie was headed by a Colonel W.F. Stirling, previously Governor of Jaffa, who had recently been appointed by Zogu as an advisor to his Interior Ministry. The British police officers who acted as inspectors and organizers were recruited by Stirling on a voluntary basis, and were employed and paid for by the Albanian government.

Meanwhile, there remained a disputed territory which prevented the finalizing of Albania's frontiers. The district now known as Sveti Naum, on the shores of Lake Ohrid, was still occupied by Yugoslav troops. The Yugoslavs claimed that Zogu had promised them the region in return for the assistance they had provided him on his return to Albania the previous December. Zogu, however, denied this and the case was referred to the Conference of Ambassadors. The matter eventually reached a settlement whereby Yugoslavia was granted Sveti Naum and the area around Mount Vermoshi, whilst Albania gained the nearby town of Peshkopije plus a few other small villages. Thus at last did Albania cease to be a mere 'geographical expression', 14 years after she became independent! [5] At the beginning of 1926, Sir Harry Eyres was replaced by Edmund O'Reilly, who became convinced that Italian involvement in Albania was a threat not only to British interests, but also to Albania's independence. Although the British had been tolerant towards Mussolini's foreign policy moves with regard to Albania, Austen Chamberlain, as British foreign secretary, felt the timing was wrong and advised Mussolini to back down. A British cruiser was despatched to Durres. Mussolini had no choice but to cease his efforts to subjugate Albania for the time.[6]

In August, Colonel Stirling resigned as head of the Gendarmerie under the pressure of too heavy a workload. He was replaced by Major-General Sir Joycelyn Percy, a distinguished military officer, who had under him eight British officers and an efficient force of around three thousand. Percy insisted that the men should receive their pay regularly, be adequately housed and equipped with proper uniform and weapons. It was only under such conditions that they would feel confidence in the Gendarmerie command and develop a sense of security, so that their loyalty would be to their Gendarmerie commander and to no one else. Above all, Percy tried to teach the officers and men that they must treat the people fairly and justly and win their confidence rather than their suspicion or hostility.[7] Despite the chronic bribery and corruption in the country, the Gendarmerie did manage to inspire a basic respect for law and order. Highway banditry actually diminished to the point where traffic could pass unmolested along the country's half-dozen or so roads.

Nonetheless, during the interwar years, Albania remained Europe's least developed and poorest state by far. The regime had made little headway in alleviating the mass illiteracy of the peasants. Although some progress was achieved with the establishment of several primary and secondary schools, and an agricultural college at Kavaje, the lack of both finance and qualified teachers meant that the standard of teaching was extremely poor.[8] The peasants, especially those in the north, who were basically self-sufficient, retired into themselves. They remained isolated in their tribal pockets, wary and distrustful of outside interference and respecting only their local leaders. Tirana remained a sleepy provincial city. Traffic consisted of horse- or ox-driven carts; the few cars belonged to foreign diplomats or government officials. For those few foreigners such as the Stirlings, and others from the diplomatic corps of the various foreign legations, Tirana offered little in the way of Western European cultural amenities. In an effort to give his capital a Western cultural air, Zogu founded a dramatic and choral society – the performances of which, however, proved an embarrassing ordeal for those unfortunate foreigners who could not find reasons to excuse themselves from attending.

The Growth of Italian Interests in Albania

In the meantime, Zogu's overt political ties with Italy began in earnest when, on 27 November 1926, the two states signed a pact pledging friendship and mutual support. The pact effectively guaranteed the Italian government's right to maintain the political and territorial status quo in Albania, together with the maintenance of Zogu's own personal regime. This was matched by an increased Italian economic penetration. Around this time, Italian companies began settling Italian colonists on the lowland plains in the south of the country. In 1926 the first three hundred colonists arrived. Although there were small pockets of economic investment throughout the country, much of it – such as the building of bridges, roads and harbour development projects – was for Italian military and strategic purposes. Nevertheless, Italy did finance a few small commercial enterprises such as cigarette and soap factories, a cement mill, tanneries and public buildings, thus capitalizing on her exclusive patronage over Albania. This was respected by the other Great Powers, Great Britain having once more lost interest in Albania – not least because the Anglo-Persian Oil Company had failed to discover sufficient reserves of oil in the country.

The signing of the Italian–Albanian pact caused some anxiety in

Athens and focused Greek attention on the still unresolved question of the Chams, which had led to increased tensions between Greece and Albania. The Greek Ministry of Foreign Affairs had serious reservations about the pact because the

> interests of the Albanians for their 'brothers' now had the backing of a more important power whose territorial ambitions extended to the territories washed by the Adriatic sea, not to mention the Ionian sea; this power could not but benefit from the existence of the Cham minority either because it was favoured by this minority, which was hostile to the Greek State, or because it [the 'important power', i.e. Italy] could always use the Chams as a counterweight to the [Greek] efforts in Northern Epirus.[9]

In an effort to settle the issue of the Chams, the Athens government had tried to gain Ankara's approval for encouraging some Chams to migrate to Turkey, in the hope that the rest would follow. Initially Ankara had been unwilling to allow the settlement of Chameria Muslims on Turkish soil, but following the diplomatic efforts by Athens, the Turkish government had agreed to allow the settlement of 5,000 Chams. However, Albanian charges directed against Greece concerning the Muslims of Chamouria gradually increased and reached their climax during the first half of 1928. In March, the Albanian Ministry of Foreign Affairs delivered to the Greek chargé d'affaires in Tirana a memorandum reiterating the Albanian charges for the 'austere measures' exercised by the local authorities against the Chams and expressing a formal protest that the Greek government did not recognize them as a 'national minority'. The Greek side argued that 'the Albanian government had no right to get involved in the domestic affairs of another country: the Chams were Greek citizens and the projection of Albania as a protector state constituted disregard of the basic elements of Greek sovereign rights.'[10] The League of Nations continued to note the Albanian protests over the treatment of the Chams but more important issues were now emerging concerning minorities in northern Europe.

Despite consolidating his power base with the Italians, Zogu was acutely aware of the many forces wishing to destroy him both internally and abroad. There followed several violent incidents culminating in the murder of Zogu's brother-in-law, Ceno Bey, in Prague in October 1927. Not surprisingly, these events triggered feelings of paranoia in Zogu. He began to see plots against him around every corner, engineered by either the Italians, the Yugoslavs, Albanian exiles or internal rivals. Having broken off diplomatic relations with Yugoslavia over the arrest of a Yugoslav accused of spying in Tirana, Zogu's fear of Belgrade forced him to even greater reliance on Italy, as his country became increasingly isolated diplomatically. As a result, on 22 November 1927, a second Pact of Tirana was signed, which enhanced the commitments of the first treaty by allowing a large Italian military mission to be based permanently in Albania. Italy agreed to sign the treaty partly because Yugoslavia and France had at that time also signed a pact, directed in part against Italy. This resulted in a substantial increase in Italian military activity in the country and, as Italian officers were attached to virtually every Albanian military unit, the independence of the Albanian army was effectively curtailed. Discontent perpetually existed within the various components of Albanian society. Apart from the constant economic grievances, Catholic mistrust of the central dominance of the north continued to be one of the most serious obstacles to Albania's unity and progress. During the winter, there began several revolts by the northern clans, each subsequently crushed by the superior forces hurriedly rushed up from Tirana.

During the years of his presidency, from 1924 to 1928, Zogu maintained complete control of the office of prime minister. A unified system of local government was established, helping to create an extensive class of civil servants, most of whom could be bought off with a bribe. The new constitution of December 1928 gave Zogu unrestricted legislative, judicial and executive powers which extended his personal dictatorship. The enforcement of law and order was seen as an essential prerequisite to the progress of the country. Zogu thus decreed the abolition of blood feuds, and prohibited the carrying of arms by all citizens except those of his own Mati tribe and their northern neighbours, the Mirdites. The remaining northern tribesmen strongly resented their disarmament, together with the curbing of brigandage (which, since they were predominantly landless, deprived them of one of their principal means of livelihood). Other plans to enhance the country's efficiency included the drainage of the malarial swamps in order to increase the amount of agricultural land. Even so, the primitive state of Albanian agriculture could not keep pace with the requirements of the ever-increasing population, which led to a constant stream of emigration – primarily to America and Turkey. In parts of southern Albania, however, especially around Korca, the standard of living was improved by the fact that many peasants were now receiving money from relatives who had previously emigrated to America.

The Proclamation of the Monarchy

Uncertain of the level of his popular support, Zogu decided that perhaps a monarchy would grant his regime more security and continuity than a republican form of government. Albania was the only Balkan country which was not a monarchy. Therefore, on 1 September 1928, Zogu abandoned his Turkic name of Ahmed, together with the 'u' from Zogu, and crowned himself as 'Zog I, King of the Albanians'. This title caused consternation in Belgrade. While the Yugoslavs had no objection to a 'King of Albania' they accused Zog of inciting irredentist tendencies amongst the Kosovar Albanians by labelling himself King of all Albanians. Nevertheless, they accorded him recognition so as not to push him further towards Italy. To instil a sense of occasion into his largely apathetic subjects a three-day public holiday was proclaimed, with firework displays and 'spontaneous' demonstrations in the major towns. An official decree stipulated that: 'The whole population must take part ... no Albanian man or woman shall sit during the demonstrations in a coffeehouse or restaurant; all must accompany the population in their manifestations.' The Catholics in the north were not keen on the idea of a Muslim king. To gain support for the monarchy, Zog granted each new army officer a step up in rank, a pay rise and a dazzling new uniform.[11] The shift from republic to monarchy nevertheless had little impact on the marginal existence of the majority of Albanians. Edith Durham accepted the widely held view abroad that the monarchy was introduced primarily to secure Italian interests. She later wrote to a friend:

> I have always thought King Zog too ignorant and uncultured to be capable of ruling rightly, and that it was for that reason that the Italians let him be made King instead of President. In order that he might be used as their tool. As President he could have been turned out and a better man elected. But as King, they had him permanently in their hands.[12]

The unfortunate Prince Wied mentioned to those who would listen that he had never formally abdicated his throne. But he waited in vain for a response, and finally gave up his claim.

The new constitution put forward in December 1928 gave the King unrestrictive legislative, judicial and executive powers, thus ensuring Zog's dominance. A rambling document of 234 articles, the constitution stated that the Kingdom of Albania was a democratic, constitutional and hereditary monarchy. There was no state religion; all creeds were equal before the law. All power was derived from the nation, and vested in the King and a unicameral parliament. Both were authorized to initiate laws. The authentic interpretation of the laws pertained to the legislative power (article 10); in practice it was reserved for the King. The election process continued to ensure that only candidates loyal to Zog stood a chance of victory, but since political parties were illegal, only such candidates ever stood for election. One hundred gold francs had to be paid to the municipality by every would-be candidate before his name was listed; few could afford this heavy fee.[13] Under Zog the government was entrusted to a single-chamber legislature under the control of a Council of State. Its members were however appointed by the King, who exercised what might be described as a fairly benevolent despotism. Members of the council were paid what were, for Albania, very large salaries – moreover, according to article 25 they could not be imprisoned for their debts. Consequently they were to a great extent dependent upon the King's favour, and tended to feather their own nests when the opportunity arose. The King would dismiss one cabinet and appoint another at will. The legislature was selected on the basis of one member to every 15,000 of the population: every 20 voters (men of 21 and over) chose one of their number to represent them in the election. In the absence of political parties, a list of the King's official candidates was issued to the electors.[14]

During the late 1920s and early 1930s, Tirana was gradually transformed from a dormant old Ottoman town into something resembling a capital city. Streets were widened and paved, as Italian architects redesigned the city. Much of the central area was completely rebuilt, the only central public building to escape demolition being the Haxhi Ethem-Bey mosque dating from 1796–7. Italian planning added a couple of hotels, a few prosperous houses such as the King's new palace, the Yugoslav and Italian legations, and public buildings in and around the central square. This monumental centre was called the Piazza Skanderbeg. Much of the domestic state budget went on public buildings during Zog's reign. In fact, of the 11 million Albanian gold francs budgeted between 1928 and 1938, 75 per cent went on the construction of public and other residential edifices in the capital, which then had a population of around 25,000.[15] Tirana's new ministry buildings housed the large number of Italian advisors who worked on public projects and 'supervised' the ministries. For example, Italian advisors sat at the Ministry of Education, where they worked to influence the school curricula to conform more closely to those of

Italy. They favoured Catholic schools, and sought to introduce Italian as Albania's second language, an ambition not realized until 1933.[16] Zog managed to hold the reins domestically, but he frequently complained that his fate was to be served by either fools or knaves. 'If intelligent and energetic, they are rogues,' he lamented, 'if honest, they are either incompetent or idle.'[17]

In order to extend his direct control throughout the entire country, Zog placed great emphasis on the construction of roads. These would aid not only trade but also the collection of taxes in previously inaccessible areas. To accelerate the abolition of banditry and blood-feuds, the remote outlying valleys were opened up by a programme of road-building. This involved cutting into the sides of the mountains with a series of serpentine zig-zags, a form of road construction which was very labour-intensive. In order to recruit labour, every male Albanian over the age of 16 years was legally bound to give ten days' free labour each year to the state. If he did not wish to do the work himself, he had to pay someone else to do it for him. Zog also toyed with the idea of land reform, but feared disturbing his close relationship with, and support from, the beys. Much of the fertile land of central and southern Albania was still in the hands of the large land-owners, whilst freeholding was mostly limited to less desirable regions. The Agrarian Reform Law of April 1930 was aimed at remedying this situation. Every bey's land was to be divided into three parts: one-third to be left under his free control, provided he worked it to its full capacity; another third to be made inalienable, to prevent him or his successors from selling out and leaving his family destitute; and one-third to be expropriated by the government and resold on easy terms to the peasants. It appears, however, that too great a time elapsed between debating the reform, passing the law, and putting it into action. What few attempts took place to expropriate the land from the beys were frustrated by diverse means. When government officials went to Fier in Muzeqe to expropriate a certain area of land, they found that the owner had so subdivided it among various members of his numerous family by antedated deeds of sale or gift that there was nothing left to expropriate. The same thing happened near Tirana, whilst at Elbasan, on learning that grazing land was to be exempt from expropriations, a certain bey evicted his tenants, burned down their houses and turned to grass all the land they had formerly cultivated.[18]

The Serbian Colonization of Kosova

In the meantime, the situation of the Albanians in Kosova continued to deteriorate. Throughout the interwar period the Yugoslav government exerted pressure on the Albanian population either to emigrate or to be assimilated. The end of Ottoman power and wartime chaos witnessed the exodus of Ottoman officials from Kosova, along with the many Albanian Muslims from urban areas who had either served in the region's civil administration or had been members of the small mercantile community. As a result, the population of Kosova had actually decreased by about 60,000 between 1913 and 1920. This vacuum was soon filled by an influx of Serbian civil, military and police officials, along with a contingent of skilled technicians to run the region's minuscule industrial structure.[19] Settlers were brought from Montenegro, Hercegovina and Lika to live in Kosova on land confiscated from Albanians, and many Kosovars subsequently found themselves homeless. Under the Decree on the Colonization of the Southern Regions of 24 September 1920, and the Law on the Colonization of the Southern Regions of 11 June 1931, the colonists were given special treatment and positions that were privileged even in comparison with the Slavs who had long inhabited the region. The settlers were granted up to 50 hectares of land, the right of free transport up to the place of settlement, the free use of state or communal forests and pastures, and exemption from any taxation for three years. Under the vague pretext of agrarian reform, land which was abandoned – or deliberately described as such – was liberally distributed to Serb and Montenegrin colonists. This 'abandoned' land included that portion left untilled during the rotation of crops. Pastures, forestry and common land used by the Albanian peasantry were seized as 'land in excess of need'. This was a particularly severe blow to those small farmers with just a few acres of land, as their livestock depended on the open pasture and commons for fodder, and the family needed the forest for fuel.

It was not only in Kosova that colonization took place. In Skopje there were in 1936 30,000 'non-local Serbian' inhabitants, who made up more than 40 per cent of the city's population. In the periphery of Skopje, over 10,000 people had been settled by the Land Colonization Decrees by the end of 1941. Pristina contained around 4,500 newly arrived Slavs, who made up 35 per cent of its population. The situation was more or less the same in the other urban centres, as the

Serbianization policy continued. According to Yugoslav statistics, in the territory of the 'southern regions' over which the agrarian directories of Peja (Pec), Ferizaj, Mitrovitca, and Skopje extended their activities, 17,879 households of colonists were settled between 1918 and 1940. Of these, 13,393 households, or about 60,000 people, settled in Kosova.[20] Djordje Krstic, chief agrarian commissioner responsible for the colonization of Kosova, pointed out that:

> through colonization, Skopje has doubled its population, Presheva has almost half its houses Serbian, Pec is full of colonists, whilst Ferizaj, they will soon dominate it completely... [He concluded that] in the Lab district of northern Kosova, the colonization had thoroughly changed the ethnic composition of the entire region in which, in 1913, there had not been a single Serbian inhabitant.[21]

Other assimilation methods included the forcing of Albanians to alter their names by adding Serbian suffixes such as -vic, -vc, or -c. They were denied the right to use the Albanian language for official matters, and all schooling was conducted in Serbo-Croat. This latter fact, however, had little effect on the lives of the majority of Kosova's population, whether Slav or Albanian. During the interwar period, only about 30 per cent of eligible children were actually receiving any education at all in the region. Over 90 per cent of the Albanian population was illiterate, and only about 2 per cent of eligible Albanians were enrolled in secondary schools. It is estimated that prior to 1939 over half a million Albanians emigrated from Yugoslavia due to the loss of their land, most going to Turkey or to the United States, and a few thousand crossing over into Albania.

On 2 March 1929 the Kosovar leader, Hassan Pristina, addressed a petition to the League of Nations in which he alleged that the Yugoslav authorities did not provide any schools for the Albanian minority in Yugoslavia – who, he maintained, were generally oppressed and deprived of their civil and political rights. The Yugoslavs replied to the Council of the League that Pristina was a revolutionary and an irredentist engaged in subversive activities against Yugoslavia, and that contrary to his claim a large number of schools existed in Yugoslavia with special classes for Albanian children. The Council of the League met to consider the matter on 18 September 1929 and decided that, in view of the vagueness of the allegations made in the petition and of the personality and antecedents of the petitioner, and considering the detailed and apparently satisfactory nature of the reply of the Yugoslav government, no action needed to be taken on the petition.[22] By now Zog was convinced that Kosova was irreversibly lost to Albania, and he therefore consistently suppressed the old Kosova Committee. Nevertheless, the issue of Kosova was ever-present. In 1931, an Italian instructor training youths in Kukes was reported by a British gendarmerie officer for impressing upon his pupils that the future of Albania lay in the recovery of Kosova, and that Italy was there to fulfil the Albanians' national aspirations. Albanians had also been approached by Italians to undertake subversive acts against Yugoslavia on the Albanian frontier.[23] The Yugoslav government remained deeply suspicious of Italian actions regarding the Balkans. Belgrade's fears that the pacts of Tirana were primarily directed against Yugoslavia were confirmed when, following the signing of the second pact, the Italian army began to lay out a general scheme of roads which were mainly directed towards the Yugoslav frontier. As one Italian officer remarked: 'Our object is to connect Durazzo [Durres] with Kossovo, and Valona [Vlore] with the heart of Macedonia – both regions within the Yugoslav frontier.'[24]

Foreign Philanthropists in Albania

During the 1920s there were no international aid programmes to provide Albania with the economic and technical assistance she needed to modernize and develop. The country was forced, therefore, to rely upon the assistance in various forms of private philanthropic agencies and individuals. One of the most important of these non-governmental ventures was the Albanian Vocational School in Tirana (AVS) or 'Shkolle Teknike'. Between 1921 and 1933, the AVS was financed by the American Junior Red Cross, the income from the various commercial activities in which the school was engaged, and some small grants from the Albanian government. In 1921, when the AVS was founded, there had been only two secondary schools in Albania and neither had offered technical or vocational courses.[25] Since there were few Albanians who possessed the technical skills required to enable their homeland to modernize, the AVS provided its students with both classroom instruction and practical experience in a broad range of vocational programmes. It operated a commercial printing press, an electric power station, an ice plant and a farm. It also undertook several construction projects, including the building of the American Legation in Tirana. Several of the school's graduates were admitted to reputable US and

European universities, and the school brought together young Albanians of different religious and social backgrounds from every region of the country.[26] From the beginning it was to be a cooperative effort, engaging the active participation of Albanian government officials, who were gradually to assume an increasing responsibility for the school until able to go on alone. Harry Fultz, the American director of the AVS, encouraged his students to 'strive to make Albania a country worth living for and, if necessary, worth dying for.'[27]

At the same time, young people were instructed in the mass exercise and close-order drills which were so favoured by other totalitarian governments of the time, especially Italy and Germany. Enti Kombetar, a nationwide compulsory youth organization modelled on that of Italy, gave 'moral, patriotic and pre-military instruction'. It swept into its fold all boys between the ages of 15 and 19, and all girls between 15 and 18. The commander-general was an Albanian responsible to the King, but the real organizers were Italian – an inspector of physical culture and an inspector of pre-military instruction.[28] The movement however never penetrated the remoter communities in the mountains of the north and south. In these areas, a few followed very basic primary schooling, after which the girls worked at home all day, whilst the boys tended to livestock or crops. It was not until 1934 that schooling was made compulsory, when the school reform law stated that 'schools are to be built in every locality where there are thirty or more children of school age'. However, this was not even partially realized until the decade following the Second World War.

There were a few foreigners who undertook charitable work in interwar Albania. Foremost amongst them was Lady Carnarvon, the mother of Aubrey Herbert. After Aubrey's untimely death in 1923, Lady Carnarvon set herself to work for Albania in his memory, and at her own expense engaged in relief work among Albanian refugees from Yugoslavia.[29] In the winter of 1926 Lady Carnarvon, whose main interest was addressing Albania's numerous health problems, came to Albania in pursuit of malarial control, organizing a medical mission in Vlore to fight malaria and establishing a hospital there with an English matron and nurse. She also financed the first public library in Albania, the Herbert Library in Tirana. It later became known as the Herbert Institute, to which the British Foreign Office made a gift of books in 1934. Another of Lady Carnarvon's projects was the founding of a village, situated near Kavaje, for the numerous refugees from Kosova. The village was also called Herbert (now Helmasi) in honour of Aubrey. The few foreigners who genuinely tried to help the Albanians were often frustrated by the response. As Edith Durham wrote:

> Poor Lady Carnarvon spent so much money – thousands of pounds – on trying to establish relations with the youth of Albania by means of the Library, the boy scouts, the trained hospital nurses and the teachers of infant welfare and got little support or gratitude. So much money has been embezzled by the Albanians that even the Library is hard to run and all the other things have lapsed.[30]

It would appear, however, that Lady Carnarvon totally misunderstood the Albanian customs, mentality and historical development of this time. The alien concepts of public libraries and boy scouts required a sense of community spirit which belonged in another world to 1930s Albania.

By the beginning of the 1930s Zog had become obsessed with his personal safety, trusting only his own Mati tribesmen. He lived in constant fear of assassination, venturing out in public only rarely. His suspicions were well founded. In 1931 in Vienna an attempt was made on his life on the steps of the State Opera House. In January of that year Zog had decided to travel to Vienna to see specialists about his poor health. Taking elaborate security precautions, his entourage installed themselves in the Hotel Imperial. On the evening of 20 February, Zog and his party attended a performance of the Vienna Opera; as the King was leaving, two Albanians shot at him. Zog hastily pulled a gun from his jacket and fired back, hitting nothing. The King's aide-de-camp, Colonel Topalaj, was killed and his minister of the court, Ekrem Libohova, wounded, but the King was unharmed. It has been claimed that this was the first of 55 assassination attempts made during King Zog's life.[31] When Zog returned to Albania there was a great show of rejoicing in the streets. It seems, however, that the exuberant crowd mostly comprised schoolchildren told to line the streets and cheer their King's return. Many of Zog's exiled opponents had organized themselves into the Bashkimi Kombetar (National Union). The would-be assassins, Ndok Gjeloshi and Aziz Cami, were members of this group. Although both held Yugoslav diplomatic passports, it seems unlikely that Yugoslavia would have wished Zog's death, as such an event would in turn have led the Italians to invoke the Pact of Tirana and send in their troops.

Italian Involvement Intensifies

The beginning of the 1930s saw an increasing upsurge of anti-Italian feeling throughout Albania. Although the Italians did contribute to economic development, they also caused severe inflation and discrimination against Albanians in the labour market. Italian immigration led to a rise in property and land prices, together with higher food prices in the major towns. At the same time, Italy had gradually begun to exert political pressure on Zog by exploiting his financial weakness. Tentative moves were made by the Italians to recover the loan granted in 1925, by maintaining that SVEA was a private company and its shareholders had to be protected – disregarding the fact that the money had been spent to secure Italian strategic interests in Albania. Zog vigorously opposed this move, though to placate the Italians he realized that some repayment was necessary. Like Fan Noli before him, Zog had been unsuccessful in gaining financial support from the League of Nations. The international community had accepted his humiliating dependence upon Italy, which by now had almost total hegemony over Albania. Nevertheless, it could be argued that Rome's patronage during the twenties had helped to prevent Albania's partition between her Balkan neighbours. In 1931 Zog obtained another Italian loan of 100 million gold francs to be repaid at 10 million a year on very easy terms, but the price extracted by Italy for their generosity was greater involvement in Albania's affairs. This included more economic privileges, the teaching of the Italian language in schools, and the admission of more Italian colonists to settle on land reclaimed from the newly drained malarial swamps.

Throughout the 1930s Zog increasingly relied on Italian economic assistance, even though Italian politicians constantly took advantage of Albania's economic and diplomatic weakness. Direct Italian subsidies had allowed the Albanian government to balance its budgets, but at the cost of the country becoming a virtual Italian protectorate. As Italy began tightening the economic screws on Albania, Zog began to fear for his country's independence. He therefore hurriedly instigated several anti-Italian gestures. Italy's proposal for a customs union was rejected, and various Italian advisors were dismissed. In April 1933 all private schools were put under Albanian control. Although this move was primarily intended to target Italian schools, the Greek minority schools in the south, where the government had forced teachers to learn Albanian, were also closed. Zog's impulsive action threw the educational system into chaos. The reckless campaign to nationalize education was especially harmful to the Graecophone villages in the south, and the Greek minority leaders immediately took their case to the League of Nations, complaining that Albania was violating the rights of the minorities agreement which it had signed in 1931. Tirana reacted by arresting many leading Greeks and thereby damaging Albanian–Greek relations. The Italians reacted by suspending all financial assistance and gradually withdrawing all Italian personnel.[32] By nationalizing the schools in what was seen as a broadly anti-Christian measure, Zog also managed to alienate both the Catholics and the Orthodox, as the majority of the schools that were closed were church-run. The state also tightened its control over the entire school system, together with increasing domination over the press.

Zog plotted ceaselessly to remain in power, resorting to extreme measures to eradicate any disloyalty. At the beginning of 1933 Hassan Pristina, one of the last remaining leaders of the Kosova Committee, was murdered in Thessalonika, almost certainly upon the orders of Zog. But the King could not so easily eliminate the mass of the Albanian peasantry, who were bitterly dissatisfied with his regime, not least with his continued failure to implement agrarian reform. In June 1934, the Italian fleet paid a sudden and uninvited visit to Durres. The Italians now began to exert such financial pressure on Zog that he was forced to resume his former relations with Italy, lest their loans be withdrawn. In August 1935 there occurred a small but significant revolt in the town of Fier, after a crowd had been falsely told that a revolutionary government had taken over Tirana. Several people joined the small group of rebels and proceeded to march on Lushnja, where they were easily overwhelmed by a large reinforcement of government troops from the capital. The movement was ill-prepared and poorly organized, yet it managed to induce alarm in Zog. It would appear that he overreacted to what was, after all, merely general resentment at some of his policies. To reassure himself that whoever was behind the revolt was eliminated he ordered the indiscriminate arrest of anyone thought to have been involved in it.

In October, in order to appease any opposition, Zog allowed the formation of a new and relatively liberal government, under the much respected former League of Nations representative, Midat Frasheri. However, this government lasted but a year, for although an improvement on the previous one it was weak and failed even to begin to implement its ambitious programme of social and agrarian reform. Following these events public confidence in the government plummeted still further, as the constant intrigue, bribery and endemic corruption placed the country in a seemingly permanent condition of instability. The public had few outlets to voice their discontent, as Albania's only two newspapers had been strictly censored. There was also a rigid penal law to silence political opposition. Despite all this, Zog was generally recognized as the only leader in Albania capable, albeit in small measure, of uniting the divergent elements in Albanian society. To many Albanians, given their tradition of loyalty to clan leadership, the notion of an autocratic monarchy was still easier to accept and understand than a democracy or a republic under a presidency. Nonetheless, between 1935 and 1936, Zog made various attempts to liberalize his regime in the hope of winning over opponents and countering his increasing diplomatic isolation. He thus allowed the press a moderate degree of freedom and permitted some political debate, though like Noli he shied away from instituting real land reform.

Before long Zog was forced to dilute his nationalistic stance and face the harsh realities of his tiny country's vulnerable economic and political situation. He thus felt obliged to adopt a few tactical reversals regarding his foreign policy. Henceforth, tentative moves were made to reduce tension with Greece by easing the restrictions on the private schools that had been nationalized in the Graecophone areas of the south. In November, Zog seized the opportunity to display evidence of Albania's cooperative attitude by voting against a League of Nation's resolution to impose sanctions upon Italy for its invasion of Ethiopia – whereupon the suspended negotiations between Albania and Italy resumed, shortly followed by a new Treaty of Accord signed in March 1936. Italian credit again flowed, though concessions too were exacted from Albania. In May Catholic schools were permitted to reopen, by royal decree, and Italian educators began to return.[33] The Italians were allowed to deepen the port of Durres so that it was able to harbour their oceangoing ships. This was in return for yet another huge, almost interest-free, loan. By the end of the year, the Italian penetration of Albania had intensified, with Italian advisors in the civilian administration as well as the military. In a desperate attempt to switch more of the country's trade away from Italy, Albania concluded trade agreements with both Yugoslavia and Greece.

In some respects, Zog's rule was mildly progressive. Although his

regime was basically secular, and he would not tolerate any interference from the church, Zog did encourage the Albanian Orthodox
community to achieve autocephalous status. Despite severe and continuous opposition from Greece, in 1937 the Orthodox Albanians succeeded in being granted a tomos of autocephaly by the Patriarch of
Constantinople. Another significant achievement of Zog's administration was the reduction of blood-feud vendettas. By 1936 the prefect
of the Mati valley told one traveller that 'whereas he used to have at
least one vendetta murder a week in his valley, now the average was
only one in six weeks.'[34] In January 1937, in order to further secularize,
modernize and Westernize his country, Zog proposed the unveiling of
Muslim women, the elimination of mixed Albanian–European cos-
tumes for males, and the construction of wooden beds to discourage
the peasants from sleeping on the floor.

In March it became a punishable offence for any woman to conceal
her face, either wholly or partially. In order to push this point home,
the King sent three of his unmarried, and unveiled, Muslim sisters
on a tour of the extreme northern section of the country – including
Shkoder, the supposed centre of remaining Muslim fanaticism in the
country. The purpose of the visit was basically to give convincing
evidence of the feasibility and practicality of having all the women of
Albania uncover their faces by revealing the charm of Zog's unveiled
sisters. The three princesses – fully arrayed in up-to-date Western
European dress, with short, tight-fitting skirts and make-up – visited
schools, churches, hospitals and market-places.[35] Although official
accounts claimed the expedition was largely successful, with very little
opposition from conservative elements, it seems unlikely that northern
Muslim women would so easily have abandoned their veils. In the
south the matter was sufficiently important to cause unrest. A stillborn revolt in May 1937 was led by a southern Muslim, Ethem Toto,
a former minister of the interior. Two main factors lay behind it: the
conservative Muslim elements of the south were strongly against the
reforms of Zog, especially the obligatory unveiling of their women;
and there was strong opposition to the renting, for the development
of oil concessions, of a considerable part of the land in the south to
the Italians, despite the fact that the land was already insufficient for
the needs of the local population.

A few months later Zog went even further in his superficial
Westernization by banning the wearing of any national costume by
men, except on national holidays. Nevertheless, it was to take more

than merely changing Albanian dress to wipe away hundreds of years
of deeply rooted tradition. Yet Zog's administration did, to some
degree, succeed in unifying the country, and in keeping Albania's
predatory neighbours at bay.

In order to ensure the stability and continuity of his reign, on 27
April 1938 Zog married Geraldine Apponyi, born in 1915 of an
American, Gladys Stewart, and an Austro-Hungarian Count, Julius
Apponyi. In his desperation to find a suitable bride, the King had
sent his sisters to Vienna and thence on to Budapest, where they
came upon Countess Geraldine Apponyi.[36] The King had been greatly
impressed by a photo of the young countess sent to him by his sisters,
and invited Geraldine to visit Tirana, whereupon he proposed to her.
The wedding was a lavish affair, and among the many wedding gifts
the couple received was a long, scarlet, supercharged Mercedes sent
by Adolf Hitler. The marriage was well received both in Albania and
abroad. After honeymooning in Durres, the couple settled down to an
opulent existence in the royal palace in Tirana, which soon became
known in England as the 'toy court'. Edith Durham commented on
an extravagant trip Zog's five sisters made to the United States: 'Why
the Princesses went to America seems uncertain. What is certain is
that the expenses have been huge and that half-starved peasants feel
it might have been better expended in Albania.'[37]

The Italian Invasion

Meanwhile, in June 1936, Count Galeazzo Ciano, Mussolini's son-in-
law, had become Italian foreign minister. After visiting Tirana for the
first time in April 1937, he advocated a dramatic move, which could
be offset against the increased prestige of the German Reich and so
raise the morale of Italy. Ciano argued for the total annexation of
Albania by Italy, which he said could provide homes for up to two
million Italians. He (falsely) believed that because Albanian public
opinion was largely against Zog, it would therefore be pro-Italian.
Another plan of Ciano's was the idea of partitioning Albania between
Italy and Yugoslavia. However the idea failed to interest the Yugoslavs,
who during the 1930s had disassociated themselves from Albanian
matters, and whose Regent, Prince Paul, remarked: 'We already have
so many Albanians inside our frontiers and they give us so much
trouble that I have no wish to increase their number.'[38] Ciano even
masterminded a bizarre plot to kidnap the King and Queen, in an

attempt to destabilize the country so that Italy had a pretext to move in to restore order. According to Geraldine, on 25 June 1938 the Italian ambassador offered the King, on behalf of his government, a yacht crewed by Italians. Zog refused the gift, fearing that the food on board might be poisoned. Instead, the King said that they would charter it to make a trip to Venice with some of his own servants. Later the King and Queen heard that, had they disembarked in Italy, they would not have been allowed to return to Albania.[39]

By the summer of 1938, the Italians controlled every essential sector of the Albanian state. Up to 170,000 Italian men were working in Albania on tree-planting, irrigation schemes and road construction. This was the core of Albania's present-day road system. The dependence on the Italian economy had increased to the extent that by 1939 Italy accounted for 92.1 per cent of Albanian exports (as compared to 68.4 per cent in the preceding year), and 82.5 per cent of imports (36.3 per cent in 1938).[40] Whilst Ciano busied himself with colonization plans, Mussolini agonized over whether to invade Albania. An attack on Albania had been discussed months previously, and as early as the beginning of February 1939 Easter week had been set as a possible date. But it was not until the middle of March that Mussolini resolved to invade. His fear of Germany was enhanced by Hitler's occupation of Czechoslovakia, and this had ended his doubts over Albania. On 25 March, Mussolini delivered an ultimatum demanding a formal Italian protectorate over Albania and the right to maintain Italian military garrisons in the country. This meant the virtual capitulation of Albanian sovereignty. Ciano described the ultimatum as:

> an accord which, though couched in courteous terms, will permit us to effect the annexation of Albania. Either Zog accepts the conditions we lay before him, or we shall undertake the military seizure of the country. To this end we are already mobilizing and concentrating in Puglia four regiments of Bersaglieri, an infantry division, air force detachments, and all of the first naval squadron.[41]

On 1 April 1939 there was a large anti-Italian demonstration in Tirana, and the angry crowd demanded weapons to fight the Italians. As the Queen was about to give birth, Zog stalled for time by accepting a few of the Italian demands. On April 4, Geraldine produced a son named Leka. The next day Italian warships appeared off the Albanian coast, and Italian planes dropped leaflets over Tirana instructing the Albanians not to resist. All Italians had been recalled from Albania and were crowding to the ports of Vlore and Durres for embarkation.[42]

As no reply came from Zog to Mussolini's ultimatum, at dawn on 7 April Albania was swiftly bombarded. Over 40,000 Italian troops landed at Vlore. What little resistance the Albanians were able to muster came mostly from Durres, where a small, poorly armed group led by a Gendarmerie officer, Abas Kupi, held out until they were overcome by sheer numbers. According to an observer:

> When the invasion took place, the main Albanian troop concentrations were above Kruja. It was intended that they defend Tirana, and when the city had fallen, retreat fighting to the Yugoslav frontier. Nearly a fortnight before, Zog had asked Belgrade whether the frontier would be available for escape, he also asked for a Yugoslav ship to take away Queen Geraldine but had no reply to either request. The Generals decided against being caught like rats in a trap, and when the Italians cleverly outflanked the Elbasan road, they moved quickly before the Greek frontier too was cut off. Giovani Giro, later leader of the Albanian fascists, approached Murat Kaloshi, of Dibra, and his brother Mushta, and offered them 20,000 gold francs to have their districts ready for a revolt against Zog. However, they informed the King, who advised them to accept the money from Giro and to get their instructions. When the plan miscarried, Mussolini began to make his demands, offering Zog a palace in Rome and the throne of a `Greater Albania' in Athens. Zog heard that Giro had given the Mirdite Chief, Gjon Marka Gjoni, 40,000 francs but when taxed, Gjoni telegraphed his loyalty to the King and asked that he might have arms to be allowed to prove it. Tirana decided not to send him any![43]

The King's first concern on that fateful day was for the safety of his family. The Queen and her two-day-old son were sent off an hour and a half before the invasion, in a caravan of cars through the mountains towards the Greek frontier. Zog then broadcast a message to his people urging them to continue the fight, but few owned radios so hardly any heard the appeal. His final desperate efforts to negotiate with the Italians having proved futile, he then made the fateful decision to follow his wife into exile.[44] The seeming impossibility of conducting guerilla warfare in the mountains made the King resolve to leave Albania as soon as possible. Before leaving the palace he went alone to the immense safe in his office and packed army boxes with gold Napoleons. According to British Foreign Office reports at the time, these amounted in worth to about £50,000 – the last of his personal fortune, made through the sale of family lands over several years. With a retinue of government members, more than five hundred officers of the high command, mayors and councillors – all in all, some two thousand people, the King crossed over into Greece. He was never to set foot on Albanian soil again.[45]

The Italian victory was swift and thorough. By nightfall on 7 April, Italy had gained what Hitler described as 'a stronghold which will inexorably dominate the Balkans'. Although there had been bitter street-fighting in Durres, which was soon overpowered, there was very little opposition elsewhere. No serious preparations for resistance had been made, and no leadership was offered. Many of the northern tribes did not lift a hand against the Italians, and the Mirdite actually disarmed Zog's retreating troops. In his diaries Count Ciano records: 'With the news of Zog's flight to Greece vanish all our fears about resistance in the mountains. In fact, the soldiers are already returning to their barracks after having deposited their arms in the garden of the Legation [the Italian Legation in Tirana].'[46] The streets of Tirana were deserted and undefended. In the capital, the crowd moved through the streets quite calmly and within days the city was decorated with Italian tricolour flags. With the King gone, Albanian morale collapsed and the few remaining fighters were soon overcome – as Zog had previously disarmed all but the official soldiers, they had precious little to continue fighting with. With the addition of another 2 million or so Muslim Albanians to the Italian Empire, Mussolini decided to erect a mosque in Rome. Count Ciano informs us that:

the Vatican was horror-struck at the idea ... but the Duce has made up his mind, and he is supported by the King, who always takes the lead in any anti-Church policy. Personally, I do not see any need for such a thing ... in so far as this proposal concerns the Albanians, we realize that they are an atheistic people who would prefer a rise in salary to a mosque.[47]

Immediately following the occupation of Albania, the Italians set about dismantling the Albanian state apparatus. Zog's monarchy and the 1928 constitution were immediately abolished and a new government was set up under a prominent landowner, Shefqet Bey Verlaci. This remained in power until December 1941, when a Constituent Assembly was convoked under Italian tutelage. The crown was then offered to King Victor Emmanuel III of Italy, who graciously accepted it. A 'personal union' between Italy and Albania was proclaimed, and Italian propaganda made much of the 'free' union between 'two equal sister nations'. Within a few weeks of the occupation a customs union between Italy and Albania was finally established – a popular move, since it caused a sharp drop in the price of imported goods.[48] Thus was established the pro-Fascist, quisling Albanian administration. To complete the colonization of Albania, thousands of Italian colonists were settled on coastal land that had been, or was in the process of being drained. All that remained of Albania's independence was its name, flag, language and the right to print separate postage stamps.[49]

7

The Second World War and the Founding of the Albanian Communist Party

Although the Italian conquest of Albania was nominally complete, sporadic fighting continued in the mountain regions, and it is extremely doubtful whether the Italian forces ever penetrated into the more remote mountain areas of the north, where, once the links with central government had been severed, the local clan leaders resumed their 'rule'. The Italians preferred to restrict their occupation to the coastal regions and the major towns, where they maintained forces which were initially adequate to protect the communications between the most important centres. Although a small number of quislings came forward to collaborate with the Italians, the majority of the Albanian people treated the occupying forces with intense hostility, and lost no opportunity to make their position uncomfortable.[1] During this period, the Albanian state was transformed into a miniature version of the Italian Fascist state. A lieutenant-general represented the Italian king, and the fiction of a constitutional monarchy was maintained. Zog and his entourage had, meanwhile, been journeying around the non-Fascist periphery of Europe – via Greece, Turkey, Romania, Poland, the Baltic states, Sweden and France – searching for a place of refuge. According to Queen Geraldine, 'at the last moment Zog would have preferred to go to Spain, but did not want to add to the worries of General Franco by him suddenly having an exiled king on his hands. In desperation, he telegraphed King George VI of England, and within hours he received a courteous reply welcoming him to Britain.'[2]

Having assured the British that he would not be a financial liability and could pay his own way, Zog and the royal party of 30-odd Albanians arrived by ship in Liverpool, and travelled thence by train to London. There they settled down to a comparatively ordered life at the Ritz hotel in Piccadilly, where they became known to the Foreign Office as 'King Zog's Circus'. The King and Queen had a third-floor suite overlooking the park, and half-a-dozen bodyguards were billeted in an upper floor. The King's gold was transferred to the Bank of England, from which the King's secretary, Mr Martini, would withdraw a thousand-pound banknote every week. King Zog was not happy with the hotel's wartime air-raid shelter; he preferred something more exclusive, and the Ritz accordingly converted the ladies' cloakroom for the Albanians' use as a private shelter. When a bomb landed in Piccadilly, making an enormous crater between the Berkeley and the Ritz, most of the royal family removed to Chelsea. But Zog stayed on in the Ritz until the spring of 1941, when Lord Parmoor's house in Buckinghamshire was put at the family's disposal.[3] Those British officials who conducted business with Zog faced the difficulty of Zog's refusal to speak English. Although Zog read and understood English perfectly, he refused to speak it, claiming that only 10 per cent of the language followed the grammar.[4] All official discussions therefore had to be conducted through an interpreter. Zog was encouraged throughout this period to keep a low profile, as the British were reluctant to recognize him officially. They were sensitive to America's distrust of British support for certain monarchies (the US being highly critical of the support the British gave to the King of Greece). After failing to pay in full the bills which had been mounting, Zog and his retinue eventually left England for Egypt at the end of the war.

In Tirana, meanwhile, the Italian lieutenant-general was assisted by a puppet Albanian legislature; although all ministers were Albanians, each had a permanent Italian advisor. All officials were required to be members of the Albanian Fascist Party, which had been founded in April 1939. It was controlled from Rome, and became the country's sole political party. Executive power was vested in King Victor Emmanuel, who exercised legislative functions through a Supreme Fascist Corporative Council. In practice, however, the Council had little legislative power. As in Italy, legislation was carried out by royal decree, the Council merely giving its formal consent to such decrees. The smaller communes and villages were still presided over by their own local officials, in deference to local sentiment, but these officials were now appointed by the central government.[5] In June 1939, the

Italian king 'granted' a constitution to Albania. Towards the end of the year, the sporadic and spontaneous resistance by Albanians had become widespread, culminating in street demonstrations, strikes, and the arrest of thousands of Albanians. A friend of Edith Durham wrote to her of the Albanians' attitude to their occupiers:

> Albanians are now not recognizing each other in the street. The hand on heart greeting has been banned because of its 'communist' implications and, as people are liable to arrest if they don't give a fascist sign, they walk past each other in the street without a word or gesture. An anti-Zog film was put on in Tirana, but Mussolini was hissed and Zog cheered. In consequence, twenty students were arrested and released next day when a students' strike was declared. Work is said to be going ahead rapidly on two military roads from Vlore to Girokaster, and from Durres to Korca.[6]

Two months later Italy, much to the annoyance of Hitler, invaded Greece from Albania, under the pretext of recovering Albanian irredentists in Epirus. Soon after the occupation, the Italians had started building roads to the borders of Greece and Yugoslavia. Rome's propaganda machine hurled fabricated accusations at Athens concerning the 'oppression' of Albanian nationals in the Greek province of Epirus. At 3 a.m. on 28 October 1939, Italy sent Greece an ultimatum – and three hours later Mussolini's armies began marching towards Greece. However, the Greeks managed with ease to push the Italians back into southern Albania. Italian military morale never recovered from this failure, which precipitated the German invasion of the Balkans in the spring of 1941, as a rescue operation for the embattled and weakened Italian army. Albanian popular opinion had initially applauded the victories of the Greeks, but the attitude changed when Athens signalled its intention of annexing southern Albania.[7] In pursuit of the retreating Italians, Greek troops entered Albania, capturing Korca in November and Girokaster in December. In the meantime, the German attack against Yugoslavia and Greece in April 1941 had abruptly transformed the military situation in the region. Following the Italian invasion of Greece, a combination of German, Bulgarian, Hungarian and Italian troops marched into Yugoslavia in 1941. At this point, the Greek armies capitulated, thus enabling the Italians finally to expel Greek troops from Albania. King Peter of Yugoslavia followed Zog's example and fled to Greece. In May, King Victor Emmanuel decided to make himself known to the Albanians by making a tour of Albania, visiting the more important towns. Whilst he was in Tirana on 19 May, several revolver shots were fired at the car in which he and the Albanian quisling prime minister, Shefqet Verlaci, were being driven. The assailant was later described by the Italian press as a Greek 'under a spell of poetic madness', who had a grudge against Verlaci. He was hanged in Tirana on 27 May.[8]

The outbreak of the Second World War had brought about, for what proved to be the last time, a brief union of Kosova with Albania during the years 1941 to 1943. In an effort to rally the Albanian people to her cause, Italy had promised the Albanians their national unity. In 1939, whilst contemplating his plans for Italian military action in the Balkans, Mussolini had thought that the Kosovars could possibly fulfil the same function as the Sudetenlanders in the German conquest of Czechoslovakia. The German–Italian agreement in Vienna of 1941 stipulated the formation of a 'Greater Albania', to include the large Albanian-inhabited areas of Yugoslavia and, to a lesser extent, Greece. Italian-ruled Albania was given control of the Kosova region, together with those Macedonian and Montenegrin lands inhabited by Albanians. The Kosovars welcomed the Italian occupation, using the opportunity to pay off old scores, especially against the Serbs re-settled there between the wars. Under these conditions, Serbs and Montenegrins were mercilessly killed by Albanians. Thousands of Slavs fled back to Serbia and Montenegro to escape Albanian attacks. The Kosovars saw the Italians as liberators who had returned to the Albanians their homeland and brought their historic aspirations to realization. Albanian-language administration, schools and media were soon established throughout Kosova. An Albanian police force was formed, and Albanians were granted once more their much-cherished right to bear arms.

The Italians were able to exploit Albanian irredentist sentiment by insisting that the unification of all the Albanian-inhabited lands was conditional upon an Axis victory. As a result of this, the most enthusiastic support for the Italian regime came from Kosova. Around this time the deportation of Serbs and Montenegrins began, as the Kosovars attempted to reclaim land lost to them by the colonization programme. Within Albania itself, however, there was considerable hostility towards the Italians. Armed resistance against the occupation had already begun. From the beginning of 1940, Albanian guerilla attacks on the Italians grew increasingly common. In August 1940 the Mirdites rose in revolt, and considerable bloodshed ensued. An estimated 4–5,000 Albanians were under arms in the Mirdite district, and about 3,000 in the Mati district. It was reported that Italian casualties were as high as 400.[9] Incidents of civil disobedience also increased. On 8 November 1941, a large rally in Korca ended in violent street-fighting with Italian carabinieri. By the end of the year, friction had developed between Verlaci and the Italians. Verlaci resigned and was succeeded by a government headed by the old Albanian nationalist, Mustafa Kruja.

The Formation of the Albanian Communist Party

During the 1920s Albania had been the only Balkan country without a Communist Party. The very first Albanian Communists had been followers of the deposed Bishop Fan Noli, and later made their way, via Vienna and Paris, to Moscow. Here they formed a National Revolutionary Committee, which later became subordinated to the Balkan Federation of Communist Parties, and thus to the Comintern (Communist International). The Comintern provided the Albanians with financial and political support. An Albanian Communist Party was officially formed in August 1928 in the Soviet Union, and members of this group were then sent back to Albania for the purpose of organizing a Communist movement there. A few cells were set up in the larger towns, but no unified party emerged. This was mainly due to the tendency of the intellectual leadership of this minute organization to break up into even smaller factions, quarrelling over trivial ideological differences. By 1941 there were no less than eight separate groups, two of which broke with the Soviet Union and became 'Trotskyite'. The most important figure at that time was Ali Kelmendi, a Gheg, who was trained in Moscow and subsequently sent back to Albania to organize the first Communist cells. Forced to flee Albania in 1936, Kelmendi fought in the Spanish Civil War and was, until his death in 1939, the acknowledged leader of the small group of Albanian Communists living in France.[10]

Fascism had little support in Albania, associated as it was with the ideology not only of the Italian occupiers, but also of the detested dictatorship of General Metaxas in Greece. The wealthy landowning beys, however, were as deeply suspicious of the Communists' plans for social and agrarian reform as they had been of Noli's and Zog's. Some were therefore inclined to be more sympathetic to the Italians, and later to the Germans. Until the end of 1941 there were just a few small Communist groups, recruited mainly from intellectuals and high-school students from the towns of the south. Because no unified Communist organization had been established, shortly after the German attack on Russia in June 1941 Joseph Broz Tito, leader of the Communist Party of Yugoslavia (CPY), under a Comintern directive, sent two delegates to Albania. These were Miladin Popovic, head of the Kosova regional Communist group, and Dushan Mugosa, and are the two men generally acknowledged as the architects of the Albanian Communist Party (ACP).[11] They were delegated by the Comintern to draft the programme and the first resolution of the fledgling Albanian party. Their most effective work was done in the organizational field, issuing instructions for the formation of party cells and the recruitment of the first members. Until this time, the number of Albanian Communists had never exceeded 150 at most. Though the Yugoslavs found total ideological confusion and bitter internal friction, they eventually succeeded in uniting the divergent Communist leaders and managed to weld together the factions that they favoured. A unified Albanian Communist Party was officially formed on 8 November 1941.

Although by March 1942 membership of the ACP stood at just 200, the Yugoslavs' effective organizational skills soon led to the formation of a number of new party cells, and the founding of local organizations. Party membership grew among young people, and among the disaffected poorer peasants who had been ignored and neglected by the prewar regime. These elements were easily recruited on the strength of Communist promises of freedom from occupation, land reform and overall social and economic change. The Yugoslavs appointed Enver Hoxha, one of the Tirana organizers of the Korca branch of the ACP, Party Secretary. Hoxha, the son of a Muslim landowner, had been born in 1908 in Girokaster, in southern Albania. He studied at the French Lycée in Korca before going to Paris, having received an Albanian state scholarship to study at the University of Montpelier. Here he had come into contact with Albanian Communist exiles, including Ali Kelmendi. He later went to Brussels to study law. In 1936 he had moved back to Albania, having obtained a degree from neither France nor Belgium, to teach French in his old school at Korca. All but one of the founding leadership of the ACP were middle-class intellectuals, the exception being Koci Xoxe, a tinsmith from Korca.

Around the same time, the first Albanian partisan battalion, Zejnel Ajdini was formed in Kosova, in the district of Urosevac. After successes against the Italians, Zejnel Ajdini grew considerably, so that it eventually had to split into two separate units: the detachment Zejnel Ajdini, for operations in Kosova; and the new detachment Emin Durak, which was to operate in Metohija.[12] The Communists' most serious activity in Kosova between the wars had been concentrated in the area around the Trepca mine, where they had helped organize a strike in 1936. The Party could also claim to have helped in organizing a protest by Belgrade University students in 1938 against a government plan (never carried out because of the war) to expel 150,000 Albanians to Turkey.[13] On the whole, however, the CPY had only a very modest foothold in Kosova, as the Yugoslav partisans failed to convince the Kosovars that there would ever be self-determination for Yugoslavia's Albanians in the postwar period. And so the Kosovars lacked any motivation to resist the Italian or the German armies, especially after the latter promised to arm them so that they could fight the Serbs.

By the end of 1941 it became apparent in Albania that non-Communists were also organizing themselves into small resistance bands. Two such groups were led by a Colonel Muharrem Bajraktari and Myslim Peza. Bajraktari, a former officer in the Gendarmerie under Zog, had been given a military post in Tirana, but soon resigned to return to his native village in the Lume region, where he organized a guerilla band. Peza, a retired regular army officer, organized a resistance band in the neighbourhood of Tirana. Both men enjoyed considerable local prestige.[14] Gradually, the small Albanian guerilla bands developed into organized movements. The first Albanian partisan units were formed early in 1942, and by late spring, due to the number of attacks on Italians, severe restrictions were enforced throughout the country but especially around Tirana. In May an unsuccessful attempt was made to assassinate the new quisling prime minister, Mustapha Kruja, whereupon the Italian authorities declared a state of siege in Tirana, and new restrictions were imposed on the Albanian populace. The police were authorized to tear veils from women in the street as a precaution against disguised guerillas, and groups of more than five persons were forbidden. Over two hundred hostages were arrested and sent to Italy. On 15 July two Albanian officers disguised in Italian uniform set fire to the tank and arms-repair factory near Tirana.[15]

The first issue of the ACP's clandestine newspaper, *Zeri-i-Popullit* (Voice of the People), appeared in August 1942. With stirring rhetoric it urged people to wage a 'popular struggle'. By the end of the summer, there was near anarchy outside the major towns. No Italians

dared visit the countryside unescorted. A large student demonstration
in Elbasan led to mass arrests. In reprisal for this and other resistance
activities, Bajraktari's native village, Ujmishte, was razed to the ground
by Italian forces. Two other villages in the neighbourhood, believed to
be harbouring patriots, were also completely destroyed by Italian
planes and artillery. As a result of such opposition, Italian guards and
garrisons had to be considerably increased. This was coupled with
much harsher retributionary measures against all forms of Albanian
resistance. In August, 16 young girls were killed and 25 wounded in
Tirana when guards opened fire on them as they demonstrated outside
a prison for the release of political prisoners. In Kruja, in September,
three youths were hanged for setting fire to the house of the quisling
premier.[16]

On 16 September the ACP decided to convene a National
Liberation Conference at Peza, 14 miles from Tirana. There, twenty
or so delegates from the various resistance groups agreed to set aside
their major differences and form the National Liberation Front (known
by its Albanian initials LNC). This was a broad united front set up,
again under Yugoslav direction, to mobilize the Albanian population
as a whole to defeat the occupiers. The delicate question of which
regime would be established in Albania after the war was raised at the
conference. The idea that a 'democratic republic' should be proclaimed
was dismissed by the Communists as inappropriate for the moment.
At the close of the conference, the delegates returned to their towns
and villages, where they began setting up national liberation councils
and partisan units. It was decided at Peza to concentrate on organizing
small *chetas* in every part of the country. There were whole areas,
especially in the north, in which the LNC had not yet penetrated.
This was partly due to the general socioeconomic and cultural
conservatism of the northern regions, but also a result of the weakness
of LNC regional committees in the north. Although the Presidium of
the LNC was Communist-dominated, non-Communists, such as Abas
Kupi and Myslim Peza were also represented in the membership. By
the end of the year, LNC partisan units were active throughout most
of Albania. The main partisan military commander was Mehmet
Shehu, the son of a Muslim priest, born in 1913. An agricultural
graduate of the American vocational school in Tirana, he later attended
an Italian military college from which he was expelled for left-wing
political activities. Returning to an Albanian officers' school, he then
left to fight in the Spanish Civil War, where he had become acting

commander of the Fourth Battalion of the 'Garibaldi Brigade' in the International Brigade. During a period of internment in France, he had become a committed Communist, and following his release in 1942 he immediately joined the partisans upon his return to Tirana. He was later generally acknowledged as Albania's most able wartime military leader.

The Emergence of the Balli Kombetar

Shortly after the formation of the LNC, the more conservative anti-Zogist nationalists became concerned about the growth of the Communist movement. They therefore decided to form their own 'National Front', the Balli Kombetar (BK, of which the adherents were known as Ballists), led by Midhat Frasheri and Ali Kelcyra. This fiercely anti-Communist nationalistic resistance movement was totally opposed to the return of Zog, and favoured the reestablishment of a republic retaining the 1941 boundaries, which would include Kosova within Albania. Many of those who formed the BK were drawn from that section of political emigrants and their offspring which had left Albania when Zog came to power in 1924, returning with the Italian occupation in 1939. The emergence of the Balli Kombetar greatly complicated the situation in Albania. As resistance to the occupying forces accelerated, so the differences between the LNC and the Ballists became more pronounced. When questioned by the Communists as to why some of their leaders who had participated in the Peza conference refused to recognize the National Liberation Front, the Ballists replied that whereas the Communists had gone to the conference as a party, the nationalists had been invited as individuals, not as members of a recognized organization. The BK therefore recognized neither the Conference nor the LNC, which they regarded as a mere front for the Communist Party. Whilst the LNC advocated a broad-based armed struggle, disregarding Axis reprisals, the Ballists favoured a more passive approach, preferring to conserve their strength until the Axis defeat appeared imminent, and then to attempt to stage a national uprising. As the BK leadership represented the prewar social order, they were naturally concerned to protect the vested interests and privileges of the landowning beys, together with their social, economic and political positions.

The announcement by the United Nations, in December 1942, of their recognition of the principle of Albanian independence added fuel to the LNC resistance movement, which rapidly gained in strength. As a result of the announcement, Mustapha Kruja's quisling government fell.[17] The conflict between the LNC and the Ballists sharpened in the period following the first National Communist Party Conference in March 1943, which was held at Labinot, near Elbasan. Here Enver Hoxha was elected secretary-general of the Party's political bureau. The agenda for this conference was based on a message from the Comintern, via Tito, which urged, amongst other things, the purging by the ACP of all fractious elements.[18] Tito's message criticized the Party's poor efforts to recruit from the peasantry, warning that victory would not be attained without the support of the peasants, as there was in Albania at this time no industrial working class to speak of. By this time party membership stood at just over 700. A major decision taken at Labinot was to establish an Albanian National Liberation Army (ANLA), to be modelled on Tito's National Liberation Army. To implement this decision, a few days after the conference closed on 22 March Svetozar Vukmanovic-Tempo, then head of Tito's partisan forces in Macedonia, arrived at Labinot to work out details for setting up ANLA's general staff and for organizing the local partisan units.[19] In April a general staff, with Fadil Hoxha as staff commander, was also set up in Kosova, but as expected it proved fairly unpopular among the Albanians. The actions carried out by the Italians, in reprisal against the military actions of these Kosovar partisan detachments, triggered demonstrations throughout the main towns of Kosova. Before long, however, Tito put a stop to the participation of the Kosovars in the liberation struggle, for fear they might move to secede from Yugoslavia.

Meanwhile, the morale of the occupying forces had begun to sink, as Italy's armies met with defeat in Africa and the battlefront drew nearer to the homeland. According to Edith Durham, the Italian army was fully stretched in its efforts to contain the escalating resistance to the occupation. Durham wrote:

In June 1943, Myslim Peza, who commanded a very mobile Partisan band in the Tirana, Durres and Kavaje districts, attacked an Italian military convoy on the Durres road. They killed 42 Italians and took 80 prisoners, many of whom declared, with tears in their eyes, that all they wanted was to leave Albania as soon as possible. Acts of sabotage are continually carried out. Telephone and telegraph wires between all the chief towns have been cut. The military engineering works at Tirana have been set on fire three times, and the office of the fascist newspaper *Tomori* has been badly bombed. The Italians revenge themselves by inflicting heavy fines on every family within three miles of an act of sabotage.[20]

The news of the fall from power of Mussolini in July was greeted as evidence of Italy's imminent capitulation. By the summer of 1943, secondary schools had to be closed because so many young Albanians were flocking to the mountains to join the LNC, in part due to the pro-LNC broadcasts from the BBC and Voice of America.

The Meeting at Mukaj and the Formation of Legaliteti

Meanwhile, the Allies were particularly concerned to unite the opposing factions and thus avert a fratricidal war in Albania. Despite strong protest from the Yugoslavs, the Allies therefore urged the leaders of the National Liberation Council and Balli Kombetar to meet, at Mukaj near Kruja. The gathering took place in August 1943, and the agreement reached provided for a joint Committee for the Salvation of Albania. Both nationalists and Communists were to fight for the liberation of an 'ethnic' Albania, which was to include Kosova. Although Hoxha, and others within the Central Committee of the ACP, believed in reaching some form of agreement with the Ballists, a disagreement soon arose over the future of Kosova. Within a few days the Communists had rejected the Mukaj agreement – presumably influenced by the Yugoslavs, who strongly objected to the term 'ethnic' Albania and to the inclusion of Kosova within a postwar Albania. They had, therefore, sent Vukmanovic-Tempo to Albania in order to bring the Albanian Communists into line. The arrival of Tempo reinforced the Yugoslav influence within the LNC, which formally repudiated the Mukaj agreement, thus weakening Allied attempts to maintain unity within the Albanian resistance. Not long after the denunciation of the Mukaj agreement, Abas Kupi broke from the LNC to form the pro-Zog nationalist movement Legaliteti, maintaining that only Zog's regime was legitimate. Kupi had support not only from the Mati region but also from many highlanders, who favoured the return of the King. Most of the northern chieftains were resentful of the southern Tosks, who were predominant in the LNC. The Gheg leaders felt they would have few opportunities for influence and, therefore, little future in an LNC-dominated postwar Albania.

The first week of September saw the commencement of a second conference at Labinot, which met to discuss the new situation created

by the events of the summer and the obvious death-throes of the
Italian occupation. At Labinot it was decided to declare the national
liberation councils the sole state power in Albania, thus thwarting any
attempts by the Ballists to seize power. The National Liberation Army
was subsequently sent to occupy all the zones and cities which had
been in the hands of the retreating Italians, and to set up national
liberation councils there. When Italy finally capitulated on 8 September 1943 the majority of the Italian soldiers surrendered to the
Germans, who by then had entered Albania from Macedonia and
Greece. However, some 2,000 enlisted with the partisans, forming
their own brigade named after Antonio Gramsci, founder and leader
of the Italian Communist Party, who had died in one of Mussolini's
prisons. The fall of Italy led many to believe the war in Albania had
ended. However, the Germans then very effectively took over the
occupation. They established themselves, as the Italians had, in the
major cities. The resistance forces, who had inherited a substantial
quantity of arms from the defeated Italians, continued to operate from
the mountains. Germany recognized Albania's 'neutrality' and made
various concessions to the highland leaders, so preventing the creation
of a Communist-dominated united front. Germany also managed to
ensure the benevolent 'neutrality' of many Ballists, and won the
assistance of a considerable number of Ghegs through their support
for the inclusion of Kosova in Albania.

In order to secure a stable Albanian administration the German
army, whose headquarters were at Elbasan, established a Regency in
place of Zog, and restored the prewar Albanian constitution. Far more
ruthless and determined than the Italian occupiers, the German army
used the same reprisal tactics that so devastated the civilian population in Yugoslavia and Greece. The army issued orders to shoot one
hundred Albanians for every German killed, and also to kill the
relatives of those who resisted their forces. In the village of Borova
near Korca over one hundred men, women and children were killed
by the Germans in reprisal for a partisan attack on German troops.
An Albanian SS division was created under the name of 'Skenderbeg'.
The actions of this division in Kosova, with its indiscriminate killing
of Serbs and Montenegrins, led to the expulsion of up to 10,000 Slav
families from Kosova. New colonists from the poorer regions of
northern Albania were then settled in Kosova.

Both the Albanian and the Yugoslav Communists believed they
could amicably solve the problem of Yugoslavia's Albanians once they

had defeated the Axis forces. The future of Kosova was to be decided in a postwar plebiscite. The Central Committee of the Yugoslav Communist Party intended to retain its Albanian minority within the new Yugoslavia, which would be a land of free nations. Consequently there would be no national oppression of the Albanian minority. Twice the Yugoslav Communists had endorsed the eventual return of Kosova, the first time in 1928 at the Fourth Party Congress at Dresden and again at the 1940 Party Congress in Zagreb. During the war, however, Tito radically revised the plan agreed upon for the future of Kosova. The right of Kosova to secede was no longer on the agenda. Self-determination was acceptable, but without mandatory secession. Following the breakdown of the Mukaj agreement, the fragile mutual tolerance that had existed between Ballists and Communists evaporated rapidly. The refusal of the Communists to argue for the return of Kosova to Albania made it difficult for the Ballists and Zogists to cooperate with the LNC in the resistance movement. But then neither could the Allies guarantee that Kosova would be a part of Albania after the war.

Allied Involvement in Albania

By the autumn of 1943, tension between the Nationalists and the Communists throughout Albania was such that civil war seemed close at hand. By then, a number of British liaison officers had been infiltrated into Albania to try to coordinate and encourage opposition to the Italians and, following their capitulation, to the German occupation. As early as 1940 the British had begun to investigate the possibilities of encouraging the fledgling resistance movement in Albania. In late 1940, a Special Operations Executive (SOE) had been set up in London, which closely observed events in Albania from Cairo and Istanbul. As in Yugoslavia, the British were prepared to support, with arms and equipment, whichever resistance group they believed was inflicting the most damage on the Axis forces. In the spring of 1943, a British military mission was sent to Albania by the Inter-Allied Mediterranean Command to work with the national liberation forces. Its main aim was to defeat the Axis forces; a secondary goal was to establish an Albanian regime sympathetic to British policies. One of the main forces behind this decision was an Englishwoman, Margaret Hasluk the widow of a famous archaeologist, who had lived in a small bungalow in Elbasan for over ten years. She had a very thorough knowledge of Albanian folklore and botany, and she had made a particular study of the Bektashi religion.[21] The Italians had been making representations for her removal from Albania for some time. Three weeks before their occupation they sent Musa Juka to demand that Mrs Hasluk leave for Greece on suspicion of being a British agent.[22] From Athens she went to Istanbul, where she certainly was recruited by the British Secret Service. Eventually, Mrs Hasluk turned up in Cairo and served as an instructor there to the British missions sent to Albania.

Between the spring of 1943 and the end of 1944, around fifty British officers were sent to Albania, the Allies wishing to send aid to whichever group was pinning down the most enemy divisions, irrespective of their political persuasions. What mattered was their motivation to attack the Axis forces. The Allied missions were therefore instructed to render assistance only to those resistance groups consistently active against Axis troops. There was evidence that the partisans were responsible for causing the vast majority of attacks on the Germans. The nationalist groups seemed more concerned to receive military aid *before* they attempted to fight the Germans, and their overall enthusiasm for active struggle appeared lukewarm at best. Both the Ballists and the partisans realised that when the Germans eventually left Albania, each would then constitute the other's main enemy. According to the senior British Liaison Officer (BLO) Julian Amery, who was attached to the Zogists, the Allied command prematurely dismissed the non-Communist resistance forces as collaborators. Another BLO concluded in a report that the nationalists (meaning all those who did not belong to the LNC) did not appear very keen to fight the Germans – and, to protect themselves from the LNC, were in fact being forced to collaborate with the enemy.[23]

In the meantime, as winter approached, the Germans set about destroying the partisans. In November 1943, around 45,000 German troops, supported by tanks and aircraft, launched a massive offensive. Their plan was to force the bulk of the partisan forces into the Vlore–Berat–Korca triangle, where they would be trapped and presumably annihilated. The partisans who managed to escape were thus driven from the centre and a good part of the north of Albania, where they had little support from the local chieftains. They then sought refuge in the southern mountains. Throughout the winter and spring, the partisans concentrated on their political activities in the towns and villages, whilst trying to contend with the savagery of the weather in the mountains. The last spring of the war brought the LNC out of its winter encirclement, and on 5 April 1944, the general staff issued orders to the partisans to go on the offensive. Towards the end of the war, however, the LNC leadership greatly feared Allied landings, believing that there was an American plan to divide up Albania and occupy much of it. Hence there was a hastily convened Congress of Permet on 24 May 1944, modelled on AVNOJ – the Anti-Fascist Council of National Liberation of Yugoslavia. The Committee elected by the Permet Congress, which was attended by 200 delegates, was recognized as the Provisional Government Executive. All previous political and economic agreements which the Zog government had entered into with foreign states were annulled, and Zog's return was barred. Thus it was hoped to present the Allies with a *fait accompli*. The Peza Conference had laid the foundations of the new state power; the Labinot Conference had authorized and centralized this power – the Permet Congress now formed the basis of the constitution of the post-war Albanian State.

At the same time, the Germans began their last great offensive against the Albanian resistance forces. On 28 May a massive attack was launched against the south. During the summer, as communications improved following the spring floods, the partisans moved northwards to challenge the Germans. By now the partisans were recruiting on a massive scale, recovering rapidly from their almost total eclipse the previous winter. There was undoubtedly a strong popular base for the LNC, although certain BLOs asserted the contrary, and there is no doubt that the LNC engaged in the overwhelming bulk of the fighting against the Axis. As in Yugoslavia, the war was fought on two fronts: a battle against domestic foes and then the wider campaign against the occupying forces. Before long the 'nationalists' were routed and, along with the Germans, driven from their strongholds. In Mirdite, the partisans destroyed the palace of Gjon Marka Gjoni as a warning to the highlanders that their patriarchal and feudal society was now at an end, and would not be tolerated in the new Albania. However, many of the Ballists and Zogists still believed, even as late as 1944, that the Allies would never allow Communism to prevail in postwar Albania. By then, however, British policy had become confused, as two distinct British missions had now emerged, each pursuing very different policies. Those attached to the partisans (Davies, Wheeler, Palmer) argued for British military aid to be withdrawn from the Ballists and the Zogists because of their collaboration with the Germans. Both Davies and Wheeler wrote of the courage and determination of the partisans. They also claimed that the fighting capabilities of the Zogists had been greatly exaggerated. Those attached to the right-wing northern movements (Amery, Hare, Smiley, McLean) argued for support to be withdrawn from the partisans for the same reasons.[24]

These BLOs were trying to keep the Balli Kombetar and Legaliteti in contention. By the spring of 1944, however, the British had decided to give assistance only to the LNC, as it was clear by then that the partisans were the principal force engaging with the Germans. Thus, despite the fact that the British mission with the Zogists continued to urge Allied Command to supply the non-Communist resistance groups, military supplies were directed to the partisans.[25] The partisans thus now received arms, money, clothing, food and communications equipment from the British. In the summer of 1944, an official LNC mission was attached to the British Balkan Command at Bari. Nevertheless, serious differences eventually arose between the British and the LNC as to their respective priorities. Like the Ballists and Zogists, Enver Hoxha's primary concern was to defeat his domestic enemies. He was therefore reluctant to destroy the country's infrastructure, which the British wanted to deny the Axis forces but which Hoxha wanted to retain for use after the war. This was one of the many factors that made Hoxha deeply suspicious of Allied intentions towards Albania. In his book *The Anglo-American Threat to Albania* he explained his conviction that the British were planning to land an army on the Albanian coast to occupy Albania after the war. Their idea, he claimed, was to obtain a permanent foothold in Sarande to complement their base in Corfu. His suspicions were not wholly unfounded. In September 1944 there occurred a rather dubious joint Anglo-American landing at Sarande, following another Allied landing further down the coast at Himara which destroyed a German garrison.

The Yugoslavs were also interested in Allied plans for the future of Albania. From 1944 onwards Yugoslav pressure on the LNC increased considerably. At the end of August, the Yugoslavs appointed a new head of their Military Mission, Colonel Velimir Stojnic, to Hoxha's headquarters. Miladin Popovic (who later met a suspicious and untimely death[26]) was withdrawn, as he was considered too friendly towards Hoxha. The Yugoslav delegation headed by Velimir Stojnic, acting under Tito's instructions, argued that Albania was too small and too weak to remain independent after the war. Albania's future would therefore be best assured by uniting with Yugoslavia to become that country's seventh Republic. Hoxha, who was first and foremost an Albanian nationalist, as were the majority of the ACP leadership, bitterly resented the Yugoslav's arrogant and patronizing attitude. Stojnic's main aide, Nijaz Dizdarevic, came not only as an organizational instructor to the ACP but also, as the war was nearing its conclusion, to assist the incorporation of Albania into Yugoslavia. Dizdarevic, (who later was in charge of the Yugoslav party's foreign policy in the 1960s) was officially an instructor, but his primary duty was intelligence-gathering.

In an interview in 1989 Dizdarevic described his responsibilities:

> In the summer of 1944 on the island of Vis, the military mission of the Supreme Headquarters of NOV [the People's Liberation Army] and POJ [The Partisan Regiment of Yugoslavia] departed for Albania to work in the Supreme Headquarters of the Albanian National Liberation Army. My duties as Secretary of the Military Mission in the final phases of the war consisted of accompanying and reporting on the Allied missions in Albania and about plans and intentions of the British and Americans towards Albania and the Balkans, learning about Albanian institutions, their military formations, the nature of their struggle and to inform the Yugoslavs as to where their strongholds were, who was arming them and what danger there was from them generally, especially in Kosova. Before the end of my stay in Albania, I was given a task that sent me to Girokaster, working to help Albanian comrades organize a centre for following events in Greece. The intervention of the British and General Skobi was directed towards the eradication of the Greek National Liberation Movement. I also had to initiate efforts to prevent the penetration of Greek reactionary influences into south Albania through the numerous Greek minority in that region.[27]

Explaining Miladin Popovic's withdrawal from Albania, Dizdarevic said:

> Popovic over-identified with the Albanians. He showed unsatisfactory firmness on some strategic questions, especially Kosova. Miladin caused problems and difficulties, making contact between us and the Albanian leadership difficult. Miladin was very close to Enver Hoxha, much closer than some individual members of the Albanian politburo. However, Miladin was killed so that he could not give his view of those relations. He suddenly began to speak about the Albanian Party being independent.[28]

It was around this time that it appeared the British would land in Albania, and Popovic apparently wanted to negotiate with them as a representative of the Albanian leadership. Dizdarevic said angrily:

'That was complete stupidity, it could be seen that he was identifying himself completely with that which he had nothing in common with.'[29]

In November 1944, a few weeks before the total withdrawal of the Germans from Albania, the Central Committee of the ACP held a plenum at Berat. The Congress of Berat corresponded with the second session of AVNOJ, held in the Bosnian town of Jajce on 29 November 1943, which had created the Yugoslav National Committee. During this meeting the Yugoslav representative, Colonel Velimir Stojnic, backed by Koci Xoxe and others, attacked Hoxha's leadership and made a serious attempt to remove Hoxha. Only after abject self-criticism was Hoxha allowed to remain as nominal party leader, and real power was now allotted to Xoxe. Although Hoxha felt betrayed, at the time he was unaware of any organized plot against him. He later believed that the Yugoslavs, in the form of Dushan Mugosa, had used his pupil Liri Gega as their agent. She was thus branded in all his later writings as a 'careerist with ambitious tendencies'. Hoxha also thought very little of the tinsmith Koci Xoxe, a member of the Korca group, describing him as non-intellectual, conceited, pretentious and easily brainwashed by the Yugoslavs. Hoxha also branded him an 'illiterate', although he admitted to respecting him because he was originally a worker. Apparently he had been elected to the leadership for this reason. According to Hoxha, Xoxe was part of the Stojnic faction; he was a 'Titoite' who had gone to Greece with Vukmanovic-Tempo as he knew Greek, but had returned from Greece a Yugoslav agent. Dizdarevic confirms this, saying of Hoxha:

> Enver was an opportunist who liked shifting responsibility onto others. It was the Yugoslav mission in 1944 that saved Hoxha from being dismissed. Before the Berat Plenum, Nako Spiru and one group wanted to eliminate Hoxha but our military mission opposed this and succeeded in protecting him. We saved him but we shouldn't be praised for it now. In May of that year he was in Permet, that was their equivalent of our AVNOJ – a meeting, where he was elected to the highest level, but in October of the same year he was supposed to be replaced. We estimated that it would be harmful for the Albanian movement so that is why we protected him, even though he made great mistakes persecuting personnel. What Popovic was to the Albanians, so Koci Xoxe was to the Yugoslavs.[30]

Hoxha believed that Colonel Stojnic had also managed to win over Nako Spiru, who had been elected to the Party's Central Committee at Labinot. Spiru apparently sent secret reports to Tito criticizing the Party and attacking Hoxha. Although Hoxha liked and respected his intelligence and bravery, he believed Spiru also suffered from 'careerist tendencies': 'He was extremely ambitious and inclined to intrigues'.[31]

The Partisan Victory

On 20 October 1944, the second meeting of the National Council was held in Berat. Here the Anti-Fascist National Liberation Council was converted into the Provisional Government of Albania. It was headed by Enver Hoxha as prime minister and minister of defence, and 11 government departments were set up. At the same time, and until the spring of 1945, Albanian partisan troops fought inside Yugoslavia helping Tito's partisans to liberate much of the southern part of that country, including Kosova. At the request of the Yugoslav Army Command, the Third and Fifth Albanian Brigades crossed into Yugoslavia as far north as Novi Pazar to fight the retreating Germans and also their Kosovar allies. (It was not until the mid-1970s that the remains of the 350 or so Albanians who died in this fighting were finally returned to Albania.) Just prior to this, the British had bombed Tirana and parachuted a number of agents into the town. As the German defeat drew near, the British insisted that only the BLOs were to be evacuated from Albania. Those Zogists and Ballists who could not manage to escape would be left to the mercy of the partisans. As a result, Abas Kupi and his officers were forced to flee Albania in a boat from the Mati coast. On 25 October, the partisans began the battle to liberate Tirana. Although the Germans had begun moving north to Shkoder, they had left behind them a full division to hold the capital until the last of their forces had withdrawn from Greece. Many hundreds of Chams who had collaborated with the Germans in Greece also fled into Albania with the retreating German army. For over two weeks street fighting raged, as every block in the capital was bitterly contested. Tirana was eventually liberated on 17 November and, to the accompaniment of a 21-gun salute and dancing and singing in the streets, Hoxha's government entered the capital. Shkoder fell on 29 November, and so all Albania was freed from Axis forces.

The Soviet Red Army took no part in the liberation of Albania, sending neither supplies nor troops. Bearing this in mind, it could be argued that, without Allied aid, the LNC could not have defeated the nationalists without a bitter and prolonged civil war. Towards the end of the war, none of the Allies were willing to offer even the slightest political commitment to Albania. They had no real policy towards the country, which was not even discussed in Moscow, Yalta or Tehran. When the British finally decided to give their full support to the Yugoslav partisans, Albania's political future was, in a sense, settled. Although the LNC partisans may have been equipped and financed by the British they were ideologically and politically guided by the Yugoslavs, who resolved their weaknesses and shortcomings, emphasized the importance of organizing the peasantry and, most crucially, curtailed their factional divisions. This does not necessarily mean that without the guidance of the Yugoslavs there would have been no Albanian Communist Party. Hitler's offensive against the Soviet Union caused great indignation amongst Albania's Communists and, given more time, the Albanians would probably have solved their ideological and administrative problems eventually to form the ACP themselves and so begin the struggle against Fascism. However, the fact remains that after the Nazi attack on the Soviet Union neither the Comintern nor Tito could sit around waiting for Albanian factionalism to end. The Yugoslavs therefore greatly accelerated the process of organizing and uniting the ACP.

The Partisan Army had the distinct advantage of having a very youthful membership, compared to that of the nationalist groups. Of the 70,000 partisan fighters, six thousand were women, whereas the nationalists rarely recruited females and so left a valuable source of assistance untapped. The partisans' superior organization and discipline, the conviction of their ideology, and their resolve to win even at the cost of the vicious Axis reprisals, underpinned their determination not only to liberate Albania but to seize power after their victory. The BK and Legaliteti did not have, in any sense, the same ruthless determination to take power. Following the collapse and destruction of the nationalist groups, the Communists were able, as there was no government in exile, to fill the power vacuum in a country left with no cohesive political institutions. The ineptitude and lack of political acumen on the part of the BK and Legaliteti meant that neither had the foresight to create even embryonic political parties. They established instead, only loose or personal resistance movements, lacking a strong and disciplined leadership. In the end, however, what was most important was the support for the partisans from the majority of the peasantry, who responded to the promise of land reform in the postwar transformation of the country. The Communists were able, therefore, to take advantage of the profound contradiction in Albanian society between the old hierarchy of power and privilege, and an impoverished peasantry.

The Kosova Uprising

Meanwhile, as the Germans withdrew from northern Albania and Kosova, the latter was annexed by the victorious Yugoslav partisans. Whatever illusions Kosova's Albanians may have had about receiving better treatment in the new Communist Yugoslavia were shattered when, in 1944, the partisans launched a large-scale military campaign in Kosova, with the objective of consolidating Communist rule in the region. They also sought to deal with all those suspected of collaboration with the enemy during the occupation. This action quickly degenerated into a persecution of the Albanians as a whole. The Kosovars' discontent mounted at the insensitive treatment they received at the hands of the Yugoslav army, the climax of which occurred at the end of October 1944 when, provoked by a Yugoslav guard, an Albanian shot and killed the guard. In reprisal, the Yugoslav commanders demanded the execution of 40 Albanians. Not surprisingly, Albanian soldiers objected to this arbitrary decision, whereupon the Yugoslav soldiers opened fire, killing around 300 Albanians. The Albanian revolt following this incident began spontaneously but quickly resulted in a general insurrection, which broke out in Urosec at the end of November 1944 and was not subdued until May the following year. The revolt spread to Gijilane, Drenica and Trepca, and some 30,000 Yugoslav troops were required to suppress the Kosovars.

Although little is known of the political aims of the uprising, the intellectual leader of the rebellion, Imer Berisha, advocated the idea of the union of Kosova and western Macedonia with Albania. Official accounts spoke of Fascists and collaborators being punished, but what was really happening was a repetition of the hideous massacres that had occurred between Serbs and Albanians during the Balkan Wars. One of the worst atrocities occurred in Tivar in Montenegro, where several hundred Albanians were herded into a tunnel which was then sealed off, so that all were asphyxiated. In February 1945 Tito declared martial law in Kosova, and a military directorate took over the administration and pacification of the area. Contingents of young Albanian men were sent to the north of Yugoslavia to participate in labour brigades. In their absence, Serb and Montenegrin military units were brought to Kosova, and presented as liberators. The behaviour of these Yugoslav partisans towards the Albanians was sharply criticized at the first Congress of the Serbian Communist Party in the spring of 1945. But by then Yugoslavia's Albanian population felt completely alienated by the violence perpetrated against them. Kosova, therefore, emerged from the war into the new federal Yugoslavia under a state of siege, her population regarded as a threat to the new state.

8

'Building Socialism' under Yugoslav and Soviet Tutelage

When Enver Hoxha set up his government in Tirana in 1944, during the immediate aftermath of the war, he maintained the appearance of collaboration with those non-Communist resistance elements which still existed and were willing to join the new Democratic Front (the renamed National Liberation Front). This organization now replaced the openly Communist National Liberation Front of the war years, but the need for concessions to patriotic, nationalistic and democratic forces in the country diminished as the Communist Party tightened its hold.[1] Thousands of BK and Legaliteti supporters fled the country, the majority settling in America. In December 1944 the state took control of industry, banking and transportation. The industrial, commercial and agricultural property belonging to those who had left the country for political reasons was requisitioned without compensation to the previous owners. The following summer, a new Albanian constitution was proclaimed which was virtually a carbon-copy of the Yugoslav constitution. The new Albanian government set about re-modelling itself to the pattern of its northern neighbour, and despite the enthusiasm and confidence of the new regime the ACP became merely an appendage of the CPY. A customs union was created in preparation for Albania's total merger into the Yugoslav Federation. The Albanian currency, the lek, which had been greatly devalued during the war due to rampant inflation, was tied to the Yugoslav dinar, and the study of Serbo-Croat became compulsory in Albanian schools. And so came about the virtual extinction by Yugoslavia of Albanian independence.

In the elections held on 2 December 1945, the Democratic Front won 93 per cent of the vote, which was no surprise since virtually all the candidates stood for the Democratic Front. Apparently a small number of 'reactionary' elements rose in opposition to the law on the elections. The most outspoken of these, Gjergj Kokoshi, demanded that candidates from outside the Democratic Front should be allowed to stand in the elections. The front's rank-and-file, however, dismissed this idea as absurd. One member, Siri Shapllo, replied to Kokoshi,

> The fact that no other group has been able to organize itself after ten months of liberation, means that the creation of such groups has not been in the interests of the people. The people are with the Front. If there are some who want to organize themselves outside the Front, let them try, but they will run up against the strength of the Front and will lose. There is nothing we can do about this.[2]

Thus, according to Hoxha, Kokoshi was left in a minority of one.

Neither did there appear to be any opposition to one of the strangest clauses in the Electoral Law, whereby the sale and use of alcoholic drinks was banned for two days prior to the elections, and for one day afterwards. Despite massive intimidation and coercion, a minuscule number of intrepid candidates did stand in opposition to the Front. As an overwhelming majority of the population were illiterate, there were no voting papers. Instead, each voter was given a small rubber ball stamped with a black eagle. This was then dropped into the voter's chosen box: a red one for the Front, and a black one for any individual candidate outside the Front. The voter had to put his or her hand into both boxes, to avoid people knowing where their vote had been cast. After the victory of the Democratic Front, a Constituent Assembly proclaimed a People's Republic, and the monarchy was officially abolished. Following that, the town of Kutshova near Berat, the centre of the oil industry, was renamed Stalin. As in Yugoslavia, Enver Hoxha's Provisional Communist Government set about dealing with 'war criminals' and collaborators, and all remaining opposition was soon mopped up. The Communist victory had realized the transference of political power from the Ghegs to the Tosks, and as around three-quarters of the membership of the ACP were Tosks, their ties to the Gheg Kosova region were subordinate to their interests in the central and southern regions. One of the first things the Albanian leadership did after taking power was to 'unify' the Albanian literary language. Since Albanian Communism had its roots in south Albania,

Tosk was imposed as the country's official language from the outset. Tosk grammar was left almost intact, while the Gheg vocabulary, which is claimed by one leading specialist to be much richer than Tosk, was 'Toskicized'.[3] As the regime hastened to consolidate its position at home, it stopped fighting actively for union with Kosova. From that time on, only verbal and written encouragement was given to the Kosovars. At the close of the war, the fate of Kosova had failed to encumber Yugoslav–Albanian relations. Both leaderships took a stand in favour of unification, so the problem of Kosova was to be resolved by its inclusion in an Albanian Federal unit. Tito had agreed, together with Stalin, that Albania should eventually unite with Yugoslavia and thereby solve, amongst other problems, the issue of Kosova.

In Kosova itself, due to their at the very least passive cooperation with the Axis forces, the Albanians were perceived as being politically unreliable and a possible threat to the stability and territorial integrity of Yugoslavia. The majority of Serbs, who regarded the region as the most potent symbol of Serbian nationalism, stressed that Kosova was an integral part of Serbia and was to remain as such. The Balkan Wars, and the subsequent liberation of Kosovo-Polje in 1913, had rejuvenated the Kosovo myth among Serbs. As a result, they consistently refused to discuss the return of Kosova to Albania. Tito did not then wish to antagonize the Serbs, Yugoslavia's largest ethnic group, or to weaken what little appeal the Communists had in Serbia by offending Serbian nationalism. However, during official talks in 1946 President Tito told Enver Hoxha that: 'Kosovo and the other Albanian regions belong to Albania and we shall return them to you, but not now because the Great Serb reaction would not accept such a thing.'[4] The Yugoslav Communist Party remained faithful to its prewar Comintern-influenced policy of trying to suppress alleged 'Greater Serbian hegemonism' by the creation of the two autonomous regions of Vojvodina, with its large Hungarian population, and Kosova, within the Republic of Serbia. In an attempt to solve the Serbian question, a compromise was reached in Article 103 of the 1946 Yugoslav Constitution, which stated that the rights and scope of the autonomous regions of Vojvodina and Kosova were to be determined by the Constitution of the Serbian Republic.

In the meantime, Albania had emerged from the war as easily the most backward country in Europe. The most pressing problem facing the new regime was the reconstruction of the country's shattered economy. The destruction caused during the war, although relatively light compared with some war-torn European countries, was wide-spread. The total number of Albanians killed is estimated at 28,000. Almost a third of all buildings were destroyed, as was over a third of all livestock; nearly all mines, ports, roads and bridges were rendered unusable, and few industrial plants were left in working order. Shelter had to be found for the thousands made homeless by the destruction of towns and villages. For many, movement from one district to another was impossible as the feeble communications network built up before the war had largely been destroyed. Transport was there-fore a real problem, as all goods had to be carried by road; until the roads were repaired, many snowbound mountain villages remained for months at a time without goods and food. To overcome these prob-lems, workers and peasants were hastily organized into brigades and battalions to repair bridges and roads and to reestablish lines of com-munication. Peasants were also mobilized to rebuild their villages and plough and sow the neglected fields. All grain depots belonging to former landowners were confiscated, and the peasants' rents and debts were cancelled. In the first days of independence, the state collected grain to prevent speculation.[5]

In August 1945, an agrarian reform law was proclaimed whereby all privately owned land exceeding certain defined limits was redistributed among the landless peasantry. Initially, the head of each family was allocated 12 acres, and the buying and selling of land was forbidden. Thus a new class of peasant farmers, grateful for the land they received, became ardent supporters of the new regime, whilst the beys lost their previously predominant economic power and found them-selves politically isolated and very heavily taxed. According to foreign reports, the United Nations' relief programme, UNRRA (United Nations Relief and Rehabilitation Administration), which replaced the immediate short-term aid supplied by Allied Mediterranean Head-quarters, was very effective. It was mainly due to this aid programme that Albania escaped a major famine. One traveller reported in the summer of 1946 that,

> Although [UN] work only commenced in August this year, much has already been done, and the warehouses of Durres and Vlore are full of goods, food, medical requirements and clothes. In the agricultural field, the work of UNRRA has been of inestimable value. It has imported quan-tities of seed wheat and also forage crop seeds, fertilizers and machinery. A number of tractors have also been imported and the Albanians taught how to use them. At first suspicious, the peasants have now begun to realize

their value. UNRRA is trying to introduce even more far-reaching improvements in agriculture, but it is a job to see that the masses get enough food. UNRRA is also importing up to 5,000 head of cattle, a number of selected animals for breeding, and about two million vines to help the recovery of the wine trade.[6]

From September 1945 to the spring of 1947, when UNRRA completed its work, Albania received a total of US$26 million of assorted goods, materials and equipment from UNRRA. Despite this generous foreign aid, everyday life in Albania was characterized by a stark austerity. There were still chronic shortages of food and consumer goods in most parts of the country, and rationing was enforced throughout 1945.

Nevertheless, there were some elements within the Party hierarchy who were highly critical of the land-reform programme. An opponent of Hoxha's in the Politburo, Sejfulla Maleshova, feared that the reforms would cause food shortages and suggested that 'We should divide the land among the poor, but must not forget the mentality of our peasants. They have had nothing at all and will be satisfied with little, and will not be interested in large-scale production. Famine will threaten us.' Hoxha asked how this could be done, to which Maleshova replied, 'We should give the extremely poor masses a minimum area, just enough to fulfil their needs, while we should reduce the land of the present owners, but leave them at least 40 hectares, They know the value of large-scale production, and will make their economies model ones and produce for the city too.'[7] Hoxha adamantly opposed this view, arguing that the peasants must be given the land due to them, and that within time the Party would have convinced the peasants that their salvation lay in large-scale agricultural collectivization. It is perhaps fortunate that at that time Albania's urban population was so small.

During 1946 severe flooding devastated most of Albania's crops. In response, and despite the fact that Yugoslavia was reconstructing her own devastated, war-torn economy, Belgrade granted much-needed economic assistance, sending food as well as providing the rails and engines for Albania's first railway. Throughout Albania *Rroft Tito* (Long Live Tito) slogans appeared alongside the abundant *Rroft Enver* signs. The Yugoslavs, however, continued to use pressure to reduce Albania to the status of a dependency of Belgrade. They exploited the country economically by paying excessively low prices for the raw materials they took from Albania. Yugoslav speculators travelled throughout Albania buying up, with devalued dinars, livestock, fruit, wool, tobacco and olive oil, which were then sold in Yugoslav markets for fifty times the price paid for them. Yugoslav intentions towards Albania were summed up by Milovan Djilas: 'With regard to Albania ... our ambitions were certainly not idealistic but inspired by a lust for power.'[8]

In the spring of 1946, the People's Assembly elected a new cabinet. Enver Hoxha was given the posts of prime minister, foreign minister, defence minister and commander-in-chief of the armed forces. He also continued to serve as secretary-general of the ACP. Koci Xoxe, on the other hand, remained in the important posts of minister of the interior and party organizational secretary. The Party purges of 'undesirable elements' began with Koci Xoxe's success in expelling Sejfulla Maleshova from the Politburo and the Central Committee, allegedly for right-wing views on internal and foreign policy and on economics. In the next year Xoxe expelled Ymer Dishnica from the Party.[9] Maleshova had argued for an independent Albanian foreign policy which would have involved closer ties with the West. The manoeuvres and countermanoeuvres had left the levers of power, for the present, firmly in the hands of Koci Xoxe and the pro-Yugoslav elements in the ACP. Xoxe was able to use his position to isolate Hoxha, as he pressed for the rapid integration of Albania with Yugoslavia. By now Koci Xoxe, who had vigorously condemned the repudiation of the Mukaj agreement, had come to be regarded as a Yugoslav vassal, a latter-day successor to Essad Pasha. That Hoxha saw Xoxe and the Yugoslavs as a threat to his leadership was made clear by his attempts to get rid of them.[10] It was against this background of fear and suspicion that the Central Committee of the ACP decided to reinforce its hold over the country by escalating the programme of nationalization and agrarian reform. Henceforth, all surplus land was turned into agricultural cooperatives or state farms, the first being in Sukth near Durres. It was hoped to transform the primitive farming methods and small-scale production, and thereby to produce enough food for what was Europe's fastest growing population. Production, however, was abysmally low because the land continued to be tilled with primitive and inefficient tools. The supply of UNRRA tractors had dried up. Originally land reform was applied mainly in the fertile areas of the Korca and Musikaja plains, where it was relatively easy to allocate land, but in the infertile mountainous areas the field sizes were so small that great difficulties arose when fair distribution of land was attempted.

Meanwhile, the British and American missions in Tirana were finding it increasingly difficult to carry out their functions. Severe restrictions were imposed on the movements of their officials, who were accused of aiding and abetting active opponents of the regime. In April 1946 Britain withdrew its mission from Albania, on the grounds that diplomatic relations between the two countries had become impossible under the prevailing conditions. Some seven months later the United States government took the same step.[11] Relations with Yugoslavia remained static, with Tirana continuing to play a subservient role to her northern neighbour. In June, Hoxha paid an uncomfortable visit to Belgrade where, as he entertainingly describes in *The Titoites*, he was shocked by Tito's arrogance and elitism, and how he was expected to be very smartly dressed to greet Tito. He described 'Tito's Court' as a place of opulence with beautiful Persian carpets and an abundance of antique furniture. The Albanian delegation was awed at what they saw. Tito wore a white marshal's uniform with a gold-embroidered collar and matching cuffs, and abundant medal ribbons on his chest to complement the stars on his epaulettes – this ensemble being completed by a huge sparkling diamond ring on his finger. Hoxha felt offended, humiliated and probably exceedingly jealous of all this excessive and ostentatious display, following so soon after the austere misery of the wartime struggle from which both he and Tito had just emerged. The small Albanian delegation felt poor and shabby in comparison to the other guests. Hoxha, who was an extremely vain man, suffered intense embarrassment after Tito had taken him, with some other guests, out into the grounds. They all sat and talked in a summerhouse, while rain fell outside and muddied the ground. When they returned to the palace Hoxha was horrified to find that the bottom of his trousers and the heels of his shoes had become smeared with mud. He blushed with shame, dragging his feet so that the heels of his shoes should not be seen.[12]

In the meantime, Anglo-Albanian relations had further deteriorated as a result of an incident which involved the British navy. Towards the end of 1945 British minesweepers had begun the difficult task of clearing the Corfu Channel of mines, despite protests from the Albanians, who had declared that their territorial waters extended three miles from the Albanian coastline. The British challenged the Albanian claims, arguing that the Channel was an international waterway. The Albanians replied on 15 May 1946 by firing at British ships in the Channel. The British then sent four destroyers from Corfu through the Channel, and on 22 October two of the ships hit mines and sunk with the loss of 44 men. As the British mine-sweepers continued to clear the area, Hoxha complained to the United Nations about foreign vessels entering Albanian territorial waters. The UN debated the issue, which was then referred to the International Court of Justice. This finally decided that the Albanian government held full responsibility for the loss of the two ships. The evidence against Albania was pretty flimsy, as the Albanians argued that they were the only country in the Mediterranean area possessing neither mines, mine-layers nor personnel trained in the handling of mines.[13] The Albanians continued to deny any responsibility as the International Court ordered Albania (by 11 votes to 5) to pay £843,947 compensation – for the value of the two ships, and to the relatives of the dead sailors. Needless to say, the Albanians ignored the demand but protested in vain for the return of a large sum of gold stolen from Albania by the retreating Axis forces, and later seized by the Allies.[14]

Yugoslav Pressure Intensifies

In the cold-war climate of postwar Europe, Albania found itself in a particularly vulnerable situation. Relations with the West were at a low point following the Corfu incident, and there was now firm American support for the renewed Greek claims to southern Albania. The Albanians therefore had little alternative but to cooperate with Belgrade, aware of Stalin's consent to Tito's domination of Albania. In July 1946, Albania and Yugoslavia signed a Treaty of Friendship, Cooperation and Mutual Aid. At the time, Tito's plans for a Balkan Federation were gathering momentum, and so a similar treaty was signed with Bulgaria. A primary goal of postwar Yugoslav foreign policy was the setting up of a Balkan Federation comprising Yugoslavia, Albania, Bulgaria and Greece. The following spring, Tito's true objectives with respect to Albania were signalled when the Yugoslav government proposed to Nako Spiru (who was on a mission to Belgrade to try to resolve the differences between the two countries) that a secret pact be signed between the two countries ensuring the protection of Yugoslav interests in Albania in the event of any change in the ACP leadership. Spiru refused to sign the pact, and his mission ended with Yugoslav–Albanian relations worse than they had been when he arrived in Belgrade. Possibly as a consequence of the failed mission, Koci Xoxe initiated new moves against his opponents in the

ACP leadership. On 20 May 1947 the Albanian government announced that nine members of the People's Assembly with known anti-Yugoslav sentiments had been arrested, tried and convicted of plotting against the state.[15]

There were, however, some financial advantages to the relationship with Belgrade. In July 1947 the Yugoslavs granted US$40 million credit to assist Albania meet her economic targets for the year. This was equivalent to around 58 per cent of the Albanian state budget. Nevertheless, resentment against Yugoslav influence was steadily increasing. The Albanian government began objecting to the Yugoslav valuation of Albania's raw-material exports, the method by which Albanian investment in joint companies would be calculated, the alleged failure of the Yugoslavs to contribute the agreed share of capital to the companies, and an apparent attempt by a joint shipping company to control Albania's foreign trade.[16] During the summer, as Tito was busy organizing the foundations of the Cominform (the information bureau of the Communist Parties) Stalin secretly invited Hoxha to Moscow. Hoxha went, and was appalled by Stalin's lack of knowledge about Albania. Stalin's ignorance was confirmed when Edvard Kardelj, Tito's foreign-policy advisor, met him around the same time. Stalin asked Kardelj questions about the origins of the Albanians, commenting, 'They seem to be a rather backward and primitive people', to which the Yugoslav ambassador replied, 'But they are very brave and faithful' – a statement that somewhat reinforced Stalin's opinion of the Albanians, as he continued, 'Yes, they can be as faithful as a dog, that is one of the traits of the primitive.'[17]

Following this generally unremarkable visit, Albania signed, naturally with Stalin's prior approval, a Treaty of Friendship and Cooperation with Bulgaria. This represented a show of independence from Yugoslavia. However, when the Cominform was set up in October 1947, Albania was the only country in the Communist bloc not invited to join, perhaps because it would have still supported Yugoslavia in any dispute, and because Stalin already anticipated serious problems with Tito. Soviet–Yugoslav relations were deteriorating over Tito's and the Bulgarian leader, Georgi Dimitrov's plans for a Balkan Federation, to which Stalin was opposed. Stalin was enraged at such a show of independent foreign policy-making by his client states, and more importantly by their lack of consultation with him. Towards the end of the year, as the differences between Moscow and Belgrade became more acute, Tito began pressing for unification

with Albania. Two army divisions and a squadron of fighter aircraft
were hastily prepared for intervention in Albania, without Stalin's
consent, under the pretext of danger to Albania from 'imperialists'
hiding in Greece. These fears were far from groundless, as the right-
wing Greek government, which then had the support of the United
States, had once again reactivated the old Greek claims to southern
Albania. Bringing Albania to heel was inconsistent with Yugoslavia's
Communist teaching about the voluntary merger and self-determination of peoples. But times were bad: the United Nations had begun
accusing Yugoslavia of intervening in the Greek Civil War, and as that
war raged on there was a real fear that Albania might possibly be
invaded by the Athens regime, with Western backing. Therefore, the
Yugoslav army divisions refrained from entering Albania but remained
poised on the border.

Gradually the factional struggle within the Albanian leadership
had become more complex and violent, and was caught up in the
deteriorating relations between the Soviet Union and Yugoslavia. By
late 1947, Xoxe and his associates, under Yugoslav direction, were
intensifying their efforts to merge Albania into Yugoslavia. Much of
the Albanian leadership, and in particular the intellectual Nako Spiru,
opposed this Yugoslav plan.[18]

In November Spiru, aware that he was about to be eliminated as a
'chauvinist', suddenly committed suicide. According to the official
Albanian version he was accidentally killed while cleaning his revolver.
It is more likely, however, that he could not stand up to the persistent
verbal attacks on him by Xoxe and the Yugoslavs. Spiru's suicide
brought Stalin's conflict with Tito to a head. In January 1948, Stalin
used Tito's behaviour towards Albania, and Spiru's suicide, as the
pretext for inviting a Yugoslav delegation, which included Milovan
Djilas, to Moscow to discuss the rapidly deteriorating Yugoslav–
Albanian situation and the dispute over Tito's controversial Balkan
Federation plan. During the subsequent discussions, Stalin remarked
to Djilas that the Soviet Union had no special interest in Albania and
that Yugoslavia was free to 'swallow' Albania any time it wished to do
so.[19] This rather confused the Yugoslavs, who interpreted Stalin's
'swallow Albania' as a provocation, and his insistence on immediate
Yugoslav–Bulgarian federation as an effort to penetrate Yugoslav
apparatuses by uniting them with already Sovietized Bulgarian ones.[20]

By now Tito was seriously endeavouring to consolidate Yugoslavia's
special influence on the other East European states, independent of

the Soviet Union. Under Tito's orders, Xoxe accelerated his drive to overthrow Hoxha and to bring the Albanian party once and for all under Yugoslav control. And so the Central Committee of the Yugoslav Communist Party sent an emissary, Savo Zllatic, to Albania to assist Xoxe in the convocation of a Central Committee meeting intended finally to overthrow his opponents. The Eighth Plenum duly met on 26 February 1948, and its proceedings reflect the extent to which the Xoxe faction nearly succeeded in ensuring a long-term Yugoslav presence in Albania. Hoxha was forced to perform self-criticism and to join in the condemnation of Spiru in order to maintain his post as secretary–general. The Plenum expelled Spiru's widow, Liri Belishova, and demoted the chief of the Albanian general staff, Mehmet Shehu. The Eighth Plenum also approved Xoxe's proposals to merge the Albanian and Yugoslav economies and armed forces.[21] Because Hoxha's position within the ACP leadership was now very weak, he stayed discreetly in the background at the height of all this factional strife. Following the Eighth Plenum, Hoxha's position was further weakened. However, fortunately for him, plans were already being made in Moscow to dismiss Yugoslavia from the Cominform. In March, Stalin launched his offensive against Tito in a series of letters accusing the Yugoslavs of every imaginable Leninist deviation.

The Period of Soviet Alignment

Much to Hoxha's relief, Yugoslavia was finally expelled from the Cominform in June 1948. This quickly led to a radical shift in alignment within the Albanian party leadership. Hoxha must have foreseen the developing rift between Tito and Stalin and decided to throw in his lot with the Soviets, as Albania became the first of the Communist states openly to attack Tito. On 1 July 1948 the Belgrade–Tirana umbilical cord was finally severed, as all economic agreements between Albania and Yugoslavia were annulled. Yugoslavia was ordered to close its information centre in Tirana, and Yugoslav personnel were given 48 hours to leave the country. Tirana henceforth was adamant in its support of the Soviet denunciations of Belgrade. The period of Yugoslav tutelage, under which Albania's status remained that of a Yugoslav sub-satellite, had witnessed the deterioration of Albania's economic situation. This was further exacerbated by the need to feed the thousands of refugees and wounded guerillas from the Greek civil war who sought shelter in Albania. Following the last desperate battles in the Grammos mountains, the remnants of the Greek Communist forces, together with the KKE leadership, had fled across the border into Albania.

During that autumn, for reasons never clarified, the Eleventh Plenum of the CPA agreed to change the name of the ACP to the Party of Labour of Albania (PLA). The Plenum also restored Belishova and Shehu to their former positions, and the latter was also appointed minister of the interior in place of Xoxe. The noose was now tightening on Xoxe, and he was finally expelled from the PLA after the meeting of the first full Party Congress held in November 1948. Tito's conflict with Stalin led to open hostility towards Yugoslavia from the Central Committee of the PLA, who denounced the Yugoslavs as traitors and Trotskyites. This, in turn, only served to strengthen Belgrade's already pronounced tendency to view all Albanians as subversive. It was Tito's independence rather than any real disagreement with foreign policy plans that caused the split between Tito and Stalin. Wishing to prevent the development of a pro-Yugoslav faction within the Communist movement, Stalin helped save Hoxha and Shehu from being purged and perhaps liquidated at the hands of Xoxe and the Yugoslavs. Although Koci Xoxe tried to save himself by launching a sharp attack on Tito, he found himself demoted within two months and arrested at the end of November. On 11 June the following year he was secretly tried, found guilty of crimes against the state, and executed. So began the relentless crushing, via a series of bloody purges, of all opposition as Hoxha moved to consolidate his position. For reasons of security and assistance, Albania continued to align itself with the Soviet Union and became Yugoslavia's harshest critic within the Communist bloc. The intended Yugoslav annexation of Albania now became impossible, and after Yugoslavia's expulsion from the Cominform, notwithstanding Stalin's scant regard for Albania or the Albanian leadership, Tirana was provided with a platform from which to reactivate the 'unsettled' question of Kosova.

Following the ruthless suppression of the Kosovars in 1945, Yugoslavia's Albanians became subject to a government-sanctioned policy of systematic persecution and discrimination. As a Western observer noted: 'Kosova became a colonial dependency, ruled, neglected and exploited by Serbs.'[22] The Kosovars suffered renewed pressures of assimilation and denationalization. A noted Albanian historian said of the period:

The Albanian language was denied equal status with Serbo-Croat. The display of any Albanian national symbols and flags and the commemoration of Albanian national holidays were prohibited. Also the teaching of Albanian history, traditions and literature was considered a nationalistic deviation.[23]

Denial of republic status for Kosova was not, as was officially suggested, merely a question of size, since the 1948 census recorded 750,431 Albanians in Yugoslavia, but only 425,703 Montenegrins, who as well as being ethnically Serbs were given their own republic. With Stalin's backing, the Albanian press began to give full coverage to the 'persecution' of Albanians in Yugoslavia, whom it incited to 'overthrow Tito'.[24] And so began the war of words over Kosova that would ebb or flow according to specific conditions relating to Yugoslavia or Albania.

At a meeting that autumn in Shkoder, Hoxha alleged that Tito was harbouring and feeding war criminals at Skopje and Pristina for purposes well known to the Albanian government. Although he maintained that the activities of his enemies were like 'the blind leading the blind', he added that Tito had assisted the escape from Albania of a few dozen enemies of little intelligence, had enrolled them into diversionary bands in Yugoslavia, and had sent them back across the Albanian frontier to stir up trouble. Subsequently, Tirana requested the Yugoslav government to extradite certain 'criminals' who had taken refuge in Yugoslavia, including Cen Elezi and Dan Kalloshi, alleging that they were 'carefully organized with hostile aims against the interests of Albania'. Fikri Dine and Muharrem Bajraktari were also mentioned as other members of this 'group of spies'. It appears, however, that the latter two were in fact not working for the Yugoslavs but for the Albanian Committee (formed by exiled BK and Legaliteti members) in Paris.[25] For Albania, meanwhile, the price of independence from Yugoslavia was further dependence upon the Soviet Union. The period of predominantly Soviet economic influence in Albania began in September 1948, when the first joint economic agreement was concluded, and it was supplemented during Hoxha's visit to Moscow in 1949. The USSR bought Albanian exports at doubled prices, and imports from the Soviet Union were delivered at half price. Furthermore, the USSR renewed all the credits previously given by the Yugoslavs.[26]

The Albanian regime faced perhaps the most difficult internal situation of any of the socialist states because of the relatively backward conditions and low standard of living. The Communist leadership attempted to deal with this situation by adopting the standard Stalinist model of a highly centralized planned economy, with strong emphasis on self-sufficiency in heavy industry. During the war, Italian mineral exploration had revealed the extent of Albania's raw material base, yet both Yugoslavia and the Soviet Union wanted the Albanians to concentrate on developing agriculture rather than their considerable mineral resources. Nevertheless, emphasis was increasingly concentrated on the development of industry. The two-year economic plan from 1949 to 1950 laid the foundation for the subsequent five-year plans. During this plan large projects were begun, such as the Lenin hydro power plant to meet the needs of the Tirana district, the Stalin textile mills and the Maliq sugar refinery.[27] In January 1949, a new system of procurement and supply was introduced by the Central Committee to improve economic relations between the town and countryside. The state guaranteed market-supplied goods at fixed prices to working people on the basis of ration cards; the barter market supplied peasants with industrial commodities in exchange for their agricultural surpluses; and the free market served those in urban town and rural areas whose needs were not met by the other two markets, either because they were not supplied with ration cards or were not engaged in cooperative agricultural production. Prices in the free market were much higher than in the others, and in this way it was hoped that money accumulated by the country's richer elements would be gradually mopped up.[28]

During the 1950s Albania embarked on an ambitious programme of electrification and industrialization. Despite protests from Moscow, greater attention was paid to the exploitation of Albania's rich mineral wealth, which included chrome, oil, nickel, coal and copper. The first five-year plan, 1950–55, which was aimed primarily at relieving acute shortages and strengthening the overall economy, proved to be far too ambitious, ignoring as it did the realities of Albania's severe lack of adequate machinery, skilled labour and a developed communication network. It did however manage to produce the Vlore cement works, a sugar-cane factory, the tobacco fermentation plant at Shkoder, and the Tirana textile combine, plus a few tractors and threshing machines. On the agricultural front the situation was even more serious. The objective of the first five-year plan was to prepare the ground and create conditions for the rapid development of collectivization. The resulting dislocation, accentuated by two consecutive very dry years, 1951 and 1952, cut grain production, as well as cattle, sheep and goat populations, between 10 and 25 per cent, and caused very acute food shortages which threatened to jeopardize the whole plan. Stopgap measures – such as a temporary halt to further collectivization, the drastic reduction of compulsory delivery quotas, the cancellation of quotas in arrears, and the free distribution of grain to peasants – had no lasting effects. Grain production continued to be erratic and always fell below target, as did the numbers of cattle, sheep and goats. Agricultural methods were still very primitive, and mechanization remained very much a dream.[29]

The Albanian state was portrayed in state publications as the 'governmental expression of the dictatorship of the working class', even if there was no working class to speak of. The PLA, released from the political and economic stranglehold of the Yugoslavs, now felt free to provide direction for Albanian society as a whole, making sure that 'true' socialist politics and leadership commanded all aspects of development. Every citizen over the age of 18 years was eligible to vote or to be elected to any elective body, including all industrial, cooperative and social organizations. These organizations were created to implement the guiding role of the Party, to strengthen its influence among ordinary people and to make sure the Party's directives were being followed. The People's Assembly was elected every four years on the basis of one representative for every 8,000 people, and was empowered, at least in theory, to appoint or dismiss the government. State power was represented at a local level by the people's councils, which represented the villages, towns and city districts. They were elected every three years on the same basis as the People's Assembly. Thus, according to Party supporters, there could not be a more democratic system. In his report to the Second Party Congress in 1952, Hoxha took the whole party severely to task in order to improve methods of leadership:

> We call meeting after meeting which go on for days on end but very little comes out of them. Many decisions are taken, but not all of them are applied. Then nearly as many decisions are taken again to carry out the previous decisions. New decisions are adopted also on matters already decided upon, but forgotten.[30]

One area in which Hoxha took a fiercely independent line was that of religion. The Albanian government frequently and openly criticized the Soviet Union and the other Communist states for their 'tolerant' attitude towards religious communities. The results of a religious census taken in 1945 had showed 70 per cent of the population to be Muslim, 20 per cent to be Orthodox and 10 per cent Catholic. Initially the Hoxha regime aimed to reduce the influence of religion and the churches. All religious bodies were brought completely under the control of the government. To achieve this, the government used various legislative acts, the elimination of distinguished clergymen who were uncooperative, and their replacement by pliant clerics. On 26 November 1949, a law was enacted requiring all religious communities to develop among their members the feeling of loyalty towards 'people's power' and the People's Republic of Albania.[31] The law, which was aimed primarily at the Catholic community, read: 'The religious communities or their branches which have their headquarters outside the state are not allowed to open branches (orders, missions, philanthropic institutions etc.) and those which exist will be closed within a month from the date of the entrance into power of this law'. The Jesuit and Franciscan orders were thus eliminated.[32] Clergymen who refused to cooperate were either imprisoned or in some cases executed. According to a document published in 1953 by the National Committee for a Free Albania, out of 93 Catholic clergymen in Albania in 1945, 10 remained free, 24 had been murdered, 35 had been imprisoned, 10 had died or disappeared, 11 had been drafted, and 3 had escaped abroad.[33]

The persecution of the Catholic clergy by the Tirana government was more drastic than that aimed at the Muslims or Orthodox, primarily because the Catholic Church in Albania was viewed as an instrument of the Vatican. Hoxha viewed Catholics as less patriotic than either Muslims or Orthodox. He later wrote:

The Catholic Church and its clergy were always in alliance with the reactionary regimes like those of Prince Wied, and Ahmed Zog, as well as with every foreign occupier of Albania, including the Austro-Hungarians, the Italian fascists and the German Nazis.... The Muslim religion and its hierarchy were not as serious an obstacle to the struggle against the Italian occupiers as the Catholic religion was. Even before the occupation of the country, but still more so after it, the hierarchy of the Muslim religion was weak, without any experience to worry us. The mosques existed. They had a hodja, but those who practised the religion were very few.... Among the Bektashi sect, also, a large proportion of the believers traditionally have displayed patriotism and have fought for the liberation of Albania. The situation was similar with the Orthodox Christian faith, too, both in the hierarchy of the church and among its believers.[34]

Despite this, in 1949 Hoxha took the precaution of replacing the Orthodox Metropolitan of Tirana, Kristopher Kissi, with (contrary to Orthodox tradition) a married priest who was a Communist sympathizer.

Finally, in 1951 the Catholic Church was forced to sever its links with Rome, in order to become a national church with its own statutes which acknowledged its complete subordination to the state. Members of the government and party officials also embarked on an intensive campaign designed to discredit religious belief and to alienate the people from religious institutions. The religious world outlook and the Communist world outlook were said to be irreconcilable, while the clergy were held up as enemies of socialism and therefore of the people. This campaign continued throughout the 1950s, and the way was thus prepared for the actual suppression of religious institutions.[35]

Following Tito's split with Stalin, and despite Tirana's realignment with Moscow, Albania was geographically very isolated and vulnerable, a fact not lost on the British and Americans who, during the late 1940s, had devised a complicated and risky plot to overthrow Hoxha's regime. The plan was to train and equip an anti-Communist force, recruited from the hundreds of Zogist and Ballist refugees who had fled from Albania after the war. They would be parachuted into the Mati area, where it was supposed there were elements still loyal to Zog who, it was hoped, could be effectively organized. There was still some residual guerilla activity against the Communists in Poland, Romania, the Ukraine and the Baltic countries, and optimists thought a victory in Albania might encourage them to greater efforts.[36] The first group, recruited from displaced persons camps in Greece and Italy and trained in Malta, was sent into Albania in 1947. Over the next two years many more groups of Albanians were sent to Malta, Cyprus and West Germany to be trained, and after training were dropped or smuggled into Albania. In 1949 the British sent a member of their secret service, H.A.R. (Kim) Philby, to Washington to work with the CIA in helping to organize the Albanian operation. However, the whole operation was a total disaster because Philby, as a double agent, was informing Tirana, via the Soviet Union, when to expect the arrival of each group. Soon after they landed in Albania, the Albanian army was waiting for them, having been notified of their exact time and place of arrival. Those that were not immediately killed were rounded up and sent for trial, where they were usually condemned to death. From the start, the whole plan stood little chance of success. After the last group went into Albania in 1952, more than

three hundred men had died in the operation. This fiasco understandably increased Hoxha's growing sense of paranoia. Henceforth,
Albanian foreign policy concentrated on preserving the country's territorial independence in the face of constant threats from the West
and from Albania's hostile Balkan neighbours.

During the 1950s, although many Czechs and Russians spent their
holidays in Durres, there were very few foreign visitors to Albania.
The only direct connection between Albania and the West was an
Italian passenger ship that provided a regular service between Brindisi
and Durres. An Austrian visitor, Anton Zischka, wrote a perceptive
account of his travels during this period. On his arrival he witnessed:

> A body of troops marching past at the frontier control, their equipment
> symbolising the more recent history of the country: Italian steel helmets,
> German rifles and camouflage, Russian officers' epaulettes. Everywhere
> people wear national costume. The old traditional patriarchal way of life
> has been destroyed, but a new one suited to prevailing Albanian circum-
> stances has not yet been discovered.'[37]

In Tirana, which by then had around 100,000 inhabitants, it appears
that life went on much as it had done before the war, despite the
Italian reconstruction of the immediate centre of the city. Zischka
noted that:

> Low houses remain unchanged since Turkish times, bazaars and half
> decayed booths of artisans, there is a continual smell of donkey manure
> and rancid mutton fat, and where hens and pigs refuse to be disturbed by
> any mere pedestrian. The embassy cars go regularly into Yugoslavia to buy
> provisions for there is a shortage not only of luxury articles, but of many
> necessities, shortages are in evidence everywhere. Most drugs are un-
> obtainable, except on the black market, and aspirin is rationed. There is
> only a surplus in raki and plum brandy.[38]

The Soviet–Yugoslav Rapprochement

In March 1953, Stalin died. His death caused immense anxiety to the
Albanian leadership. They had lost their protector and had now to
wait to see if Stalin's successors would provide the same security
from Albania's many predators. Whilst the struggle for power was
going on in Moscow, Hoxha decided to strengthen his position in
Tirana through some quick ministerial shuffling. Mehmet Shehu duly
became the new deputy prime minister. The following year, he took
over the prime ministership from Hoxha, who remained First Secre-

tary of the Party. More than half of the 53 members of the Central
Committee of the PLA were related. By now only three of the original
Albanian Central Committee – Hoxha, Jakova and Spahiu – were still
members; the latter two had already been demoted and were purged
in 1955.[39] Following Stalin's death, Yugoslav relations with Moscow
began to improve, and – despite vigorous objections from Molotov –
the new Soviet Party Secretary, Nikita Khrushchev, visited Belgrade.
Soviet foreign policy analysts believed that if Yugoslavia were wooed
back into the Soviet bloc, discipline might be restored to a seriously
disunified Eastern Europe. Khrushchev's visit was of great significance, for it finally shattered the myth that a Communist's first loyalty
must be to the 'first land of socialism'. A year later Tito visited
Moscow for the first time since 1946, and was received as a hero.
Throughout Eastern Europe 'Titoites' were preparing to be rehabili-
tated, while in the Soviet Union a policy of de-Stalinization had
begun. At the 20th Congress of the Communist Party of the Soviet
Union in February 1956, Khrushchev gave his notorious report 'On
the cult of the individual and its consequences', which was an all-out
attack on Stalin ... accusing him of the greatest 'arbitrary cruelty'.[40]

Following this congress, Khrushchev began pressurizing the Albanians to reexamine their attitude towards Tito and the sentences which
had been pronounced against Koci Xoxe, Tuk Jakova and other anti-
party elements, on the grounds that these were errors committed
'under Stalin's cult of the individual'.[41] The continued improvement
in Moscow–Belgrade relations was perceived by the Albanian ruling
elite as a serious threat to the country's independence. In reconciling
with Yugoslavia – Albania's perceived principal enemy – the Soviet
Union had ignored Albania's vital national interests.[42] Nevertheless, at
the Third Party Congress in May 1956 Hoxha had little choice but to
begrudgingly follow the Soviet line and change his policy towards
Yugoslavia by announcing that all accusations were unjust and Albania
would establish friendly relations with Yugoslavia. In reality, however,
the Albanians resisted Soviet and Yugoslav pressure to rehabilitate
Koci Xoxe and other supporters of Yugoslavia, which Hoxha must
have realized would only serve to hasten his own demise. He managed
to survive this period due to his undoubted tactical brilliance and
singleminded ruthlessness, aided by Albania's isolated position, its
backwardness and marginal importance, as well as the growing tensions
in Hungary and Poland.[43] The post-Stalin leadership in Moscow had
clearly calculated that the financial costs of supporting the Albanian

economy now far outweighed the country's political or strategic importance to the Soviet Union. The immediate effect on Albania of Khrushchev's rapprochement with Tito was increased unemployment and a reduction of goods coming into the country from the Communist bloc, although this was partly offset by China suddenly granting a long-term loan to Albania, together with 20,000 tonnes of wheat, 100,000 metres of silk, 2,000 tonnes of rice, and 2,000 tonnes of sugar as a gift to the Albanian people.[44]

Around this time, according to the Albanian regime, Tito masterminded a counter-revolutionary conspiracy within Albania that was discovered shortly before the Third Party Congress of the PLA on 25 May 1956. Dali Ndreu and Liri Gega were accused of participating in the plot and were arrested trying to flee into Yugoslavia, where apparently a resistance group was being formed. In an effort to secure external support for his regime, Hoxha paid a visit to China in October 1956, and the foundations of Albania's subsequent alliance with Peking were laid during this trip.[45] If in 1948 Hoxha was rescued by the Tito–Stalin conflict, so in 1956 the Hungarian uprising saved him from disgrace and almost certain death. The Russian invasion of Hungary in November 1956 shattered Tito's plans for continued Soviet–Yugoslav rapprochement. In the wake of the Soviet suppression of the Hungarian uprising, Hoxha and Shehu quickly set about removing their remaining opponents within the party leadership. An abrupt communiqué announced that Liri Gega, a member of the ruling Politburo, her husband Dali Nreu, also a Central Committee member, and the Yugoslav-born Major Bulatovic had been shot as 'foreign spies'. Khrushchev later revealed that the Soviet leadership had at that time asked the Albanians to spare the life of Gega, on the grounds that she was expecting a child, a request that probably served to confirm the well-founded suspicion that she had been involved in a Soviet-sponsored attempt to overthrow Hoxha.[46] Hoxha had continued to have serious misgivings over Soviet policy ever since the rapprochement with Tito and the discrediting of Stalin. As a result, he acted cautiously, whilst searching around for another patron.

The Albanian regime remained on its guard, watching with suspicion Khrushchev's relations with the Yugoslavs. Hoxha certainly had plenty to be suspicious about, and claimed that when the Russians sent oil 'experts' and 'geologists' to Albania they made two reports: an accurate one, with exact and positive data on discoveries of different minerals; and a false one, which alleged that the prospecting had yielded negative results. The first report was sent to Moscow through the KGB centre, which was called the Soviet Embassy in Tirana; the second report was sent to the Albanian Ministry of Industry and Mines.[47] Having weathered the storm of the Hungarian revolution, Khrushchev was anxious to improve relations between Yugoslavia and Albania as discord continued to prevail throughout Eastern Europe. Consequently, he courted the Albanians with promises of financial and material aid. Late in 1957, Moscow granted Albania a 160-million-rouble loan and the East European satellites followed suit. During the second five year plan (1956–60), the Karl Marx hydroelectric plant was constructed on the Mati river, an oil refinery was built at Cerrik, and canneries opened at Vlore, Elbasan, Korca and Shkoder.[48]

By 1958–9, later known in Albania as the Golden Years, when capital was pouring into Albania from all over the Eastern bloc, there was also a steady increase in Chinese credits to Albania. All this resulted in rapid Albanian economic growth and a transformation in literacy, health, education and general living standards. A social-security system had been established in 1953, with old-age and disability pensions made mandatory. From 1950 to 1959 the number of physicians increased from 129 to 378, and medical practices from 67 to 125. Malaria was practically eliminated, owing to the continued draining of the swamp lands in the western regions of the country. The University of Tirana was established in 1957, following the merger of several colleges, and many Albanian students went to the Soviet Union and Eastern Europe. Opposition to the government was muted, owing to the widespread power of the regime, the weakness of the Albanian intelligentsia, and the rigid control the Party exercised over all publications, including those concerned with literary and cultural matters. The Writers' Union served only to publicize the Party's will. But by the end of the 1950s in the agricultural sector collectivization was pushed ahead at breakneck speed, leaving in its trail widespread dislocation bordering on chaos, and reducing bread grain production to only 23 per cent of its 1957 level.[49]

In the meantime, the situation in Kosova had not improved. Throughout the 1950s the Albanian government continued to utter the occasional half-hearted and vaguely patriotic statement concerning Yugoslavia's Albanians. In 1958 Mehmet Shehu commented:

> Had we not raised our voice in defence of our Albanian brothers in Kosova, Montenegro and Macedonia, we would have betrayed Marxism–Leninism.

> We are not at present asking that Kosova be joined with Albania, but the same mother that gave birth to us, gave birth to the Albanians of Yugoslavia. We demand that the Yugoslav government grant the Albanians all the rights pertaining to them as a national minority.[50]

This meaningless rhetoric did little to help the Kosovars. The Serbs continued to hold all the top state and party positions and to dominate all aspects of cultural and economic life in Kosova. For the Soviet Union it was disruptive and troublesome that Albania refused to fall in line with the other Eastern bloc countries. The Russians tried to appease the Albanians by presenting them with a fine new film studio in Tirana where, in 1958, *Tana,* the first Albanian film, was made – a love story set on a collective farm.

At the end of May 1959, Khrushchev paid a two-week visit to Albania to show how important he considered the tiny Balkan state – and to try to render the country more dependent upon the Soviet Union. The Albanian leadership believed that Khrushchev's main reason for coming was that the Americans were building rocket bases in Greece and Turkey and he sought to do the same in Albania. During his visit, Khrushchev pressured the Albanians not only to improve their relations with Yugoslavia, but also to focus their economy on the growing of citrus fruits rather than concentrate on industrialization and the expansion of their oil industry. Hohxa noted, 'In Sarande he advised us to plant only oranges and lemons for which the Soviet Union had great need.' Khrushchev advised Hoxha 'not to waste your land and marvellous climate on maize and wheat. They bring you no income. The bay tree grows here ... plant thousands of hectares of bay because we shall buy it from you.' 'He went on talking about peanuts, tea and citrus fruit ... in other words', wrote Hoxha, 'he wanted Albania to be turned into a fruit-growing colony which would serve the revisionist Soviet Union, just as the banana republics in Latin America serve the United States of America.'[51] Khrushchev's visit was clouded by an atmosphere of mistrust, which culminated in a hurried departure two days earlier than scheduled. Disgusted by Khrushchev's patronizing attitude, Hoxha began to show common interest with the Chinese, as his defiance of Moscow became more pronounced. By the autumn of 1959, China's open hostility to Moscow's foreign policy began to show itself. It was Peking, not Tirana, which initiated the rift with Moscow in June 1960. Thereafter, Hoxha had no choice but to declare his colours on the side of Peking.[52]

9

The Retreat into Isolation

Although the Albanian leadership had a new pride and confidence, bred of being courted by both the Soviet Union and China, it remained cautious and deeply suspicious of the motives and actions not only of declared enemies but also of so-called 'protectors'. At the end of May 1960, Khrushchev had had a meeting with the Greek Liberal leader, Sophocles Venizelos, who had complained about the treatment of the Greek minority in southern Albania. Khrushchev had promised to discuss the question of internal autonomy for northern Epirus with the Albanian delegation at the forthcoming Bucharest Conference to be held in June. Having already resumed contact with the Yugoslav regime in the interests of his 'peace offensive' in the Balkans, Khrushchev now seemed to be cultivating the Greeks. Albania interpreted the gesture as representing implicit Soviet support for Greek territorial claims on southern Albania; since a state of war still existed between Albania and Greece, Albania feared once more for the security of her 460-mile land border with Greece.

By the middle of 1960, Albania's relations with the Soviet Union had deteriorated further. Differences arose between China and the Soviet Union at the Bucharest summit in June. Here Albania solidly backed the Chinese, openly questioned Soviet dominance among the socialist states and accused Khrushchev of revisionism. Feeling angry and betrayed by Khrushchev, neither Hoxha nor Shehu had attended the meeting at Bucharest and had instead sent Albania's number three, Hysni Kapo. After Bucharest, Khrushchev launched a concerted attack to force the Albanians back into line by ordering the termination of much-needed grain shipments to Albania. At the time, Albania was suffering from famine caused by a series of droughts, floods and earthquakes, and had only fifteen days' supply of wheat in storage. Almost immediately the Chinese stepped in and sent a large consignment of wheat, which they bought in France and had shipped to Albania. There followed a series of dismissals of pro-Soviet Albanian party officials, including Liri Belishova, a secretary of the Central Committee.[1] Belishova, along with her family, was interned for 30 years, accused of being involved in a Soviet plot to overthrow the Albanian leadership. The Soviet chief engineer for the construction of the Tirana Palace of Culture (a 1959 gift from Moscow to Albania) suddenly left for Moscow in October, taking all the construction plans with him. He never returned. Moscow claimed that the Albanians by April of that year had so increased their demands on its size that its cost had risen by two-and-a-half times.[2]

By now Albania had begun to play a significant role in the deepening Sino-Soviet rift, which centred on their longstanding border dispute and policy differences towards the West and the Third World. In November another Communist summit was held in Moscow, attended by delegates from 81 parties from all over the world. This time, Hoxha and Shehu attended. Again, the central issue was the Sino-Soviet conflict, and once more the Albanians sided with China. They accused Khrushchev of having abandoned the ideological and political struggle against 'imperialism'. In fact, Hoxha's speech so vehemently denounced Khrushchev that even the Chinese delegates looked embarrassed. Hoxha and Shehu left the summit early, travelling overland via Austria and Italy rather than risk an 'accident' in a Soviet plane. They never again returned to the Soviet Union. This was Hoxha's last public journey outside Albania. At the Moscow Conference Hoxha had felt cornered and was by then convinced that Khrushchev was out to destroy him. His apparent paranoia was somewhat justified, since there had been at least three significant postwar threats to Albanian sovereignty. Before the break with Stalin, Tito had certainly planned for the incorporation of Albania into Yugoslavia. From 1949 to 1953 the British and Americans had attempted to overthrow Hoxha's regime; and during the period 1960–61 Khrushchev was undoubtedly intending to isolate Hoxha and thereby increase Albania's territorial vulnerability. Following the Moscow Conference, Albania's relations with the Soviet bloc deteriorated sharply, Albania becoming a small but persistently irritating problem for Khrushchev.

In January 1961, Moscow sent the experienced apparatchik, Josif Shikin, as ambassador to Tirana. His task was to smooth relations and to appeal to the Albanian leadership to mend its ways.

By 1961 the Albanian Communist Party had been thoroughly purged and the small ruling group, led by Hoxha and Shehu, were more convinced that they now commanded loyalty. Thus the regime was able to deal effectively with any emerging opposition. During the PLA Congress, the country's third five-year plan (1961–65) was announced and Khrushchev's advice was pointedly ignored as the Albanians decided to concentrate on industrial rather than agricultural development. This was the last Albanian party congress attended by the Soviet Union. The ever-widening conflict with Khrushchev was highlighted by the failure of Hoxha and Shehu to attend the important Warsaw Pact Conference in March 1961. There followed a steady withdrawal from Albania of Soviet-bloc personnel, finance and equipment, including eight submarines from Vlore. A number of Albanian ships which were undergoing repairs at Sebastopol were also impounded by the Soviets. The Soviets had made vigorous efforts to retain some presence at the Vlore base, which was their only port in the Mediterranean. Soviet and East European embassies were drastically reduced, and their promised credits for the 1961–5 five-year plan were promptly cancelled. In May, the show trial of Moscow-trained Rear Admiral Teme Sejko opened in Tirana. Together with other officials, he was charged with involvement in a plot supposedly organized by the Greeks, the Yugoslavs and the American Sixth Fleet to overthrow the Albanian regime. The defenders were found guilty and four of them, including Sejko, were shot.[3]

Hoxha now benefited from the fact that his country had no common land frontier with the Soviet Union. In other words, what had been a source of grave anxiety in 1948 became a positive asset in the 1960s.[4] His defiance, however, caused great financial hardship and seriously disrupted Albania's economic planning. The planning for the 1961–5 five-year plan had relied heavily upon the delivery of Soviet and East European industrial equipment and spare parts; also the majority of Albania's commercial and agricultural imports and exports were geared to Eastern-bloc countries. Apart from China's economic assistance, in these precarious and explosive political circumstances Albania was in greatest need of political protection against further attempts to overthrow the regime. Albania had experienced great pressures, intimidation, and interference by Yugoslavia and the

Soviet Union: Hoxha was determined to preserve Tirana's autonomy in domestic and foreign affairs, and the alliance with China was an attempt to achieve that objective.[5] For China, the benefits of the alliance evidently outweighed its costs. Although an economic liability on the already burdened Chinese economy, Albania was an important political asset. Albania could serve as a beachhead in Europe, from which Peking could potentially challenge Moscow's dominance in Eastern Europe.[6] Thus China granted Albania a loan of US$125 million, which more than matched the cancelled Soviet and East European loans for Albania's third five-year Plan (1961–65). The loan – estimated to be the largest ever extended by Peking up to that time – was intended to pay for the purchase of equipment for 25 industrial plants, tractors, agricultural machinery, consumer goods and other products.[7]

The Break with Moscow

By late summer, Chinese specialists and credit had begun to move more conspicuously into Tirana. The Albanian leadership carried on as if nothing had happened, as they were technically still members of the Soviet bloc, albeit banished to its farthest reaches. In September, however, the mood of the leadership was captured in a defiant speech by Hoxha:

> The imperialists, the Belgrade revisionists and all the enemies of our Party and people have tried by sword and fire, by plots and blockades, to strangle our Party and subjugate our people. These enemies think they can easily liquidate Albania because it is a small country. But they have miscalculated … because they have come up against a rock-like impregnable fortress, heroically defended by a brave people and Party. Those who tried to dig a grave for Albania have fallen into the grave themselves.[8]

On 25 November 1961 the Soviet ambassador was withdrawn from Tirana, due to the alleged restrictions which the Albanians had placed on his activities. The complete break with Moscow finally came after the Albanian Central Committee issued a declaration charging Khrushchev with dividing the International Communist Movement, and of speaking against the will of the Soviet People. Unwilling to tolerate Albania's 'different road to socialism', the Soviet Union officially severed relations with Albania in December 1961. This was an unprecedented development between socialist states. The move had serious repercussions for the Albanian economy, as the Soviet Union immediately ceased deliveries of the spare parts of equipment it had been supplying.

A major reason behind the Albanian leader's defiance towards Moscow was his extreme nationalist outlook. Hoxha, like Mao Tse-Tung, believed that Khrushchev was defying the world Communist movement by suppressing individual nationalisms and that in this he was deviating from true Marxist–Leninist practice. Hoxha was not prepared to compromise with Khrushchev on the role of Stalin or the rehabilitation of Koci Xoxe. Claiming that Khrushchev was developing a personality cult himself, Hoxha still maintained (quite wrongly) that Stalin had been the protector of Albanian national interests against Yugoslavia. He described Khrushchev as 'the greatest counter-revolutionary charlatan and clown the world has ever known'. Khrushchev in turn called Hoxha a 'leftist, nationalist, deviationist'. A speech by the Hungarian foreign secretary, Janos Kadar, labelled the Albanians 'Trotskyists'. Albania's ruling group managed to survive the rift with Moscow by initiating a series of bloody purges, in which the anti-Hoxha, pro-Soviet elements were eliminated. By 1962, of the 31 members of the Central Committee elected at the first Congress in 1948 only 9 survived: 14 had been liquidated and 8 forcibly 'retired' from political life. Those who survived were bound together by the traditional ties of clan loyalty and their common complicity in the ruthless purges. Among the 61 Central Committee members were 5 married couples ... and no less than 20 persons related to one another as sons-in-law or cousins.[9]

As the majority of the population were still subsistence farmers, often living in remote and isolated communities, their ability effectively to challenge the regime in Tirana was extremely limited. The main duty of the secret police, the Sigurimi, was to monitor and then eliminate any opposition to the government. The Sigurimi operated a reign of terror by covering the entire country with a network of informers. Children were taught to spy on their own parents, and the web of informers was so tight that there was no chance of an organized dissident movement materializing. The Sigurimi also controlled the prisons and labour camps, the most notorious of which were Burrel, Vlocisht and Spac. Conditions inside these institutions were appalling; inmates were routinely tortured and starved of decent food and medical care. Thousands of people were either imprisoned for political crimes or exiled to remote villages where they were treated as outcasts by the local peasants. Many of those imprisoned were indeed anti-Communists, but whole families could also be exiled simply because one member told an anti-Hoxha joke or was found listening to foreign broadcasts. A person was not condemned alone; his or her whole family would also be sent away. In some cases the exiles were told to build their own villages. This was the case with the squalid and remote village of Gradishta in southern Albania. Gradishta, which was home to around 70 exiled families, was built from nothing in 1954 by the first group of exiles to arrive. The exiles suffered the physical misery of long arduous hours working in the fields with very meagre food rations, together with the psychological isolation of being totally shunned by local people.

Meanwhile, by the spring of 1962, Sino-Soviet relations had steadily worsened as Khrushchev continued to court Yugoslavia. The visit to Belgrade by Soviet Chief of State, Leonid Brezhnev, infuriated both the Chinese and the Albanians, who declared: 'the Brezhnev visit constitutes a link in the chain of Khrushchev's aims to achieve a rapprochement with the Yugoslav revisionists, to co-ordinate with them a new revisionist course to split the Socialist camp and liquidate Socialism.'[10] Following Khrushchev's fall from power in 1964 no major changes were made to the substance of Soviet foreign policy, and the new Brezhnev–Kosygin leadership continued to irritate China through its policy of coexistence with the West. During this period, Chinese aid to Albania steadily increased. Whereas Soviet aid had been limited to light industry, food and infrastructure, the Chinese gave Tirana assistance to build up heavy industry and thus a real base for long-term self-reliance.[11] As a result, several major industrial projects were completed during the third five-year plan. These included the Engels and Stalin hydroelectric plant, and the copper and iron smelting plants at Gjegjan and Elbasan. Also during this period many of the country's main reservoirs of water were built by the cooperatives. Nevertheless the new plan, with its exaggerated emphasis on industry at the expense of agriculture, contained the same fundamental error which had caused the failure of the previous two five-year plans. Here again industry and mining together were allocated 4.2 times the budget of agriculture. Even when allowing for the fact that some industrial projects, such as the artificial fertiliser factory, were essentially agricultural in aim, the plan remained unbalanced, with industry getting the lion's share of investment and agriculture completely under-resourced.[12] China's credits, however, amounted to only one-fifth of the previous Soviet credits, and the impact on Albania's finances caused by the break with Moscow was severe, forcing the government to adopt a policy of strict austerity. The situation was aggravated by Albania's rapid population growth. The country's birth-rate in the mid-1960s was around 33 per thousand – one of the highest in the world – and consequently the country, with a population of about two million, faced a constant grain deficit. Better healthcare had led to a fall in the infant mortality rate, contraception was non-existent, and abortion was illegal. This conformed with the prevailing view in most socialist states that a high birthrate would inject youthful vigour into their newly industrialized economies.

In Kosova Gradual Reform Awakens Albanian National Awareness

A turning point in the status and role of Yugoslavia's Albanians came in 1966 with the fall of Alexander Rankovic, a leading proponent of Serbo-centralism who was vice-president of Yugoslavia and heir-apparent to Tito. Rankovic and his Serbian entourage in the federal government were allegedly behind serious irregularities in the Yugoslav Security Police, UDB-a (Uprava Drzavne Bezbednosti), for which Rankovic was held directly responsible. In 1956 the UDB-a had confiscated the weapons of the Albanian population of Kosova, provoking widespread resistance. Using the pretext of suppressing Albanian irredentism, the security police regularly put pressure on Albanians to emigrate. Between 1954 and 1957 some 195,000 Kosovars left Yugoslavia, and by 1966 the figure had reached 235,000. Rankovic's activities were not subjected to supervision or review because of his political status. As a result, he was able to transform the Security Police into a strongly centralized organization based largely in Serbia and consisting mainly of Serbs. Thus, the dismissal of Rankovic from his leading state and party functions was a heavy moral and psychological blow to those Serbs who had worked continuously to maintain a degree of Serbian supremacy in Kosova. For the Kosovars, the event was a milestone in their campaign for the assertion of their national rights. Serbs however, viewed the affair as an attack on their nation and its position within Yugoslavia. Rankovic's dismissal led to more open discussion of the persecution suffered by Albanians. Even Tito referred to Rankovic's police as 'dogmatic elements', and after visiting

Kosova in 1968, he offered the Albanian leaders more autonomy, economic aid, promises of reforms, and the appointment of more Albanians to responsible positions.

However, by removing police pressure and granting more concessions to the Kosovars to ensure their loyalty to Yugoslavia, the government had unwittingly assisted the Albanians in becoming more conscious of their rights and strengths. This in turn fuelled militant Albanian nationalism, which culminated in the events of November 1968 when serious riots broke out in Kosova. Although the majority of Albanian demonstrators demanded republic status for Kosova within Yugoslavia, a significant minority called for the union of Kosova with Albania. Not surprisingly, republican status for Kosova was not even remotely on the agenda for the Serbs. They considered such a demand to be the first step towards complete secession from Yugoslavia and union with Albania.

The agitation soon spread to neighbouring Macedonia where, in the Tetovo region, the demonstrators again demanded the incorporation of the Albanian areas of Macedonia to form, with Kosova, an Albanian republic within Yugoslavia. The Albanian areas of Macedonia had not been included in the Kosova autonomous region after the war for geographical as well as political reasons. The Sar mountains form a formidable barrier between the two areas, making communication difficult. Nevertheless, in order to accommodate Macedonian nationalism, the CPY divided the Albanian population in the Tetovo area from those in Albania. By splitting them up, especially after the 1944–5 rebellion, it became easier to control the Albanians as a whole. The Tetovo region contained a 50 per cent ethnic Albanian population. A Macedonian republic diminished and deprived of its Albanian population would be more liable to Soviet-inspired propaganda and infiltration from Bulgaria, which still harboured claims over Macedonia dating back to the 1878 Treaty of San Stefano.

To appease the Kosovars Belgrade took concrete steps to amend the constitution, giving back some, albeit small, measure of autonomy and allowing the Albanian national flag to be flown. Whilst Tito fully supported the proposals for constitutional reform, he was equally adamant in opposing the establishment of a Republic of Kosova. Instead Kosova was upgraded from regional to provincial status. In 1969 a new university was founded in Pristina, and Albanian textbooks were imported from Tirana. Kosova was given priority over other regions in the distribution of central funds, but this resulted merely in piecemeal and cosmetic improvements which had little effect on the lives of ordinary people.

Albania's Cultural Revolution

Meanwhile, the April 1967 military coup in Greece had caused concern in Tirana, as the new Greek regime began uttering numerous, if vague, allusions to northern Epirus, referring to the inhabitants of Girokaster and Korca as 'our brethren'. However, like Venizelos before them, the Greek Colonels had to turn their attention to more serious international problems. The main focus of Greek foreign policy was Turkey and the problem of Cyprus. Yet more unsettling for the Albanian regime was the unexpected Soviet invasion of Czechoslovakia in 1968, whereupon Albania officially withdrew from the Warsaw Pact. Aware that the affiliation with China did not include any military alliance, Albania was from now on to include self-defence in her programme of self-reliance. Reflecting the panic the Albanian leadership must have felt, an estimated 400,000 concrete pill boxes were hastily constructed at vast expense throughout the country.

As it became clear that China's geographical remoteness was not adequate protection from the dangers close at hand, the Albanian leadership tried to get on more friendly terms with their immediate neighbours: Italy, Greece, Romania and Yugoslavia – the latter suddenly finding itself transformed from national enemy number one to a potential ally against Soviet aggression. The departure of Alexander Rankovic had paved the way for a resumption of dialogue between Belgrade and Tirana. Both leaders regarded the Soviet intervention in Czechoslovakia as an ominous sign and were forced to reappraise their foreign policy. The Albanian leadership also began to widen its sources of economic assistance, as the enormous geographical distance between China and Albania made the export of Albanian produce to China highly unprofitable. In a bid therefore to diversify trade Tirana concluded a new trade agreement with Italy, and the Italian airline, Alitalia, opened up a route from Rome to Tirana. Italian engineering and agricultural specialists were also invited to Albania. An Albanian ambassador was appointed to Vienna, and trade agreements were established with many other countries.

During the late 1960s, in the wake of China's Cultural Revolution, Albania introduced numerous new policies. A series of propaganda campaigns were aimed primarily at the emancipation of women, the

abolition of religion and the reduction of an over-inflated bureaucracy. The regime also hoped to quell popular dissatisfaction and
thereby eliminate any 'revisionist' opposition that might threaten the
PLA's power base. Hoxha appeared to have a genuine interest in transforming the status of women. At the Fourth Congress of the Women's
Union in 1955 he linked their oppression with backward customs
enforced and institutionalized by religion. He told the audience:

> The canons of the Sheriat [Sharia] and of the Church, closely connected to
> the laws of the bourgeoisie, treated woman as a commodity, a thing to be
> bought and sold by the male ... just as the bourgeoisie had made the worker
> into its proletarian, so had the savage ancient canons of the Sheriat, the
> Church, feudalism and bourgeoisie, reduced woman to the proletariat of
> man.[13]

In February 1967, in a speech on the 'further revolutionization of the
Party' Hoxha warned: 'The entire Party and country should hurl into
the fire and break the neck of anyone who tramples underfoot the
sacred law of the Party in defence of the rights of women and girls.'[14]

During the immediate aftermath of the war, the conscription of
women into the labour force had contributed to solving the country's
initial labour shortage. Women, in theory, now had equality with men.
But in reality, although they could no longer be sold as men's property,
they now became the property of the state. Women continued to work
as long hours in the fields as they had done before the war. As in
Romania, they were denied the right to control their fertility, since
abortion and contraception were illegal. This was in line with party
policy to try to increase the population. The birth-rate reached its
highest point in 1955 at 43.8 per thousand, and slowly declined to
30.6 per thousand by 1975. Meanwhile the death-rate continued to
decline, reaching a mere 7.2 per thousand by 1975. The subsequent
rise in population greatly exacerbated the already severe housing
shortage, leading to cramped and squalid conditions. In practice it
was in their traditional role as mothers that women were most prized
under the Hoxha regime, just as they had been in prewar days. For
producing 6 children a Mother's Medal was awarded; for nine, the
Glory Medal and for 12, the Heroine Mother's Medal. There also
remained a great contradiction in the attitude of many men, who may
have accepted women's new role in public life but continued to regard
women as subservient to men in the domestic sphere.

The concerted attack upon religion was another aspect of the drive to destroy traditional attitudes. Amongst other things, religion was blamed for impeding social advancement by condoning arranged marriages of children, ordering people's lives and conflicting with the movement for the emancipation of women. The Party's relentless war against such 'backward manifestations' culminated in the closure of the majority of the country's 2,169 religious buildings, a few of which were converted into cultural centres, sports halls, theatres, and storage depots. A report in the Official Vatican newspaper *L'Osservatore Romano* on 26 April 1973 stated:

> Places of worship either no longer exist or have been transformed into dance halls, gymnasia, or offices of various kinds. Scutari [Shkoder] cathedral has become the 'Sports Palace'; a swimming pool has been constructed in place of the presbytery and sacristry; the artistic bell-tower that soared above it has been raised to the ground. The ancient canonry chapel at Scutari, used as a baptistry among other things, has become a warehouse for tyres. The church of St Nicholas in the Catholic district of Rusi has been transformed into flats for factory workers. The church of the Stigmatine Sisters has become a lecture hall, the one of the Institute of the Sisters of St Elizabeth is used as the headquarters of the political police. The national sanctuary of Our Lady of Scutari, 'Protectress of Albania', has been pulled down. On its ruins there now rises a column surmounted by the red star.[15]

This article was prompted by the news that a priest, Father Shtjefen Kurti, had been executed by firing squad for having baptized a child at Lushnja. Father Kurti was in fact first sentenced to death in 1945, having been charged with 'spying for the Vatican'. This sentence was commuted to life imprisonment, and 18 years later he was released from prison. He then returned to parish work, but when the government declared all religious practices to be illegal he took a secular job as a clerk in a cooperative. Soon after this soldiers arrived to destroy Father Kurti's parish church, and he fought them with his fists. For this offence he was sentenced to a further 16 years' imprisonment, but he continued to exercise his priesthood secretly, and during the early part of 1973 a woman prisoner asked him to baptize her child. The ceremony took place privately, but news of it reached the authorities, who once again put the 70-year-old priest on trial and later handed him over to a military firing squad. He was said to have been found guilty of 'subversive activities designed to overthrow the state'.[16] Although many of the smaller churches and mosques were totally demolished, those religious buildings of great historical or architectural interest, such as the beautiful Ethem Bey mosque, with its graceful minaret in the very centre of Tirana, were preserved as part of the people's traditional heritage.

Secular festivals were substituted for the traditional religious observances. It can therefore be argued that Hoxha outdid even Stalin and Mao by officially banning the practice of religion and the sale of religious books and icons. Yet, although Albania had proclaimed itself the world's first totally atheist state, it could not claim to have eradicated all religious beliefs and practices. Effectively, it drove them underground: mass was celebrated secretly, and many continued to listen to religious programmes broadcast by radio stations in Italy and Greece. In 1971 there were still services held in a very few churches, although their congregations had severely dwindled by the end of the decade. 'It is for old people', one foreign visitor was told, 'who pray for rain, but everyone knows it's meteorology, not God, which brings rain. We laugh at these old people, but we don't harm them. They have been left behind, no one worries about them anymore.'[17] One by-product of the regime's anti-religious policy was its concern with the question of people's Muslim and Christian names. Parents were actively discouraged from giving their children names that had any religious association or connotation. From time to time official lists were published with pagan, so-called Illyrian or freshly minted names considered appropriate for the new breed of revolutionary Albanians.[18] One such name which became quite popular was Marenglen, a corruption of Marx, Engels and Lenin.

Reforms were also instigated throughout the educational system, with the aim of eradicating any remaining Soviet influence. The burgeoning bureaucratic machine was reduced by cutting the number of ministries from 19 to 13. The number of departments within each ministry was also reduced. The several thousand party and government employees who were made redundant were switched to what was called 'productive work' – this meant manual labour in most cases. Many writers and artists were also sent to work in factories and collective farms.[19] In order to rid themselves of 'reactionary and bourgeois' styles of writing and thus reach out to the masses, writers and artists were encouraged to 'purify the mind by soiling the hands'. However, much as the Albanian leadership applauded China's Cultural Revolution as a 'valuable contribution to the theory and practice of scientific socialism', they were careful to avoid the social disruption, chaos and excesses which characterized Mao's programme in China.

The country's development programme continued apace. The fourth five-year plan (1966–70) witnessed the construction of the Mao Tse-Tung textile mill near Berat, a plastics factory in Durres, and various other new industrial projects. Around 200,000 hectares of drained land were turned over to agriculture. The Chinese continued to supply the country with wheat until the Albanians, with advice and help from Chinese experts, were able to produce just enough grain to feed their country's growing population. Agricultural collectivization was also finally completed, despite strong opposition from the largely Catholic population of the northern highlands who were amongst the fiercest opponents of the Communist regime. For Hoxha, this was one of the positive aspects of abolishing religion, as he hoped to eliminate the bond of Catholicism linking the northern tribes. Their traditional clan-based loyalties had to be broken if the Communists were to secure control of the north. The social, industrial and agricultural policy changes of the Communist regime gradually eroded many of the traditional family, tribal and regional loyalties. The large patriarchal family, in particular, was under constant pressure and was fast disappearing. In those rural areas where it continued to survive, its head lost most of his former power, prestige and respect.[20]

During the 1970s, Yugoslav–Albanian relations witnessed a gradual rapprochement as a result of the threat posed to the two countries by the Soviet invasion of Czechoslovakia and Belgrade's gradual devolution of power to the Kosovars. The development of cultural contacts with Albania was encouraged, and it was hoped that the concessions to Albanians in Kosova could help the process of 'bridge-building' with Albania. An ever-growing number of Albanian publications were allowed in the province, reinforcing the Kosovars' perception of their Albanian identity. Their discovery of the preeminent role of their forefathers during the struggle for Albanian independence from the Ottomans intensified their sense of being Albanian. The Serb and Montenegrin population, however, felt threatened in this new environment, which seemed to be fast losing what little remained of its Slav character. They began moving away from Kosova in increasing numbers. In February 1974, Yugoslavia's new constitution considerably narrowed the powers of the Federation while extending those of the republics and autonomous provinces. For the Kosovars this meant that self-government now replaced the almost permanent state of emergency, as the new constitution accorded them their own judiciary, legislation and administration. The autonomous provinces now had a veto on all issues that affected them, so that the Belgrade leadership no longer had full control over republican affairs. Serbian prestige suffered, and during the mid seventies, a working commission of members of the Serbian Party travelled throughout Kosova gathering arguments and lists of Serbian grievances against this enhanced provincial autonomy in what became known as the 'Blue Book'. This sought to return to Belgrade control of the province's judiciary, police, defence and economic policy. Given that acceptance of these aims would certainly have involved a new bout of repression in Kosova, and inevitably also the rehabilitation of the Rankovic administration and its admirers, the document received a hostile reception from the federal leadership. Although the 'Blue Book' was suppressed and never publicly discussed, its very existence allowed the issue of provincial autonomy to smoulder beneath the surface of Serbian politics.[21]

Meanwhile, Sino-Albanian relations continued to drift along as both Tirana and Peking reevaluated their foreign policies. In October 1970 Albanian basketball players visited China – where, according to a Chinese account, many of them were

> too excited to sleep and talked deep into the night: 'We love Chairman Mao as we love Comrade Enver Hoxha' they said. On the morning of 2 October, the Albanian athletes arrived at the China–Albania Friendship Commune outside Peking, to be greeted by the beating of drums and songs. Like the commune members, the Albanian comrades put on work aprons, went to the fields and began picking cotton. Chairman Mao said: 'A bosom friend afar brings a distant land near. China and Albania are separated by thousands of mountains and rivers but our hearts are closely linked.'[22]

The Chinese, however, were not so popular in Albania, as one foreign visitor noted:

> By 1971, few industrial areas were without a population of Chinese, they have settled down well but the natives are not enthused about them: 'They are not like us, they are ugly, they have disgusting habits,' such are the common criticisms. What sort of habits?: 'Picking their noses, things that offend us,' you are told.[23]

The Chinese community kept very much to itself. Work contracts were usually for six months to a year, rarely more, and the workers were housed in flats in a self-contained quarter of Tirana with their own restaurants. One of the largest Chinese industrial projects to be constructed in Albania was the ironworks at Elbasan, employing over

8,000 people. Chinese influence could also be seen in the form of flocks of Peking duck on the state farms, the silkworm production on cooperatives in the Shkoder region, and the appearance on hillsides of bamboos and agaves to supply the raw materials for the basket and string industries.

One area where the Communist regime did make significant progress was in the field of education. Before the war Albania was the only country in Europe without a university. From 1945 the campaign against illiteracy was relentlessly waged by enrolling thousands of people in night schools, where they progressed from elementary classes to secondary courses. Many probably wondered if perhaps literacy was a mixed blessing as, following a hard day's work, they had to attend the obligatory courses for all on Marxism–Leninism, plus texts and lectures on dialectical and historical materialism. Nevertheless, the virtual eradication of illiteracy must be considered one of the most impressive achievements of the Hoxha years. By 1963 every man and woman in the country was obliged to complete eight years of elementary schooling. Before they could embark on higher-education courses, all secondary-school graduates were required to complete a one-year work placement, so they could 'keep in touch with the masses'. The participation of students in physical work such as railway construction, terracing or planting trees would, it was hoped, discourage such bourgeois tendencies as idleness and intellectualism. The then secretary to the Central Committee, Ramiz Alia, reporting to the Sixth Plenary Session of the Party on the problem of binding intellectuals to the socialist spirit said:

> Because of their tendency to divorce mental from manual labour, because of their position and the role they play in leading and organizing work and of the individual nature of that task, intellectuals are susceptible to alien bourgeois and revisionist attitudes and ideology. They are inclined to detach themselves from the masses, to overrate their ability and talents, to slip into postures of egotism and self-conceit, to consider that they alone are capable of directing and leading. We must see that our intellectuals study Marxism–Leninism, the teachings of our Party and Comrade Enver Hoxha.[24]

'Revisionism' was seen as a cancerous growth within Marxism.

Some notable improvements were also made in the field of health-care, with free medical treatment available for all. Hospitals, clinics and sanatoria were built, and the average life expectancy increased from 54 years in 1950 to 67 years by 1970. As with all other aspects of life, entertainment was strictly controlled by the state, and had to be immune from 'decadent', 'bourgeois' and 'revisionist' ideology. In the process, writers and artists had to become mere deliverers of official propaganda. A notable exception was the writer Ismail Kadare, whose novels largely managed to evade official censorship. This is perhaps because some of his work was published in France and England, and such international recognition saved his work from suppression. The New Albania Film Studio – which had begun operating in 1952 and at first showed mostly newsreels and documentaries – in 1959 created the first large-scale Albanian opera. It was called *Mrika*, and its theme was the construction of the great Karl Marx hydro-electric plant. Mrika was the heroine who led the mass mobilization of workers to capture saboteurs sent to the country from Yugoslavia and Greece to blow up the dam.[25] Before long, however, it became necessary for Albania to begin producing her own films, as those from the Soviet Union and Eastern Europe, together with their literature, were increasingly being deemed decadent and bourgeois, and therefore unsuitable. In 1972 a sketch at the Opera House was enticingly entitled: 'How Khrushchev Unfurled the Banner of Discord and Betrayal'. The regime left no aspect of Albanian life or culture untouched, as all means of communication and information were tightly controlled by the Party. Even the work of Albania's greatest poet, Father Gjergj Fishta (1871–1940), whose writing is chiefly concerned with the social values of the old peasant society and with religious themes, was totally banned. Thus Albania became an excessively dull and barren cultural desert.

There was naturally widespread resistance, especially among young people, to this lack of cultural and intellectual freedom. A common response to the stifling dullness and restrictions of daily life was shoddy workmanship or absenteeism from work. There was also much theft of state property, and bribery was rife (a legacy of Ottoman days). Chronic fatigue, stress and boredom thus characterized average daily life under the Hoxha regime, as people retreated into their own private lives. By 1972 Tirana had 150,000 inhabitants, yet still not much had changed in the sleepy Balkan capital. A foreign visitor noted in 1971: 'In Skenderbeg Square the lonely traffic cop sleeps on his feet, and jumps to attention to greet a car like an old friend if it happens to pass by twice in the same day.'[26] Until 1991, no private cars were allowed in Albania; except for leaders and other dignitaries, people travelled, when permitted, in decrepit old buses, by train, bicycle pony or ox-cart. At first cars had been made available to individual citizens on a points system, as in the Soviet Union, but owners of cars began charging those without cars for lifts, and there was keen competition to get one's name higher up on the list. This was seen as generating the kind of selfish bourgeois ethics rooted in private possession. All cars were, therefore, withdrawn and gathered into pools from which collectives could take what they needed for work or recreation. Public transport was virtually free.[27] Naturally, cars were available for the use of leading party cadres and bosses.

The population was kept as ignorant as possible of conditions outside Albania. Until the mid-1970s foreign travel was forbidden, except for the Party elite, and foreign visitors were strictly controlled. Hoxha's contempt of capitalist society was summed up in a speech which also hinted at the pride he felt in Albanian national culture: 'Why should we turn our country into an inn with doors flung open to pigs and sows, to people with pants on or no pants at all, to the hirsute, longhaired hippies to supplant their wild orgies, the graceful dances of our people.'[28]

The Break with China

From mid-1970, relations between Albania and China began gradually to decline. The Albanians had always had great problems trying to decode China's intentions through the veil of secrecy that shrouded China's actions. Hoxha began to sneer at Chinese polemics. Commenting on the Romanian delegation to China in 1971, Hoxha reflected: 'Mao received Ceausescu saying to him: "Romanian comrades, we should unite to bring down imperialism." As if Ceausescu and Co. are to bring down imperialism!! If the world waits for the Ceausescus to do such a thing, imperialism will live for tens of thousands of years.'[29] The Chinese also began to reassess their commitment to their tiny Balkan ally in the light of China's gradual emergence from isolation. As China's diplomatic relations and foreign aid programmes to the Third World intensified, the Albanians were informed that they could not rely indefinitely upon Chinese assistance and were advised to seek aid from Western nations.

Albanian–Chinese relations became increasingly strained, especially after China's rapprochement with the United States. When President Nixon visited China in February 1972 the Albanian media completely ignored the visit. Hoxha strongly disapproved of China's new attitude towards Washington and began cautiously to realign Albania's foreign policy. While sharing Peking's concern about the Soviet threat, Tirana did not believe there was a significant decrease in the US threat to warrant – as Chinese policy pronouncements then reflected – the transformation of Washington from primary adversary to a lesser one. Hoxha maintained that the two superpowers were equally dangerous and refused to differentiate between their 'imperialist' policies.[30] A conflict developed between the PLA and the military establishment after several high-ranking officers, together with defence minister Beqir Balluku, were arrested for conspiring to seize power through a military coup. Balluku, his chief of staff Petrit Duma, and the head of the army's political directory, Hito Cako, were accused of setting the army against the Party by opposing Hoxha's concept of a 'people's army', arguing instead for the development of a modern, professional army, whose first loyalty was to the general staff rather than to the PLA leadership. This idea was anathema to Hoxha, who as First Secretary to the Party was also commander-in-chief of the army. He consequently moved swiftly to ensure the PLA's control over the military by ordering the trial and execution of 'the traitorous, counter-revolutionary group' of Balluku and his associates. In October 1974, Mehmet Shehu was appointed defence minister.

After his experiences with the Yugoslavs and then the Russians, Hoxha was on the lookout for signs from China that the relationship was ending. The increasing ideological alienation led to the dwindling of Chinese aid, which consequently had an adverse effect on Albania's economy. Industrial projects ground to a halt as desperately needed materials and machinery failed to be delivered. Sino-Albanian relations went from bad to worse following the death of Mao in September 1976. The Albanian leadership was further angered by the invitation issued to Tito by the new post-Mao leadership to visit China. This was seen as a direct snub to Hoxha. Towards the end of the decade, Albania ceased to be the valuable political asset to China it had been during the 1960s. Mao's heirs, who now disregarded ideological compatibility in their search for new alliances against the Soviet Union, preferred to court Tito as their most important Balkan ally. Albania had also become an economic liability, and in July 1978 China finally terminated her aid programme. All Chinese advisors were recalled to Peking, and Albanian students returned to Albania. Following the break with China, a policy of maximum self-sufficiency was proclaimed. It involved reliance on internal manpower and material resources, and the implementation of a strict savings regime. The

PLA sought to create the impression that the People's Socialist Republic of Albania, as the only real 'socialist' country in the world and faced with an all-round 'imperialist-revisionist' blockade, had no alternative but to go it alone.[31]

Concern about national sovereignty was, as always, the key factor for determining Albanian foreign policy. From this point on Albania had to renounce all ambitious development programmes, but by then the country had become self-sufficient in cereal grain production, oil and electricity, which it even exported to Yugoslavia. Albania was reduced to a degree of self-imposed ideological and political isolation for which there is hardly any modern parallel. As the rest of the world, with the exception of her Balkan neighbours, continued to ignore Albania, the country retreated into almost total seclusion, forgotten behind its formidable, lonely mountains. The few visitors to the country came primarily on business and trade union delegations, as tourism was deliberately kept very small-scale. For the first time in her modern history, Albania was without a foreign 'protector'. Hemmed in by the potential menace of predatory neighbours, there was every justification for Hoxha's anxiety, unease and suspicion. He began to make threatening noises to confirm to anyone who may have had doubts as to the alert state of the country: 'They will never catch us asleep, we will never be lacking in vigilance, let everyone understand clearly: the walls of our fortress are of unshakable granite rock.'[32]

Riots in Kosova Strain Albanian–Yugoslav Relations

Towards the end of the decade, relations between Albania and Yugoslavia entered upon a new phase of slightly improved cooperation. The death of Tito in 1980 caused only mild concern in Tirana, as Yugoslavia's new collective leadership stressed that it wished to maintain the improved relations with Albania. In November 1979 former Yugoslav foreign minister Milos Minic had declared:

> We do not treat Albania as a small country but as one of our most important neighbours, with whom we can only share a common destiny.... Whatever befalls Yugoslavia will befall Albania too, in relation to security. Therefore, it would be in the interest of the two countries, of the nations and nationalities of Yugoslavia and of the peoples of Albania, to strengthen and to develop friendly cooperation.[33]

Cultural and economic ties therefore increased. Apart from trade agreements, every month five to ten groups from Albania visited

Kosova. An increasingly large number of Kosovars had also begun to visit Albania, and heavier tourist traffic was planned for the near future. Those Kosovars who did visit Albania at this time, however, were shocked at the level of poverty they witnessed there. This was reflected in a saying then common amongst Kosovars: 'The streets of Tirana are so clean because the Albanians have nothing to throw away.' The Kosovars were not all enamoured of Enver Hoxha's condescending attitude towards them either. Another widely heard saying in Kosova – 'Enver Hoxha should remember that he is a head of state and head of a party, but not the head of a nation' – showed how unrealistic were the claims made by many Serbs, who stated that the immediate goal of all Kosovars was secession and unity with Albania.

In February 1981, two protocols in the film industry were signed in Pristina between Kosovofilm and the New Albania Kinostudio, which agreed on the joint production of films from 1981 to 1985. Superficially at least things looked relatively rosy for Kosova. Nevertheless, the numerous concessions made to the Kosovars remained relatively meaningless. Edvard Kardelj, one of Tito's closest advisors, had warned back in 1977 that if the Party failed to adopt a resolute policy that would narrow the economic gap and tranquillize interethnic tensions, then Kosova would explode into violence.[34] Large amounts of credit had been pumped into Kosova via the Special Fund for Economic Development, yet the province continued to slip further behind the other Yugoslav federal units. The policy of levelling economic inequalities had been, as far as Kosova was concerned, a complete failure. There was little point pouring money into Kosova if it was not going to be more evenly or wisely distributed. A disproportionately high share of central government funds had been directed into the administrative sector, which grew much faster than did the province's industrial output. A quarter of all employed Kosovars were well-paid government employees, who enjoyed the privileges of good housing, cars and other symbols of material wealth and were naturally resented by less well-paid workers and unemployed graduates.

One of the major unresolved problems that needed to be addressed was the opposition of the Serbs to any further devolution of power to the Kosovars. Little or no effort had been made to discuss the quite different demands and expectations of both Serbs and Albanians in the reality of the existing situation. Nevertheless, few people could have been prepared for the violence of the uprising that erupted in Kosova during the spring of 1981. To contain the riots, as in 1968, tanks and up to 30,000 troops were deployed in Kosova. A curfew was imposed throughout the province, which was viewed as a military occupation by the Kosovars. The central authorities reacted with excessive force to stabilize the situation. Belgrade reported that 11 people had died, but Albanians claimed that almost 1,000 were killed. The subsequent trials, purges and dismissals of Albanians in all walks of life resulted in a steady accumulation of frustration, bitterness and anger. The Federal Secretary of Internal Affairs, Stane Dolance, commented: 'Albanian irredentists are now showing their true face, they no longer talk about a republic but say "Long live Enver Hoxha." It is quite clear that what is really involved is the integrity of the Yugoslav State, this is why we call it a counterrevolution.'[35] The fact that the problem could only be contained by a such a massive show of force fuelled the view held by the regime's hardliners that the regional party was initially responsible for the breakdown of communications between Pristina and Belgrade. The Kosova leadership, though, agreed with accounts given by foreign observers about the true nature of the unrest: the riots were not nationalistically inspired but were economically and socially motivated.

Events in Kosova again directly influenced other Albanian-inhabited areas. This was especially the case in western Macedonia where, in July 1981, police and territorial defence units were put on alert after the Albanian population had made repeated calls for language equality and the establishment of an Albanian university in Tetovo, demands which the Skopje government refused point-blank to consider. In Macedonia there had been a far more intensive campaign against Albanian national culture than in Kosova. An initiative had even been launched in early 1981 to ban the use of the Albanian flag in Macedonia.[36] At first the regime tried to play down the riots by persuading the public that they had been caused by the 'dirty work' of traitors and were unanimously condemned by local Albanians.[37] Nevertheless, this façade could not be maintained for long, and admission of the scale of the violence led to immediate criticism of the entire previous policy by the League of Communists of Yugoslavia towards Kosova.

As Kosovar leader Mahmoud Bakali resigned, the provincial leadership admitted that their past policy in Kosova has been erroneous in failing to address the region's major problems. Bakali was succeeded by his predecessor, Veli Deva, who had constantly criticized 'Greater Serbian Chauvinism' in Kosova. The appointment of Deva suited

Belgrade, as he was respected amongst the majority of Kosovars. Deva's main task was to preserve Kosova for Yugoslavia. Many Serbs were talking of 'past mistakes', an implicit criticism of Tito without actually mentioning his name. It was felt that his successors now had to face the consequences of Tito's liberal policies towards Tirana. For some time the Yugoslav leaders were therefore reluctant to identify Tirana as the source of the troubles. There was no direct proof of Albania's involvement, and because of her acute isolationist position, it was important to Albania that the situation in both Kosova and the rest of Yugoslavia be stable. Initially, Yugoslav officials put the blame for the unrest upon foreign enemies in the West. But once Albania's party newspaper *Zeri-i-Popullit* condemned the Yugoslav's handling of the crisis, blame was rapidly shifted on to Tirana, and Albanian–Kosovar cooperation came almost to a standstill. Both Yugoslavia and Albania had been engaged in powerful ideological competition for influence over Albanians on both sides of the border. Pristina's radio and television stations were overloaded with cultural programmes produced in Albania, while Radio Tirana reached 60 per cent of Kosova territory.

The departure of the skilled Slav element from Kosova left fewer Serbo-Croatian cultural and educational initiatives for the Albanians. The net emigration of Slavs from Kosova has been estimated at 102,000 in the decade 1971–81, with a further 30,000 between 1981 and the autumn of 1987.[38] This exodus served to reinforce Serbian national anxieties, and Serbs began to boycott Albanian shops and bakeries, cutting their sales by as much as 85 per cent. A similar pattern developed in Macedonia and Montenegro. In a dramatic appeal, the Serbian Party Central Committee called for a halt to the exodus of Slavs from Kosova. An observer noted that if the current exodus were to continue, it could stir Serbian nationalist agitation throughout Yugoslavia, creating new animosity in already strained relations among Yugoslavia's nationalities. This is the real reason why the Serbian leaders warned so dramatically against a revival of nationalism.[39] The war of words with Tirana escalated after an Albanian report questioned Yugoslavia's territorial integrity by saying: 'The London and Versailles Treaties which settled the frontiers between Yugoslavia and Albania can no longer be imposed to the detriment of the Albanian people.'[40] These were strong words, followed up in June by a *Zeri-i-Popullit* editorial entitled 'The Events in Kosova and the Secret Soviet–Great-Serbian Collaboration', which drew attention to the deceptive silence of Moscow about the Kosova riots. It concluded that Moscow had calculated that the Serbian strong hand would soon be used in the rest of Yugoslavia, causing repercussions throughout the Balkans and hence for NATO via Italy and Greece. It rightly concluded that the weakening of the Yugoslav federation would strengthen Bulgarian demands for Macedonia.[41] It is not clear why the Albanian leadership chose this moment to go on the offensive and open itself to the fury of Belgrade, but this sort of reporting contrasted markedly with Tirana's previous policy of seeking to minimize the broader significance of previous disturbances in Kosova in the interests of Albania's overall political and security interests regarding Yugoslavia. As a result, Belgrade promptly severed Kosova's cultural links with Albania, and Albanian textbooks were banned. In November 1981, the Central Committee of the LCY met to discuss Kosova. A major report was delivered by Dobroslav Culafic, secretary of the CC Presidium, who admitted that the main cause of the 'troubles' was erroneous policy in the past, especially concerning vital sectors of social, economic and cultural life.[42]

The Deaths of Mehmet Shehu and Enver Hoxha

In the meantime, Hoxha's health had begun to deteriorate rapidly. He could no longer make lengthy public speeches, and his visits out of the capital became less frequent. Mehmet Shehu seemed the most likely candidate to succeed the ailing Hoxha, having been generally regarded as number two to Hoxha's leadership. Through his power base in the Sigurimi, Shehu had managed to consolidate his grip on the mechanisms of the state. However, signs had recently begun to indicate that Shehu was slipping out of favour. In April 1980 he was relieved of his duties as minister of defence during a government reshuffle, but managed to retain the post of prime minister. As Albania faced mounting social problems and economic slowdown in the wake of the break with China, Hoxha had apparently decided that Ramiz Alia was better equipped than Shehu to carry the heavy responsibilities and burdens that his own successor would inherit. Alia was seen as less unpredictable and extremist than Shehu. Hoxha, according to his wife Nexhmije, 'had much faith in and deeply appreciated his close collaborator, Comrade Ramiz Alia, in whom he saw a revolutionary embodying the ability, courage, wisdom and determination needed to carry forward the complete construction of socialism at the head of the Central Committee of the PLA'.[43] Plans were thus set in motion to get rid of Shehu, who seemed unlikely to step down voluntarily. On 18 December 1981, there came the astonishing announcement that Shehu had committed suicide whilst 'in a state of nervous crisis'.[44] This followed Shehu's subjection to severe criticism for arranging the betrothal of his son to a woman whose family had, it was alleged, collaborated with the occupation forces during the war. Because of this Shehu was accused of attempting to create a scandal which would undermine the Tirana regime.

Since Shehu's main power base had been the military and the Sigurimi, Hoxha quickly instigated sweeping purges of a number of military and Sigurimi officers who were supporters of Shehu. According to his nephew, Luan Omari, Hoxha was badly shaken for several days following Shehu's death. It was generally believed, however, that either Hoxha himself shot Shehu or that his bodyguard was responsible. This does not seem too improbable, especially as almost a year after Shehu's death Hoxha announced to a bewildered Albanian populace that Shehu had all along been a multiple agent, in the pay of the British, Yugoslav, American and Soviet secret services. Nevertheless, Hoxha would have had many other less dramatic means of disposing of Shehu. It will probably never be known exactly what happened to Shehu or why Hohxa turned so venomously upon his former legendary general. But it is generally assumed that the two had opposing priorities regarding the economy. Hoxha insisted on maintaining the principle of self-reliance, whilst Shehu argued for more economic interaction with the West. By this time, however, the Shehu faction had been completely purged, and all potential opposition to Hoxha's chosen successor was now eliminated. Shehu's wife Fiqret was sentenced to 25 years in prison, and the core leadership was reduced to Hoxha and his wife, Ramiz Alia and Adil Carcani. Hysni Kapo had died in 1979.

Following a long illness, Enver Hoxha died on 11 April 1985, aged 76. According to an official medical communiqué,

> Comrade Enver Hoxha suffered since 1948 from the illness of diabetes, which as the years passed caused extended damage to blood vessels, heart, kidneys and some other organs. In 1973, as a result of these damages, he suffered disorders of heart beating. In later years the grave heart insufficiency developed. A year before he suffered ischemic insult of brain with transitional nemiparesis.[45]

There followed eight days of official mourning, during which Hoxha was buried in Tirana's cemetery of the martyrs of the homeland. For over 40 years he had ruled his tiny state isolated in its remote corner of the Balkans. His complex and contradictory personality had forged a unique and lonely path for Albania, and left its imprint on every aspect of Albanian life. Although the country benefited from improved agriculture, industry, and in particular health and education, such initiatives were overshadowed by a horrific legacy of brutal repression, the full story of which has yet to be told. The Albanian people had been cowed into a fearful state of submission, which led them, like their country, to withdraw into themselves with their thoughts kept secret, paranoid and suspicious of all around them.

For Hoxha, the single most important issue had been that of the survival, not only of Albania's sovereignty, but also of his small ruling clique. This had meant eliminating all real or potential rivals. Hoxha's policy of trying to practice 'socialism in one country' was totally impractical for Albania. The best he could manage was a policy aimed at mere survival. When Albanian leaders proudly declared that their economic growth was due only to Albania's own efforts, and that Albania did not owe a penny to anybody, this ignored the fact that every time the Albanian leadership shifted allegiance from one country to another, it automatically wrote off all debts to its former ally. The debt to China alone has been calculated as amounting to US$5 billion.[46] Hoxha's regime not only impoverished the economy; it all but destroyed the intellectual life of the country, and far from healing the north–south divisions it actually widened the gulf between the Gheg and Tosk regions. Hoxha will be bitterly remembered for all these things within Albania, but internationally he will be recalled primarily for the violent, ruthless nationalism with which he defied Tito, Khrushchev and then Mao. Shortly before his death, in a speech to commemorate the 40th anniversary of the liberation, Hoxha made a final denunciation of 'the Titoites, the Soviet revisionists and those of the countries of Eastern Europe and Mao-Tse-Tung's China which had ulterior, hostile, enslaving aims. We tore the mask from them and told them bluntly that Albania was not for sale for a handful of rags, or a few roubles, dinars or yuan.'[47]

The End of Communism and the Path to Democratic Pluralism

Hello Europe, I hope we find you well.
Dr Sali Berisha, to the crowd in Skenderbeg Square
following his election victory in March 1992

When news of Hoxha's death reached the Albanian people there was a stunned numbness throughout the country, and virtually everywhere signs of grief and mourning. Aware of the brutality of Hoxha's regime, many outside observers may have been surprised, but as one elderly Albanian explained: 'When a father beats his son, the child cries, but still clings to him as the only protector he knows.' Two days after the death of Hoxha, Ramiz Alia was elected First Secretary of the PLA. Alia was born in Shkoder, of Kosovar parents, on 18 October 1925. He had joined the Communist Party in 1943, and in 1948 was elected to the Party's Central Committee. As he steadily moved up through the party ranks, he held prominent positions in the youth organization and the Central Committee's Office of Propaganda. Following a course of study in the Soviet Union, Alia became a candidate member of the Politburo in 1956, later to be elected a full member, and also a member of the party secretariat. Far less charismatic than Hoxha, Alia had managed to survive the various purges by keeping a relatively low profile. Although he wished to convey a sense of continuity during the late 1980s, Alia's government began gradually to distance itself from the Hoxha legacy. In March 1986, Hoxha's wife Nexhmije became chair of the Democratic Front, a mass organization of the PLA in charge of organizing elections and maintaining internal security. However, she exerted little influence.

There followed cautious attempts at decentralization and liberal-ization. A more flexible foreign policy led to improved relations with a number of European countries. In his speech to the 9th Congress of the Party of Labour in November 1986, Alia spoke of the

> freedom-loving, democratic, and peace-loving aspirations of the European peoples. Guided by the principles of equality, non-interference in internal affairs, territorial integrity and national sovereignty, our country maintains normal relations with most of the European countries and is trying to develop them in favour of the common interest. With France, Austria, Switzerland, with Sweden and the other Nordic countries, our relations are developing in positive directions. We believe that with joint efforts ways can be found to carry our concrete collaboration further.

The stress Alia put on the phrases 'non-interference in internal affairs' and 'territorial integrity' appear to have been more for the benefit of Albania's Balkan neighbours than any distant north European state. Albania's relations with its immediate neighbours, Yugoslavia and Greece, had progressed somewhat during the late 1980s, although renewed trouble in Kosova once more threatened cooperation with Belgrade. Relations with Greece had been improving following bi-lateral negotiations in 1984. Furthermore, in 1987, Greece decided to end its formally held position of being in a state of war with Albania. This 'state of war' had been in existence since 1945. Nevertheless, the status of the ethnic Greek minority in southern Albania remained a sensitive issue.

In February 1988, Albania participated in the Conference of Balkan Foreign Ministers in Belgrade, the first official meeting of all six Balkan states in more than 50 years. Through its involvement, Albania accomplished a goodwill gesture, reassuring its neighbours, especially Yugoslavia, of the country's willingness to help establish a general framework of cooperation in the region. During the early 1980s, Yugo-slavia had become one of Albania's major trading partners, and any ideological differences between them tended to be played down. This was especially so in the case of Kosova. Ever since the riots there in 1981 the situation had remained tense, until matters entered a new dimension in 1987 with the dramatic rise to power in Serbia of Slobodan Milosevic. Milosevic was able to exploit the Kosova situa-tion in a series of mass rallies, where he spoke of the Serb nation's historic task of preserving its unity. Throughout Serbia he was greeted with cries of 'Srbija je ustala' (Serbia has arisen), to match the call from Zagreb 'Hrvatska je ustala' (Croatia has arisen). The façade of 'brotherhood and unity' amongst the people of Yugoslavia had by now evaporated as Yugoslavia began its tortuous journey towards disintegration.

The Albanian leadership showed its concern by issuing the following statement:

> The PSR of Albania has clearly expressed that she is for relations of good neighbourliness with Yugoslavia, for a stable and independent Yugoslavia, and that its peoples live in harmony with one another and with equal rights. Albania also expressed this desire at the meeting of Foreign Ministers in Belgrade, which marked a positive step towards understanding and confidence in our region. But it is a pity that winds are blowing precisely from the organizing country where this hopeful meeting was held that destroy this climate.[1]

Throughout Kosova a mood of apprehension prevailed, and in November 1988 some 100,000 Albanians gathered in Pristina to demand the reinstatement of two Kosovar party leaders who had been forced to resign. This was matched by a million Serbs demonstrating in Belgrade against alleged maltreatment of Kosova's Serbs by their Albanian neighbours. In February 1989, Serbia's National Assembly passed the controversial constitutional amendments which effectively handed back Kosova to Serbian control. A state of emergency was declared following serious rioting which left 28 Albanians dead and many more wounded.

Albania reacted to the violence in Kosova with stronger language than usual. *Zeri-i-Popullit* accused Yugoslavia of brutally oppressing the Kosovars. Tirana also warned that Belgrade's policy in Kosova would jeopardize the increased spirit of Balkan cooperation that had been painstakingly built up over the previous year. Many Serbs generally believed that Tirana was encouraging Kosovar dissent, in preparation for moves to create a 'Greater Albania'. Unification with Kosova would not have been in Tirana's interest, and would certainly have destabilized Albania. Although the Albanian leadership had often used the situation in Kosova as a way of deflecting domestic discontent, the new administration of Ramiz Alia realized only too well that seventy years of separation had enhanced the many social and psychological differences between the internationally isolated Albanians and the relatively cosmopolitan Kosovars. The two countries' strongly contrasting ideopolitical systems had left the predominantly Muslim Kosovars free to practice their religion, quite in contrast with the situation of enforced atheism in Albania. Nor would Albania's agricultural collectivization have appealed to the Kosovars, who worked their own land. Albania's leadership, valuing their country's ideological purity above national unity, therefore limited their interests in Kosova to cultural influence. Albania never appealed to international forums on behalf of the Kosovars, and when members of illegal Kosovar groups sought shelter in Albania they were promptly returned to the Yugoslav authorities.

Albania embarked on mildly reformist policies, for social and economic reasons, a year or so before the collapse of the Communist regimes in Eastern Europe in 1989. Nevertheless, the example of the 1989 revolutions, especially the rapid fall of the regime in Romania (and more particularly the sight of Nicolae Ceausescu's bullet-riddled body), must have signalled to the Albanian leadership that its survival rested on an immediate ending of the old policy of international isolation and self-sufficiency and a public acknowledgement of willingness to undertake reforms. The Albanian population may have been isolated and imprisoned within their frontiers, but they were fully aware of what was happening in the outside world as they avidly watched Italian, Greek and Yugoslav television. The impetus for change came initially from the intelligentsia and from within the PLA itself – particularly its increasingly educated elite. As they watched the popular movements in Eastern Europe pressing for change it became increasingly obvious that the PLA could not expect to hold on to its monopoly of power indefinitely.

The first signs of stirring among Albania's intellectuals appeared in late 1989, with the publication of a novel criticizing human-rights violations by the Ministry of Internal Affairs. The author, Neshat Tozai, was careful not to criticize the PLA directly, but the reader could easily infer from the novel that the ultimate responsibility for the repression lay with the country's Communist leaders. Other intellectuals took advantage of what appeared to be a mild relaxation of the PLA's controls in the cultural sector to express views that until then had been anathematized by the ruling party.[2] At the same time, Ismail Kadare, the country's foremost author, during a literary conference vigorously criticized the government's interference in literature, arguing that no government could either grant or deny a writer's freedom to create.[3] In November the first gesture towards political liberalization appeared, when an amnesty for certain political prisoners was announced. The pace of reform quickened as the pent-up anger, frustration and despair of 45 years exploded in a number of demonstrations and strikes during the spring of 1990. In January, anti-government demonstrators in Shkoder were violently dispersed by the security forces, but further demonstrations were reported during the month. The Sigurimi responded by intensifying its activities against opponents of the regime. There then followed the Ninth Plenum of the Central Committee of the PLA, which met to approve a 25-point reform plan proposing greater decentralization of the economy, bonuses for workers in some key industries, pricing changes and some decentralization of party authority (which would enable local organizations to appoint all but the most senior officials). Increased supplies of food and consumer goods were also promised and enterprises were to be allowed to sell some surplus goods on the free market. Nevertheless, Alia continued to reject the idea of a multi-party system, claiming that it was not appropriate for Albania. The population, however, thought otherwise.

In response to continued popular pressure for more radical changes, Alia announced proposals for reforming the political system, including redefinition of the role of the PLA, and a new electoral procedure requiring the presentation of at least two candidates in every constituency. In a major reversal of previous policy, religious worship was now to be tolerated, although Albania was officially to remain an atheist state. The announcement in May that the practice of religion was no longer an offence prompted thousands of people to attend the first legal Catholic mass for 23 years in Shkoder. Christian celebrations were permitted throughout the country, and Muslims also celebrated their services as mosques too were gradually reopened. Although it was mostly elderly people who participated in these first religious ceremonies, curious youngsters gathered to watch in silent amazement at the strange antics of their elders. Meanwhile, the People's Assembly approved further measures of liberalization. In the hope of redressing widespread human-rights violations the Ministry of Justice, which had been abolished in 1965, was reestablished and the penal code revised. This considerably reduced the number of crimes carrying the death penalty. It was also agreed to make passports available to the general population, in theory for purposes of foreign travel. In practice, however, Albanian poverty and the immigration policies of most Western countries put severe limitations on the exercise of this new freedom.

Despite the increasing liberalization there was further unrest in July 1990, when security forces violently dispersed anti-government demonstrators in Tirana. Immediately following the violence, four Albanians sought asylum in the embassy of the Federal Republic of Germany and, over the next few days, several thousand others followed their example and sought refuge in other foreign embassies. The dramatic scenes were reminiscent of the previous summer's rush by East German families into the West German embassy in Prague that sparked the fall of Communist rule throughout the Eastern bloc. In response to this crisis an emergency meeting of the Central Committee took place, resulting in personnel changes in various ministerial positions, including the dismissal of the leading conservative, Simon Stefani, as minister of internal affairs. However, most of the changes that had taken place so far affected the government rather than the real centre of power, the Politburo. (Stefani, for example, although removed from the Ministry of Internal Affairs, remained a member of the Politburo.) The refugee crisis was finally resolved when some 5,000 Albanians were allowed to leave the country, assisted by a multinational relief operation coordinated by the United Nations, and watched worldwide by curious television viewers. While foreign observers debated whether the embassy siege was the result of an organized political opposition, Ramiz Alia appeared on state television and denounced the refugees as 'disorientated persons, vagabonds, demagogues and café speculants'.

In conjunction with domestic policy reforms, there were some significant changes regarding foreign affairs. In July, the restoration of diplomatic links with the Soviet Union was announced, following talks in Washington on the resumption of diplomatic ties with the United States. The US government, however, showed some reluctance to restore relations until it was assured that multi-party elections would be announced. Diplomatic representatives from Britain and Albania also met, but Albania continued to insist on the return of the gold seized by the British at the end of the Second World War (which by 1990 was valued at around £20 million), before any diplomatic ties could be resumed. This was one of Europe's oldest diplomatic disputes, prompting President Alia to accuse consecutive British governments of remaining 'in a Cold War mentality'. Eventually, however, both parties agreed that arguments over the confiscated gold should be postponed until after the resumption of diplomatic ties, which were finally restored in May 1991.

Relations with Yugoslavia were meanwhile becoming increasingly strained, as the systematic erosion of Albanian civil and human rights in Kosova continued apace. In July 1990, the Serbian government had gone as far as amending their republic's constitution so as to remove the legal basis for Kosova's autonomy. Kosova's parliament was suspended and direct rule was imposed from Belgrade. With the exception of the Albanian-language paper *Bujku*, the newspaper offices were taken over by Serbian journalists after the sacking of their Albanian colleagues. The Rilindja publishing house came under Serbian management, and ceased printing any Albanian material. Serbian journalists also occupied Kosova's radio and television stations, leaving no broadcast media in the Albanian language. At the same time, the Kosovars established an Assembly of the Republic of Kosova with headquarters in Zagreb, where it was decided to hold a referendum on Kosova's sovereignty. Although they were forced underground, the activities of the various Kosovar political groups could not be prevented by the Serbian authorities. The most important of these was the Democratic Alliance, with over 700,000 members, headed by Dr Ibrahim Rugova. The Kosovars had now lost any pretence at having a stake in the future of Yugoslavia. They had little choice but to try to go it alone.

The Emergence of Independent Political Parties

Meanwhile, as the process of change in Albania gathered momentum, the credibility of Alia's reform programme suffered a reversal when 54-year-old Ismail Kadare, feeling that he would be freer to publicize Albania's plight abroad, sought asylum whilst in Paris in October 1990. Kadare's defection was a major blow for Alia and a clear indication that Kadare was critical of the limitations of the reforms being implemented. In Paris the author declared, 'The promises of democracy are dead.'[4] The timing of the defection also caused severe embarrassment to the Albanian government, which was in the midst of hosting the Balkan Foreign Ministers' Conference. Many young people, especially students, felt betrayed by Kadare's departure, which seemed to focus their sense of isolation and despair. Continuing their demonstrations in Tirana, the students now demanded better living conditions and the introduction of a full multi-party system for the forthcoming elections to the People's Assembly, scheduled for February 1991. In a hasty television address to the nation, Alia warned of the risk of 'democracy' being stillborn, leading to instability and anarchy. Nevertheless, support for the students grew rapidly, and on

11 December, fearful of the growing unrest, the Central Committee of the PLA finally agreed to legalize independent political parties.

The formation of the Democratic Party of Albania (DPA), the first legal opposition party since before the Second World War, was announced the next day (12 December 1990). Led by economist Gramoz Pashko, and Dr Sali Berisha, a cardiologist, the DPA announced that it wished to see the provisions of the Helsinki Final Act (which provided for the self-determination of peoples using the freedom to vote in multi-party elections) as the basis for Albanian society. The DPA leaders also demanded that Albania should abide by the four principles of the Paris Charter (signed by members of the CSCE – all European countries except Albania - in Paris in late 1990): a free-market economy, self-determination, free elections and the right to own private property. The Council of Ministers granted the DPA one million leks and a loan of US$50,000 to help defray their expenses. The DPA also received a considerable amount of money from the Democratic League of Kosova in Switzerland and Germany, together with a large sum from Albanian groups in the United States. The first opposition newspaper, *Rilindja Demokratike* (Democratic Revival) appeared and was relatively assertive in its anti-Communist stance. Reflecting public demand for new political debate, its first print-run of 50,000 sold out completely within hours. By March, the DPA membership had risen to some 60,000, against the PLA's estimated 130,00 members (a significant drop from the figure of 147,000 given at the Ninth Congress of the PLA in 1986).

The announcement of the new party came amidst yet more violent unrest in Shkoder and other towns, where students burned Hoxha's books and attacked government buildings. Security forces were sent to quell the trouble. The leaders of the DPA appeared on television and appealed to the people for restraint and patience so as not to hinder the pace of reform. The demonstrations seemed to be a spontaneous expression of frustration, by a people who had been promised fundamental reforms, yet were seeing few results. Shortages of consumer goods (most of which still resembled props from early 1950s film sets) and the rationing of basic foods and commodities had led to bitter discontent and demands for far more radical changes. The government, unable to satisfy public demand, responded feebly by dismissing the more conservative officials, including Nexhmije Hoxha who resigned from the presidency of the Democratic Front. She was replaced by Adil Carcani, a hardliner from Girokaster who had become prime minister in January 1982 and was now chairman of the Council of Ministers. Addressing the Council in December, Alia announced that the PLA must now 'deviate from many of the principles of socialism'. The core of his speech examined the PLA's expressed goal of 'full integration within Europe', with a cautious but significant remark regarding the status of Stalin and people who styled themselves 'loyal Stalinists'. The Council of Ministers agreed that 'historic circumstances have changed since the time when it was decided to honour J.V. Stalin in our country', and decreed that Stalin's name and statue should be removed from state institutions and public places. The dismantling not only of the cult of Stalin but also of that of Hoxha was a prerequisite for reform in Albania. It was striking that when Alia spoke at the 10th Plenum of the Central Committee back in April 1990, he had mentioned Hoxha only four times in a long and very thorough speech. By the standards of the PLA this could almost have been interpreted as a snub to Hoxha, and perhaps preparation for a significant reappraisal of his official place in Albania's history.

Domestic Unrest Intensifies

The beginning of 1991 saw the country in the grip of strikes throughout the mining and public transport sectors. These only ended after wage increases were agreed and full legislation granting the right to strike was adopted by the People's Assembly. The strikes were followed by the second round of government personnel changes in less than six weeks, in which Fatos Nano and Skleqim Cani, both reformist economists, were appointed deputy premiers. Following threats from the nascent opposition to boycott the forthcoming elections unless they were postponed, the government announced that they would now take place on 31 March, instead of 10 February. In a gesture aimed at stemming the growing support for the DPA, the government, trying to retain the political initiative, announced the release of more than two hundred political prisoners. In a radio statement, President Alia also declared that the government proposed to free all remaining political prisoners. The move was made in a forlorn bid to dilute the influence of the DPA, in effect by coopting many of its policies.

In the meantime, Albania's relations with Greece had deteriorated due to the exodus of more than 5,000 members of Albania's Greek minority, who since late December had been crossing the border into northern Greece. Although the majority had passports, the Greek embassy in Tirana was reluctant to issue more than a minimum of visas, fearing that Greece might be overwhelmed by large numbers of ethnic Greek Albanians. The Albanian Government estimated that the officially recognized minority in the southern provinces numbered 50,000, but Greece had long claimed a figure of 300,000 or more (all of whom would be eligible for Greek citizenship if they crossed the border). To defuse the crisis the Greek prime minister, Konstantin Mitsotakis, was invited to Tirana, where he sought to discourage a further exodus by urging ethnic Greeks to remain in Albania and keep faith in the reform process. However, most of the potential refugees appeared to have little confidence in the changes under way in Albania. Instead, not knowing when they would get another chance to leave the country, young Albanian men, clutching little parcels containing meagre food supplies, continued to trek southward over the Grammos mountains into Greece. Thousands more who gathered in border villages preparing to cross found little resistance from the once-feared border guards now that the penalties for attempting to leave the country, which had been up to 20-year prison sentences, were no longer in force.

The spring of 1991 was a time of political crisis and chaos in Albania, with many observers predicting military intervention. Everywhere there was a sense of the absence of government control in a country where, hitherto, all decisions of importance had been made by the PLA. Students in Tirana were now upping their demands, calling for the resignation of the ministers of foreign affairs, interior and justice. Demonstrations at Tirana University in early February developed into a hunger strike involving both students and lecturers – their demands included the removal of the name of Enver Hoxha from the university and an end to the compulsory study of Marxist–Leninist theory. A week later several thousand people marched to the centre of Tirana and pulled down the giant statue of Enver Hoxha in Skenderbeg Square. There was some violence as security forces attempted to disperse the protesters, who were astounded at the ease with which the ten-metre-high statue came down. Perhaps the regime itself was just as hollow? Within hours, statues of Hoxha were brought down in Durres and Korce. In response to the growing unrest, Alia declared presidential rule. Yet again he denounced the demonstrators as 'vandals', and announced the formation of a new government and the establishment of a Presidential Council. Undeterred, the demonstrators continued the next day with an orgy of book-burning, as bonfires engulfing a constant supply of portraits of Hoxha and official literature were lit in the streets surrounding Skenderbeg Square.

The tense political situation resulted in yet more concessions from the authorities, including the removal of Hoxha's name from the university. This, combined with increased force from the security forces, bought a temporary end to the rioting. The underlying tensions of pent-up frustration and resentment, however, remained. Shortly afterwards, a group of officers loyal to Hoxha established a 'Commission for the Defence of the Homeland' and demanded that the statue of Hoxha be reerected. The PLA district and local committees hurriedly organized pro-Hoxha rallies, the most successful being in Berat, where groups of 'Enverists' took an oath before the national flag. Other 'activist unions' proclaiming loyalty to Hoxha's ideology staged demonstrations in several southern towns. Clashes between Communists and their opponents were now occurring throughout the country. At this point, it was the status of Hoxha that remained the main focus of the conflict between the youth-led anti-Communist opposition in the towns and the older conservative Communists who controlled the security forces and were stronger in the provinces, especially in the south around Berat and Girokaster. Increasing industrial unrest added further to the country's woes. The government hurriedly moved to dampen the dissatisfaction in the industrial sector by conceding pay rises and better working conditions, and promising yet further wage increases in the rest of the economy. These promises were to prove impossible to implement, however, as the state was all but bankrupt. Alia was thus merely hoping to buy time. By now many in the party leadership were fearful of mass violence erupting in the major population centres. Precautionary measures were hastily adopted by the military and security forces to forestall a coup. Ammunition available to the Sigurimi was rationed and, capitalizing on the Kosova issue, a sizeable section of the army was deployed far to the north on the Yugoslav border.

In early March a new crisis began. With the social and economic life of the country in collapse and foodstuffs about to be exhausted, thousands of Albanians attempted to flee to Italy. The 20,000 or so would-be emigrants, mostly unemployed young men, commandeered ships in the ports of Vlore and Durres and sailed to the Italian port of Brindisi. The Italian navy was rapidly ordered to prevent ships from docking, and the Albanian authorities placed the ports under military rule to prevent more refugees from hijacking ships. Italians were shocked by television pictures of thousands of hungry and destitute Albanians, dressed in ragged 1970s clothing, roaming the streets of Brindisi. Italian premier Giulio Andreotti, proposed that Italians should 'adopt' refugees and take them into their homes. He offered to be the first to do so. However, few Italians took up the challenge and the Albanians remained huddled in groups amid puddles of urine and water on the windswept docks. Doctors at Brindisi's only hospital began treating hundreds of cases of scabies, dysentery, hepatitis and serious malnourishment. Initially, the Albanian government adopted a passive attitude to the mass exodus across the Adriatic, perhaps not wanting to discourage so many anti-Communists from leaving the country before the coming elections. However, after Rome had demanded that Tirana act to stop the flow of refugees, and announced that all but a handful were to be repatriated, the Albanian government declared the port of Durres a military zone and ordered police and the army to move into the town to halt the gathering of potential refugees. Had these alarming upheavals in Albania occurred a year previously, they would probably have aroused Western sympathy of the sort extended to the Romanians during the dramatic fall of the Ceausescus. Now, however, the plight of the refugees was treated as little more than a curious side-show, completely overshadowed by the Gulf War.

The March 1991 Elections

Following emergency talks between the government and opposition parties, it was agreed that workers would refrain from striking until 1 May, in exchange for delaying the elections until 31 March. Thus the opposition were given more time to organize for the polls. Other smaller parties also began registering for the elections, the most prominent of which were the Republican Party, the Agrarian Party, the Ecology Party and the Democratic Union of the Greek Minority (OMONIA). The PLA and its affiliated organizations, such as the Democratic Front, the Union of Working Youth of Albania, the War Veterans' Committee and the Women's Union, nominated 644 of the 1,074 registered candidates. By the last week of March, Albania was gripped by election fever. The world's media, together with 260 international observers, descended on Tirana. The capital's two decent hotels were soon crammed to capacity. Albanians invited foreign journalists to sleep on the floors of their already cramped apartments. Virtually every report that appeared in the Western press included the phrase: 'last bastion of Stalinism set to fall'. Many articles also described how 'backward' and 'primitive' Albania was, caught in a 'time-warp' which gave the visiting journalists more of a culture shock than most Third World countries.

With wages as low as US$20 a month, and unemployment at around 40 per cent, the DPA campaign promised a transformation of living standards. This was to be brought about by EC membership, Western financial aid and jobs in Italian and German factories. Albanians began eagerly to plan which family members would be going abroad and how much money they were likely to be sending home. The walls of Tirana were soon covered with DPA campaign posters including symbols which echoed those of the European Community. One even showed Albania as an extra star on the EC flag. As for the smaller parties, the most important was the Republican Party, with a manifesto similar to that of the DPA but inclining more to the right. It promised a gradual programme of land privatization relying on foreign investment, in contrast to the DPA's advocacy of rapid privatiz-ation and an immediate transition to a free enterprise system. The Ecology Party, with its minute membership, campaigned on issues of social harmony and environmental protection rather than on political or economic issues. OMONIA, while supporting democratic changes, campaigned on issues specific to the Greek minority. The Agrarian Party promised to raise the living standards of the country's pre-dominantly rural population, which comprised almost 60 per cent of the population.

Despite the unrest which preceded them, Albania's first multi-party elections for six decades took place peacefully. Almost 97 per cent of the 1.9 million people eligible to vote did so, the highest level in any multi-party election in Eastern Europe. In the first round of voting, the PLA won 162 of the 250 seats in the Assembly. The DPA won 65 seats, including 17 of the 19 seats in Tirana, and some 40 per cent of the votes cast. The opposition won all the urban constituencies, while the rural population, who were wary of change and anxious for their security, voted overwhelmingly for the PLA. A crucial factor in the defeat of the DPA was the widespread belief that it would priva-tize and redistribute the land, while the PLA had promised to protect the peasantry from privatization. Further rounds of voting took place on 7 and 14 April in the electoral districts where no candidate had won an absolute majority during the first round. In these rounds the DPA won 10 seats, the PLA 7 and OMONIA 2. Overall, the PLA won a total of 169 of the 250 seats in the People's Assembly, just over the two-thirds majority (167 seats) required to adopt a new constitution. The DPA won 75 seats and OMONIA 5. The PLA fared best in the Tosk-inhabited south, where Communist sympathies remained strongest. The most surprising result was the failure of Alia to win a seat in the People's Assembly. He won only 36 per cent of the votes cast in his Tirana constituency and became another victim of the urban electorate's determination to rid themselves of the Communists. Alia's humiliating defeat shocked the population. A reporter for the Austrian daily *Die Presse* described the news of his defeat as hitting Tirana like a bomb. It claimed that people had cried, including some of his critics, and that there had been 'no overwhelming joy'.[5]

Apart from being defeated on the land issue, the opposition suffered because of its recent formation, and due to poor infrastructure throughout Albania it lacked the transportation and communication necessary to disseminate its views widely and quickly. The DPA also complained of a lack of media representation and of persistent psychological pressure to vote for the PLA. The DPA leadership contradicted the consensus among the international observers by claiming that the elections had been conducted amidst a climate of fear. Most independent Western observers, however, attested to the overall fairness of the elections, claiming that fraud and manipulation were minimal. They admitted the PLA's control of election scrutineers in some rural areas and domination over the media, but concluded that the PLA's victory was largely the result of the lack of a developed and informed political culture. Sali Berisha won a resounding victory in Kavaje, an anti-Communist bastion south of Durres, which now called itself 'Albania's capital of democracy'. Youths in lorries drove up and down Kavaje's main street shouting, 'Freedom! Democracy!' Berisha later told reporters that 'Morally, we are the winners. This is the real end of Communism in Albania.' The results were in some respects similar to those in other former one-party Balkan states, where many rural voters were wary of change while the better educated urban population was impatient for swift and fundamental reforms. There was an immediate reaction to the PLA's victory in Shkoder: peasants coming into the town to sell their produce were beaten by town dwellers blaming them for ensuring the Communist victory. Hundreds of young people demonstrated in Shkoder on 2 April against alleged incidents of fraud and intimidation during the elections. When security forces attempted to disperse the crowd, four people were killed and many injured by shots fired by the police.

With the elections over and won, it seemed possible that conservative elements within the PLA, including the military, would try to arrest the process of reform. Indeed, to placate the professional members of the armed forces, it was decided to reintroduce ranks which had been abolished in the 1960s. Following the violence in Shkoder, Alia appealed in parliament to the DPA for a 'national salvation coalition government', so as to defuse 'unnecessary political antagonisms'. However, his proposal was rejected by the opposition, who insisted that those responsible for the shootings in Shkoder be brought to trial. Initially, Alia had been perceived as a strong politician who favoured dialogue; he was seen by many as the motivating force behind the reforms, which were strongly opposed by conservatives in all the state security organizations. Even non-Communists credited Alia with resisting the pressure from conservatives within the PLA to halt the reform process, and for this reason the DPA was reluctant to stage an open confrontation with him. Many credited Alia with avoiding bloodshed by making repeated concessions to the reformists. It seems, however, that Alia remained severely compromised by the close relationship he had had with Enver Hoxha.

The new People's Assembly first convened on 10 April, but opposition deputies refused to attend until those responsible for the deaths in Shkoder were identified. The Assembly reconvened a week later, after the DPA had ended its boycott, and a parliamentary commission was established to investigate the Shkoder shootings. It reported, within a week, that the police were to blame for provoking violence from initially peaceful demonstrators. The new constitution, not surprisingly, contained many structural changes, including the establishment of political pluralism and the renaming of the country. The People's Republic of Socialist Albania now became simply the Republic of Albania. The constitution made no reference to Marxism–Leninism as an ideology, nor to the 'leading role of the PLA' that had been previously enshrined. The state was defined rather vaguely as 'democratic and juridical, based on social equality, the defence of freedom, and the rights of man'. The right to private property was endorsed, as was the right to strike, to demonstrate and to emigrate. Instead of a presidium of the People's Assembly, an executive president of the country was to be elected by two-thirds of the votes cast in the

People's Assembly. Ramiz Alia was elected to this new post by an overwhelming majority, but all the opposition deputies abstained.

Communism in Retreat

Following his election as president, Alia resigned as First Secretary of the PLA, in accordance with the new constitutional amendment which prevented the president from holding office in a political party. He also resigned from the Politburo and the Central Committee of the PLA. In early May the People's Assembly, trying to strengthen their shattered morale, approved a new government headed by Fatos Nano. Although all the new ministers were PLA members, the programme presented to the Assembly by Nano envisaged fundamental reforms, including extensive privatization and a rapid shift to a market-based economy. However, the new government faced immense problems amidst a fast disintegrating economy, with inflation running at around 260 per cent per month, and over 70 per cent of the workforce idle. As soon as the 'no-strike policy' had expired in mid-May the newly established independent trades unions organized a general strike in which around 300,000 workers from all sectors of the economy participated. As the country plunged into political uncertainty, the strikers demanded unrealistic pay rises of up to 100 per cent. In a national radio appeal for an end to the stoppages, Alia admitted that the country was paralysed: 'I appeal to all to return to work as the sole possibility to save the country and ourselves from the fatality of failure. The situation is extremely grave. Economic and political life are almost at a standstill.'

As the general strike moved into its fourth week, the government appealed again for the establishment of an interim coalition 'caretaker' government until fresh elections could be held the following year. With so little experience of multi-party politics, it was no surprise that the DPA initially refused to enter a coalition with the Communists. They feared being discredited in the eyes of their staunchly anti-Communist supporters. It seems that they eventually agreed to join the coalition only in response to the country's critical socio-economic situation, and on condition that the new government would act merely as an interim administration until another general election took place. By now, the PLA leadership realized that their last chance to enforce their authority had passed. They were unable to utilize their two-thirds majority because the party was disintegrating and, more importantly, the psychological will to hold on to power had gone.

Kosova Votes for Independence

Meanwhile, in Yugoslavia the Kosova Assembly held a presidential election on 24 May 1991. Ibrahim Rugova was duly elected President of the Republic of Kosova with 99.5 per cent of the vote. On 30 September, Kosovars voted in a referendum overwhelmingly to endorse Kosova as a 'sovereign and independent state'. As expected, these events were declared illegal by Belgrade and the intimidation policy against the Kosovars accelerated. By the end of the year, more than 75,000 Kosovars had lost their jobs; these included at least 6,000 teachers who were sacked for refusing to give up the Albanian, in favour of a Serbian-imposed, curriculum. As a result, over 400,000 Albanian pupils boycotted classes, attending instead, wherever possible, secret underground schools set up by unemployed teachers. Due to continued economic migration, by 1991 Serbs and Montenegrins accounted for just 9 per cent of Kosova's population. In an effort to reverse the region's ethnic distribution, Belgrade offered favourable credits, housing, and where possible, jobs to those Serbs and Montenegrins willing to settle in Kosova. By March 1992, however, less than two thousand Serbs had taken up the offer, and most of these were refugees from Albania's minute Slav minority.

In the wake of the continued disintegration of Yugoslavia, there was little employment for either Slavs or Albanians as the economy had all but collapsed. In a move to reaffirm once more their tentative hold on Kosova, the Serbian leadership set up the Serbian Bloc for the Colonization of Kosovo in Pristina. Its aims were to place high-level pressure on the administration to accelerate the Serbian colonization of Kosova. In order to accommodate more Serbs, the authorities began requisitioning apartments belonging to Albanians who had either departed or been evicted. Since the start of the fighting in the former Yugoslavia, an estimated 350,000 ethnic Albanians had left the country. The Serbian Orthodox hierarchy was by now so convinced that war-clouds were thickening over Kosova that Patriarch Pavle took the precaution of ordering the relics and icons in the church of Gracanica to be taken to Belgrade for 'restoration'. The escalating conflict in Yugoslavia, with war in Croatia and the threat of fighting in Bosnia-Hercegovina, meant that Albania's politicians could no longer ignore the fate of the Kosovars. Fearing a massive influx of Kosovar refugees, the Tirana government issued statements containing by far the strongest criticism yet of the policies of Kosova's Serbian leadership. Albania's armed forces were placed on alert following reported incidents between Yugoslav and Albanian border guards, and in October Albania officially recognized the Republic of Kosova as a sovereign and independent state. This gesture, it was hoped, would spur on further international recognition of Kosova.

With a real risk of spill-over from the war in Yugoslavia, the Albanian government was acutely aware that its country's defences relied on worn-out Soviet weaponry, vintage Chinese guns and 400,000 useless concrete bunkers. Moreover, the Albanian army had no funds or technology to buy or manufacture new weapons. A measure of how vulnerable the government felt regarding the war to the north was noted in the publication, for the first time, of the country's military capability. The report by the army's chief of staff, Kristaq Karoli, stated that the Albanian armed forces consisted of 35,000 troops, 500 tanks, 700 artillery pieces, 95 fighter aircraft and 70 small boats. Given these figures, it seemed somewhat unnecessary for Karoli to assure a conference in Vienna that Albanian military training was strictly defensive in nature. Defence Minister Alfred Moisiu explained that the military was now looking westward for help in strengthening national security:

Joining the North Atlantic Treaty Organization [NATO] or establishing military relations with its member states seems to be a necessity for our country. But affiliation with NATO will take time and does not depend only on us, so we are rather working towards a bilateral cooperation aiming at integrating ourselves with the military structures of the European Community.[6]

The Government of 'National Stability'

In Tirana, the Democrats were congratulating themselves as the general strike succeeded in its primary objective of bringing down the government. On 4 June, Nano's government resigned. The next day, Ylli Bufi, previously the minister for food under Nano, was appointed chairman of the Council of Ministers, leading a new 'Government of National Stability' which included 12 non-Communist Ministers approved by the legislature. The PLA held 12 portfolios; the DPA gained 7; and the Republican Party, the Social Democratic Party and the Agrarian Party shared the other 5 among them. The new government immediately agreed to pay rises of 15–18 per cent for all state workers, and announced a fresh investigation into the Shkoder killings. The Tenth Congress of the PLA, convened on 10 June, marked the beginning of an official reevaluation of Albania's past, at a time when the very survival of the party was at stake. The delegates to the Congress had to decide on what measures to take next as Albania slid deeper into economic and social despair. They hastily approved fundamental changes to the structure and ideology of the party. The PLA was renamed the Socialist Party of Albania (SPA), and Fatos Nano was elected president of a new Managing Committee which replaced the Central Committee. There was a thorough purge of the party leadership, with nine former members of the Politburo expelled from the PLA and others demoted. The ideology of the party was also reformed: the new party manifesto stated that the SPA would be a modern progressive party, committed to democracy, social justice and economic reform. This provoked clashes between reformers and conservatives within the party, who chanted the traditional Communist slogan: 'Enver's Party – Always Ready.'

The hardliner Xhelil Gjoni, one of three party secretaries who led the PLA after Alia had resigned as First Party Secretary, delivered the keynote speech to the Congress. He engaged in unprecedented public criticism of certain aspects of Hoxha's rule, referring to Hoxha's supposed infallibility and to the personality cult that surrounded him, and claiming that his fellow party and state leaders had profited from these aspects 'in terms of authority and privileges'. Gjoni's concluding remarks on the question of Hoxha's leadership demonstrated how difficult it was to evaluate his place in postwar Albanian history:

> There is one thing that can definitely be said – Enver Hoxha was not mistaken in his stand on freedom and independence. He was a popular leader who knew how to unite the people and how to rouse them. Let the historians deal with the mistakes, and let him remain the inheritance of our Party and of his country. It is for the common good to avoid discussions that would divide us. Enver Hoxha should be accepted for what he was. It is our duty, knowing the values he stood for, not to confuse them with his mistakes. We should demand of Enver that which he could and should have done, and not what we would have had him do.[7]

By summer 1992 the economic situation showed no signs of improvement, and a further 10,000 Albanians attempted to emigrate to Italy. As with previous attempts, the majority were unemployed and

complained of lack of food at home and administrative chaos throughout Albania. The Italian authorities, who were still trying to cope
with previous destitute Albanian arrivals, ordered the forcible re-
patriation of the new influx of refugees. In Albania there was a
dramatic shift of the rural population to the towns, owing to the
absence of appropriate legislation, which had left many peasants,
especially those in the mountainous areas, with little or no land.
Thousands of peasants began to settle in and around Tirana, which
by July had a population approaching 500,000, 30,000 people having
arrived during 1991.[8] Those peasants who remained in the countryside were hoarding any food they produced, thus contributing to the
country's overall food shortage. In September, the deputy prime minister, Gramoz Pashko, appealed at a meeting in Brussels of the Group
of 24 industrialized nations (G-24) for emergency food aid. The G-24
responded by providing more than US$150 million in emergency aid,
and some five hundred Italian soldiers were sent to Albania to help
with the aid distribution.

In a belated attempt to prevent further chaos in the countryside,
the National Stability Government introduced long-awaited legislation
on the privatization of land and replaced the people's councils (local
administrative organs) with multi-party bodies. The decision to grant
peasant families the private use of up to one acre of cooperative land
resulted in a free-for-all. Some collective farm members were report-
edly seizing land on the basis of pre-collectivization boundaries, while
others were left without any land to cultivate. The rural chaos could
not have come at a worse time: following four successive years of
drought, the land-grab coincided with what should have been harvest
time. By the end of the year the country was in an appalling state. In
Tirana around 20,000 people rallied not only to celebrate the first
anniversary of the pro-democracy protests, but also to protest against
the dire shortages of essential foods and fuel. It was a particularly
severe winter and everywhere people began to chop down trees for
fuel. These included the magnificent stately elms, planted in Zog's
time, which lined all the country's main roads and provided much-
needed shade during the summer months. Soldiers and police had to
restore order in the northern Kruje district after hungry crowds
stormed food banks. The panic set in after Prime Minister Ylli Bufi
announced that current food supplies would only last one more week.
This led to frenzied rioting in the town of Lac, where mobs ransacked
a food-processing plant, as well as bakeries, restaurants and other

food stores. During the rioting two people were killed, one of them a policeman.

In December, DPA Party Chairman Sali Berisha charged the SPA with deliberately obstructing the reform process in the countryside and instigating the current vicious crime wave and refugee crisis. He called for DPA members to resign from the coalition government, and 7 ministers promptly pulled out of the 21-member Cabinet. This occurred whilst Gramoz Pashko was having talks in London with the International Monetary Fund (IMF). Pashko was furious, and immediately cut short his trip and returned to Tirana. It was then that he acknowledged the split in the Democratic Party. Pashko criticized Berisha for breaking up the government, saying that the move would lead the country into even further anarchy and chaos. The same week saw the arrest of 71-year-old Nexhmije Hoxha, who had been expelled from the party in June. She, along with others, was charged with corruption. And so began the series of witch-hunts, mixing corruption with politics, that would so preoccupy the country's leaders over the next few years. As the new year was ushered in, Albania's immediate future could not have appeared bleaker. The deepening crisis caused Prime Minister Bufi to resign. Alia hoped to restore some measure of stability to the government by appointing former food minister, Vilson Ahmeti, as the new prime minister of the caretaker government. Alia then signed the decree for fresh elections to be held on 22 March.

The March 1992 Elections

In the meantime, the situation in the former Yugoslavia had deteriorated sharply, following international recognition of Croatia's and Slovenia's independence in January 1992. This led directly to the escalation of the conflict into Bosnia-Hercegovina. There was a corresponding tightening of Serbian control in Kosova, and at the end of January a large rally was held in Tirana in support of the Kosovars. Demands were made within Albania for more forthright government action on the issue of Kosova, and Serbian warnings against Albanian involvement in Yugoslavia became more strident. Berisha told DPA supporters of one of their party's aims: 'Our brothers, living in their territories in the former Yugoslavia and wherever they are: the DPA will not stop fighting until her great dream of uniting the Albanian nation comes true.'[9] This was a provocative statement to make at such a sensitive time, but Berisha, like many politicians in Europe, believed that now three of the former Yugoslav republics had international recognition, Kosova's turn might also come. Himself a Gheg, Berisha attached greater priority to unification with Kosova than did many Tosk politicians. On 20 March the Democratic Party held a huge rally to close its election campaign in Skenderbeg Square. Berisha and other DPA leaders spoke to an estimated crowd of 100,000, urging them to unite for real democracy in the forthcoming election. At the same time the new Albanian Communist Party, which had been formed in December 1991, warned of 'danger on the doorstep' as a result of the 'counter-revolution taking place in the country'. The party appealed to the electorate to follow the 'teachings and instructions of the genius, Enver Hoxha, who contributed to the freedom, independence and sovereignty of the homeland as nobody before in the history of this nation.'[10]

On 22 March the DPA finally swept to victory in the elections with 62 per cent of the votes, compared to just 25 per cent for the SPA. On this occasion 90.35 per cent of eligible voters cast their votes. On 29 March the DPA consolidated its landslide victory by scooping up all 11 seats at stake in the second round of voting. This time the SPA won only 6 seats, all of them in the south, their traditional power-base. The DPA now had a total of 92 seats in the new 140-seat parliament – just one short of a two-thirds majority. The Socialists gained 38 seats; the Social Democrats, 7; and the Human Rights Union Party, 2. The Socialist Party accepted the election results and suggested that its defeat was due to the fact that 'even in Albania the electorate was influenced by the present European trend towards the political right'. The party's chairman, Fatos Nano, claimed that there were some irregularities during the electoral campaign and on the election day, but that they did not alter the final results. He wished the DPA good luck in solving the problems in store for them.[11] Thus ended almost five decades of Communist rule.

On 4 April, President Alia announced his decision to resign from office. Dr Sali Berisha, from the northeastern district of Tropoje, became Albania's first non-Communist president since Zog (elected to the presidency by a large majority in Parliament as the only candidate). Berisha then appointed the new government, headed by a 53-year-old archaeologist, Alexander Meksi. The DPA held the premiership and 14 ministries, including the key ministries of finance, the interior, foreign affairs and defence. Independent technocrats were appointed to run the ministries of industry and justice. The Social Democrats and the Republicans held one portfolio each. The Socialists, whose number of seats in the 140-member parliament shrank in the elections to 38, were not represented in the new government. The new, youthful and inexperienced cabinet faced such a daunting panoply of ills that without extensive foreign investment and unconditional loans the long-term future of the new government was open to question. Berisha had now to satisfy the high expectations he had created during the election campaign by claiming that foreign investment would increase dramatically if the remaining Socialists were ejected from the government. He had also openly implied that immigration quotas to EC countries would be available to Albanian workers if the Democrats won. As it turned out, neighbouring Macedonia was the only country, albeit not a recognized one, actually to invite Albanians to visit. Even this invitation, however, was limited to visits of just 32 hours, and only to residents of Pogradec, a centre of Orthodoxy 80 miles southeast of Tirana. Muslims were also allowed to cross the border, providing they could prove they lived in Pogradec. And so on 26 April, thousands of Albanians flooded into the little Macedonian town of Struga after the border was temporarily opened for the first time since 1948, in a goodwill gesture for the Orthodox Easter. The day-trippers returned to tell awestruck relatives and friends of the amazing consumer goods they had seen.

A few days later, the new government carried out its first priority task. The body of Enver Hoxha was quietly exhumed from his hero's tomb and reburied in a public grave in a suburban cemetery. The bodies of 12 other former senior Communist officials were also removed from the Martyrs' Cemetery on a hill overlooking Tirana. The exhumation was carried out in secrecy in the early morning and under heavy guard. Hoxha's lead coffin was removed from his concrete and marble mausoleum, and only close relatives took part in the reburial. The rapid dismantling of the one-party state had brought about the almost total breakdown of state authority, resulting not only in the collapse of the economy, but also in an escalation of serious crime. With no laws controlling the ownership of weapons, the crackling of pistols or rifles, and occasional machine-gun fire, frequently disturbed the still Tirana nights. Incidents of robbery and rape increased dramatically, and foreigners were advised to travel around the country with an armed guard. On a visit to Albania, the leader of the Social Democratic Party for Kosova, Shkelzen Maliqi, was attacked by a gang of youths, robbed of his personal possessions, and stripped of his clothing, and was forced to wait in a car until someone fetched him a pair of trousers. Such crimes only served to enhance the already bewildered population's sense of insecurity, as well as acting as a serious deterrent to foreign investment. The ill-equipped police force, suffering from lack of confidence, indifference and in many cases from acute fear, was unable to cope with the anarchic situation.

There seemed no escape from the country's escalating spiral of woes. Realistically, Albanians could expect no immediate release from their abject poverty. By the Democrats' own admission, the rebuilding of the country's devastated economy would be a long, slow process. Revenue from hard-currency exports such as oil, chrome and electricity had dramatically declined, and the severe lack of raw materials in combination with outdated technology had left industry paralysed. The old Chinese-built factories were by now rusted, gutted hulks. Although at first their redundant workforce was paid 80 per cent of their former wages to soften the blow of mass unemployment, state reserves were soon exhausted, and as the first step of their austerity programme the new government announced that the jobless would receive just 60 per cent of their former wages, with a further reduction after six months. Agricultural production was in a state of chaos due to the uncontrolled seizure of state-owned cooperative land and property. The peasants, realizing that state authority had broken down, had also begun demolishing cooperative buildings and seizing the bricks, livestock and implements for their own dwellings. Naturally, this greatly exacerbated the overall economic decline in the countryside, home to two-thirds of the population. But even with up to 70 per cent of cooperative land back in private hands, agricultural production could only hope to remain at subsistence level, owing to the acute shortages of seeds, fertilizers and machinery.

Gloom and despair now typified Albanian rural life, as most peasants had a little milk or cheese to sell but were otherwise jobless and without income. The young wanted to get out at any cost and did not mind where. They continued to drift towards Tirana and the ports in search of the prosperity and freedom promised them. At the beginning of July, in yet another bid to flee the country, around 6,000 Albanians tried to commandeer ships in Durres. Police also reported dragging people from fishing boats in Vlore. The attempted exodus was triggered by the discontinuation of unemployment benefits for state workers, thus effectively cutting off the income of around 20 per cent of Albania's workforce. A general air of unrest soon prevailed throughout the country as the desperate population was, by now, almost entirely dependent on foreign food aid. Although Operation Pelican, the Italian-organized food aid programme, had successfully prevented mass starvation, it could hardly be seen as a permanent solution to the country's food shortages.

The Democratic 'Dream' Fades

By the summer of 1992 support for the ruling Democrats was already beginning to wane. In local elections held on 27 August the DPA saw their share of the vote plummet from about two-thirds to around a half. The Socialist Party of Albania was the surprise beneficiary, capturing several key DPA strongholds. Against the social hardship caused by the government's tough economic reforms, the Socialists promised to slow down the reform process, and were regarded by many as the only defence against the huge job losses and social deprivation that people had begun to experience. Initially, Albanians had expected quick returns from their investment in democracy, much as they had done from the Young Turk Constitution in 1908. However, their growing political maturity was producing a crisis of confidence, and disenchantment with the democratic process was in turn leading to rising social discontent. Frustration grew as the promised job prospects and progress in living standards failed even marginally to materialize. As the country sank further into economic ruin, and war-clouds threatened in the north, the government turned its attention to the settling of old scores.

On 12 September, former president Ramiz Alia was put under house arrest, accused of corruption. The cause of his sudden arrest could be traced to his outspoken articles in the socialist newspaper, *24 Hours*, in which he criticized the government for having lowered the standard of living since it came to power. At the end of December, five former Communist Party and police officials were jailed for up to 20 years for ordering the fatal shooting of the four demonstrators in Shkoder in 1991. By then virtually the entire former Politburo was under arrest and awaiting trial on charges of stealing from the state. These included 72-year-old Nexhmije Hoxha, who was sentenced to 11 years in prison at the beginning of February 1993, charged with misappropriating 750,000 leks (the equivalant of $75,000) in state money between her husband's death in 1985 and the end of the old regime in 1990. There was, however, a noticeably subdued reaction to these events from the Albanian people. Although the horrors of the Hoxha years were still sufficiently clear for many Albanians to feel the need to 'cleanse' the country of Communists, many saw the purges of former leaders as directing attention away from the real and acute problems facing the country. As Albanians watched the country's politics being reduced to a struggle between personalities who end-lessly disputed the roles their opponents had played in the former regime, many began to argue that the DPA did not have the mo-nopoly on democracy that it claimed. Gagging opponents could do little to help heal the country's deep social, economic and political divisions, nor could it help develop a democratic political process that had no previous roots in the culture.

By the summer of 1993, the forces which had striven in the past to divide the Albanians along religious and political lines had again come to the fore. Missionaries and clergy with religious and educational funding from countries all around the world (including Iran, Egypt, Saudi Arabia, Greece, America and the Vatican) campaigned for the minds and souls of the Albanian people. Émigrés, especially the sons and daughters of those who had fought for Balli Kombetar or Legaliteti as opposed to the Communists during the Second World War, re-turned to reclaim what they had lost more than half a century before. A spirit of dogmatism and revenge rather than reconciliation was emerging, and this contributed to an overall climate of intolerance. Some degree of cooperation with former Communists was unavoidable, especially given that a sizeable number of Democrat politicians had until so recently been Communist Party members themselves, a phenomenon applicable to virtually every East European country and to the republics of the former Soviet Union. The Albanian govern-ment's most pressing task, therefore, was to concentrate on healing the bitter rifts between young and old, rural and urban, Gheg and Tosk, opposition and Communist, that now characterized the society.

As a result of such a lack of internal cohesion, Albania was sending out confused and contradictory signals to the international commu-nity – which, given the violent reemergence of the national question in the Balkans, could not now ignore this once-forgotten fragment of Europe. Together with a firm process of national integration, political stability in the southern Balkans had become a prerequisite for foreign investment, economic growth and future prosperity in Albania. Dependent above all on the ending of the war in the former Yugoslavia, and the resolution of a series of complex issues concerning the fate of Albanians living in Kosova, Montenegro and Macedonia, stability in southeast Europe has proved an elusive prize. At the time of writing, it appears that these matters are unlikely to be settled without further conflict. It is Albania's tragic misfortune that she should emerge from such an extended period of isolation into a Balkans seething with as many national grievances and rivalries as when the Albanian state was proclaimed in 1912.

Notes

Introduction

1. A detailed account of this period can be found in Harding, A., 'The Prehistoric Background of Illyrian Albania', in Tom Winnifrith (ed), *Perspectives on Albania*, London, 1992, pp 14–28.

2. Hill, S., 'Byzantium and the Emergence of Albania', in Winnifrith (ed), *Perspectives on Albania*, p 48.

3. Wilkes, J., *The Illyrians*, Oxford, 1992, p 273.

4. Hammond, N., 'The Relations of Illyrian Albania with the Greeks and the Romans', in Winnifrith (ed), *Perspectives on Albania*, p 39.

5. Skendi, S., *Balkan Cultural Studies*, Boulder, 1980, p 151.

6. Nicol, D.M., *The Despotate of Epirus 1267–1479*, London, 1984, p 251.

7. Nicol, *The Despotate of Epirus*, p 142.

8. Logoreci, A., *The Albanians, Europe's Forgotten Survivors*, London, 1977, p 29.

9. Hobhouse, J.C., *A Journey Through Albania, Travels in South Albania and Epirus 1809–1810, Vol 1* New York, 1971, p 139.

10. Treptow, K.W., 'The Albanian Rebellion of 1481', *Albanian Life*, no 48, issue 2, 1990, p 32.

1. The Nature of Ottoman Rule and the Rise of the Great Pashaliks

1. Jelavich, Charles and Barbara, *The Establishment of the Balkan National States, 1804–1920*, Washington, 1977, p 12.

2. Zürcher, Erik J., *Turkey – A Modern History*, London, 1993, p 17.

3. Norris, H.T., *Islam in the Balkans, Religion and Society Between Europe and the Arab World*, London, 1993, p 244.

4. The Vlach until recently lived as semi-nomadic pastoralists. They speak a Romance language and claim descent from the ancient Thracians. Today they live as shepherds and traders in the more mountainous regions of the southern Balkans. They are almost entirely Eastern Orthodox in religion.

5. Pollo, Stefanaq, and Puto, Arben, *The History of Albania*, London, 1981, p 94.

6. Hobhouse, J.C., *A Journey Through Albania, Travels in South Albania and Epirus, 1809–1910*, New York, 1971, p 131.

7. Zürcher, *Turkey – A Modern History*, p 17.

8. Skendi, S., *Balkan Cultural Studies*, Boulder, 1980, p 208.

9. Skendi, S., *The Albanian National Awakening*, New Jersey, 1967 p 8.

10. Hobhouse, *A Journey Through Albania*, p 131.

11. Odysseus, *Turkey in Europe*, London, 1900, p 401.

12. Mehmet Ali was an Albanian born in Kavalla (now in northern Greece), who had come to Egypt as an officer in the Albanian contingent of the Ottoman expeditionary force against the French. In 1803 he became leader of that corps and established himself as the *de facto* ruler of Egypt. In 1808 he was officially recognized as governor of Egypt by the Sultan.

13. Pollo and Puto, *The History of Albania*, p 100.

14. Shupp, P.F., *The European Powers and the Near Eastern Question, 1806–07*, New York, 1931, p 278.

15. Plomer, William, *The Diamond of Janina, Ali Pasha 1741–1822*, London, 1970, p 24.

16. Shupp, *The European Powers*, pp 278–279.

17. Ibid., p 282.

18. Ibid., p 288.

19. Norris, *Islam in the Balkans*, p 125.

20. Babinger, F. Von, *The Sphere*, no. 1525, 13 April 1929 p 63, quoted in Norris, *Islam in the Balkans*, p 132.

21. A description of the Bektashi sect can be found in Norris, *Islam in the Balkans*, and also Margaret Hasluk, 'The Non-Conformist Muslims of Albania', *Contemporary Review*, CXXVII, May 1925.

22. Plomer, *The Diamond of Janina*, p 24.

23. Lear, Edward, *Journals of a Landscape Painter in Greece and Albania*, London, 1965, p 142.

24. Ibid., p 159.

25. A detailed account of the *Tanzimat* Reforms can be found in Zürcher, *Turkey – A Modern History*.

26. Lear, *Journals of a Landscape Painter*, p 77.

27. Ibid., p 96.

28. Jelavich, *The Establishment of the Balkan National States*, p 99.

29. Swire, Joseph, *Albania, The Rise of a Kingdom*, New York, 1971, p 36.

30. *Antologji e Letersise Shqipe*, Tirana, 1955, p 85.

31. Frasheri, Sami, *Was war Albanien, Was ist Es, Was wir Es werden?* Vienna, 1913, p 46.

32. Zürcher, *Turkey – A Modern History*, p 76.
33. Skendi, *The Albanian National Awakening*, p 35.
34. Hobhouse, *A Journey Through Albania*, p 131.
35. Skendi, *The Albanian National Awakening*, p 132. For the full text of the memorandum see F. Lippich, *Denkschrift über Albanien*, Vienna, 20 June 1877, pp 8–9.

2. Political and Cultural Moves to Consolidate the Albanian National Movement

1. Skendi, Stavro, *The Albanian National Awakening*, New Jersey, 1967, pp 41–2.
2. Zürcher, E.J., *Turkey – A Modern History*, London, 1993, p 85.
3. Skendi, *The Albanian National Awakening*, p 45.
4. Pollo, Stefanaq and Puto, Arben, *The History of Albania*, London, 1981, p 125.
5. Durham, Edith, *The Struggle for Scutari*, London, 1914, p 159.
6. Knight, Edward, *Albania, A Narrative of Recent Travel*, London, 1880, p 44.
7. Ibid., pp 84–5.
8. Ibid., p 68.
9. Ibid., p 117.
10. Odysseus, *Turkey in Europe*, London, 1904, p 401.
11. *Correspondence on Negotiations on Rectifying the Greek Frontier, 1879*, Presented to both Houses of Parliament by Command of Her Majesty, London, 1879. Memorandum against annexation to Greece by the Janina delegates, page 65, no. 101, Preveza, 28 January 1879.
12. *The Times*, 31 January 1879.
13. *Correspondence on Negotiations*, Efforts of Moukhtar Pasha, Commissioner to the Porte, to excite Albanians against annexation to Greece. M. Delyani to M. Gennadius. Communicated to the Marquis of Salisbury by M. Gennadius, 19 February 1879, Athens.
14. *Correspondence on Negotiations*, Petition by members of the Albanian League against annexation to Greece, addressed to the Marquis of Salisbury. Despatch from Vice Consul Blakeney, page 105, no 157, February 28 1879, Preveza.
15. Hobhouse, J.C., *A Journey Through Albania, Travels in South Albania and Epirus, 1809–1810, Vol I*, New York, 1971, p 70.
16. Ibid., p 88.
17. Knight, *Albania*, p 115.
18. Ibid., p 259.
19. Ibid., p 202.
20. Skendi, *The Albanian National Awakening*, p 193.
21. Ibid., p 201.

22. Vasa Effendi, *La Vérité Sur L'Abanie et les Albanais, Etude Historique et Critique*, Paris, 1879, p 98.

23. *Histori e Shqiperise*, Tirana, 1984, p 37.

24. Hasluk, Margaret, 'The Non-Conformist Muslims of Albania', *Contemporary Review*, CXXVII, May, 1925, p 601.

25. Skendi, *The Albanian National Awakening*, p 118. Dora d'Istria was born in Bucharest in 1829, the daughter of the Romanian Prince Michael Ghika. She died in Florence in 1888.

26. Ibid., p 249.

27. Ibid., p 231.

28. Ibid., p 155.

29. Ibid., pp 159–160.

30. Palmer, S.E., and King R.R., *Yugoslav Communism and the Macedonian Question*, Connecticut, 1971, p 7.

31. Skendi, *The Albanian National Awakening*, p 212.

32. Miller, W., *Travel and Politics in the Near East*, London, 1898, pp 206–8.

33. Odysseus, *Turkey in Europe*, p 385.

34. Miller, *Travel and Politics*, p 211.

35. Ibid., p 393.

36. McManners, John, *Lectures on European History, 1789–1914*, Oxford, 1977, p 293.

37. Bridge, F.R., *The Habsburg Monarchy Among the Great Powers 1815–1918*, London, 1990, p 141.

3. Albanian Independence and the End of Ottoman Rule

1. Durham, Edith, *High Albania*, London, 1985, pp 222–3.

2. Ibid., p 300.

3. Ibid., p 327.

4. Ibid., p 328.

5. Skendi, Stavro, *The Albanian National Awakening*, New Jersey, 1967, p 379.

6. Micic, D., 'The Albanians and Serbia during the Balkan Wars', in Kiraly, Belsk., and Djordjevic, Dimitrije (eds), *East Central European Society and the Balkan Wars*, New York, 1986, p 166.

7. Durham, *High Albania*, p 106.

8. Ibid., p 270.

9. Bridge, F.R., *The Habsburg Monarchy Among the Great Powers, 1815–1918*, London, 1990, p 226.

10. Durham, *High Albania*, p 275.

11. Trotsky, Leon, *The Balkan Wars, 1912–1913*, New York, 1980, p 123.

12. Durham, *High Albania*, p 294.

13. Ibid., p 347.

14. Swire, Joseph, *Albania, The Rise of a Kingdom*, New York, 1971, p 63.

15. Ibid., p 69

16. Skendi, *The Albanian National Awakening*, p 162.

17. Swire, *Albania*, p 92.

18. Ibid., p 93.

19. British Foreign Office Handbook No 17, London, 1920, pp 44–45.

20. Swire, *Albania*, p 96.

21. Durham, *Albania*, pp 88–9.

22. See a further account in E.C. Helmreich, *Diplomacy of the Balkan Wars, 1912–1913*, Cambridge, Mass, 1938, p 47.

23. Mikic, D., 'The Albanians and Serbia', p 168.

24. *Histori e Shqiperise, 1900–1919*, Tirana, p 58.

25. *The Memoirs of Ismail Kemal Bey*, London, 1920, p 369.

26. Bridge, *The Habsburg Monarchy*, p 317.

27. Tucovic, Dimitri, *Serbia and Albania*, Belgrade, 1914, pp 107–8.

28. Trotsky, *The Balkan Wars*, p 267.

29. Crampton, Richard, *The Hollow Detente, Anglo-German Relations in the Balkans 1911–14*, London, 1979, p 76.

30. Ibid., p 83.

31. Kontos, Joan F., *Red Cross Black Eagle, A Biography of the Albanian–American School*, New York, 1981, p 5.

32. Crampton, *The Hollow Detente*, p 87.

33. Durham, Edith, *Twenty Years of Balkan Tangle*, London, 1920, p 237.

34. Swire, *Albania*, pp 78–9.

35. For a description of Shkoder during the Montenegrin occupation see Edith Durham, *The Struggle for Scutari*, London, 1914.

36. *Report of the International Commission to Enquire into the Causes and Conduct of the Balkan Wars*, Carnegie Endowment for International Peace, Washington, 1914, p 418.

37. Mikic, D., 'The Albanians and Serbia', p 186.

38. Lt. Col. Reginald Rankin, war correspondent of *The Times*, *The Inner History of the Balkan War, Vol 1*, London, 1914, pp 326–7.

39. Zürcher, Erik J., *Turkey – A Modern History*, London, 1993, pp 113–14.

40. Crampton, *The Hollow Detente*, p 99.

41. Jelavich, Charles and Barbara, *The Establishment of the Balkan National States, 1804–1920*, Washington, 1977, p 221.

4. The Reign of Prince Wied and the First World War

1. *Foreign Office Handbook*, No 17, H.M. Stationery Office, London, 1920, p 50.

2. Ibid., p 70.

3. Ibid., p 97.

4. Swire, Joseph, *Albania, the Rise of a Kingdom*, New York, 1971, p 177, reproduced in *Radnitchke Novine*, 22 October 1913.

5. Crampton, Richard, *The Hollow Detente, Anglo-German Relations in the*

Balkans 1911–14, London, 1979, p 126.
6. Jelavich, Charles and Barbara, *The Establishment of the Balkan National States, 1804–1920*, Washington, 1977, p 77.
7. Crampton, *The Hollow Detente*, p 128.
8. PRO.F.O. 371/1892 85635 4799 2.2.19147.
9. Durham, Edith, *Twenty Years of Balkan Tangle*, London, 1920, p 261.
10. Swire, *Albania*, p 184.
11. Helmreich, E.C., *The Diplomacy of the Balkan Wars 1912–13*, New York, 1938, pp 420–21.
12. Durham, *Twenty Years*, p 259.
13. *Foreign Office Handbook*, p 70.
14. Swire, *Albania*, p 212.
15. Jelavich, *The Establishment of the Balkan National States*, p 318.
16. Rankin, Lt. Col Reginald, war correspondent for *The Times*, *The Inner History of the Balkan War, Vol 1*, London, 1914, p 315.
17. Laffan, R.G.D., *The Serbs, The Guardians of the Gate*, New York, 1989, p 227.
18. Swire, *Albania*, p 245.
19. Unpublished letter from Edith Durham to Harry Hodgkinson, 11 January 1939.
20. Swire, *Albania*, p 276.
21. For a detailed account of the development of the Katchak movement, see Limon Rushiti, *Levizja Kacake Ne Kosove 1918–1928*, Pristina, 1981.
22. Peacock, Wadham, *Albania, the Foundling State of Europe*, London, 1914, p 217.
23. Pollo, Stefanaq, and Puto, Arben, *The History of Albania*, London, 1981, p 174.
24. Jelavich, *The Establishment of the Balkan National States*, p 319.
25. Swire, Joseph, *King Zog's Albania*, London, 1937, p 90.
26. Fischer, B.J., *King Zog and the Struggle for Stability in Albania*, New York, 1984, p 25.
27. Official Journal of the League of Nations, December 1921, 1191, quoted in Swire, *Albania*, p 335.
28. Swire, *Albania*, p 291. See also the Amnesty International archives on crimes perpetrated against Albanians in Kosova during the period 1921–4.
29. Emmert, T.A., 'The Kosovo Legacy', *Serbian Studies*, vol 5, no 2, 1989, p 21.

5. Political Instability and the June Revolution

1. PRO.F.O. 371/5726 XC3801 C 9287. May 6.1921.
2. Official Journal of the League of Nations, December 1921, 1185; quoted in Joseph Swire, *Albania, The Rise of a Kingdom*, New York, 1971, p 335.
3. PRO.F.O. 371/5726 XC3801 No.8–Archives. April.1.1921.
4. PRO.F.O. 371/5726 XC3801 No.8–Archives. April. 1.1921.

5. Swire, *Albania*, p 408.
6. *Black Lambs, Grey Falcons, Women Travellers in the Balkans*, ed. J. Allcock and A. Young, Bradford, 1991, p 95.
7. Swire, Joseph, *King Zog's Albania*, London, 1937, p 101.
8. Lane, Rose Wilder, *The Peaks of Shala*, London, 1922, p 62.
9. Swire, *King Zog's Albania*, p 105.
10. Swire, *Albania*, p 354.
11. Fischer, B.J., *King Zog and the Struggle for Stability in Albania*, New York, 1984, p 30.
12. PRO.F.O. 371/13711 3896/75. 9/12/29.
13. PRO.F.O. 371/5726 XC3801 No.8–Archives. April.1.1921.
14. Fischer, *King Zog*, p 35.
15. Kontos, J.F., *Red Cross, Black Eagle, A Biography of the Albanian-American School*, New York, 1981, pp 45–6.
16. Swire, *Albania*, p 407.
17. PRO.F.O. 317/5726 XC3801 No.8 Archives. 1.4.1921.
18. Kontos, *Red Cross, Black Eagle*, p 63.
19. Swire, *King Zog's Albania*, p 18.
20. Swire, *Albania*, p 429.
21. Jelavich, Barbara, *History of the Balkans, Twentieth Century*, Cambridge, 1983, p 179.
22. Kontos, *Red Cross, Black Eagle*, p 22.
23. PRO.F.O. 371/37135. 196824/103.
24. Kontos, *Red Cross, Black Eagle*, p 28.
25. Lane, *The Peaks of Shala*, pp 141–2.
26. Michalopoulos, D., 'The Moslems of Chamouria and the Exchange of Populations Between Greece and Turkey', *Balkan Studies*, vol 27, no 2, 1986, pp 305–6.
27. Michalopoulos, 'The Moslems of Chamouria', pp 306–7.
28. Fischer, *King Zog*, p 67.
29. Pollo, Stefanaq, and Puto, Arben, *The History of Albania*, London, 1981, p 195.
30. Swire, *Albania*, p 444.

6. The Consolidation of Zogu's Regime and the Italian Ascendancy

1. PRO.F.O. 371/37135 196824. 103.
2. Kontos, J.F., *Red Cross, Black Eagle, A Biography of the Albanian-American School*, New York, 1981, p 78.
3. Fischer, B.J., *King Zog and The Struggle for Stability in Albania*, New York, 1984, p 57.
4. Swire, J., *Albania, The Rise of a Kingdom*, New York, 1971, p 457.
5. Ibid., p 458.

6. Fischer, *King Zog*, p 95.

7. Oakley-Hill, D.R., 'The Albanian Gendarmerie, 1925–1938, and its British Organizers', in *Albanie*, Published by the Comité National-Democratique 'Albanie Libre', 1962, p 405.

8. For a description of the setting up of the Agricultural College at Kavaje, see A.E. Fusonie: 'An Experiment in Foreign Agricultural Education in the Balkans, 1920–1939', *East European Quarterly*, vol VIII/4, 1974/5, pp 479–93.

9. Michalopoulos, D., 'The Moslems of Chamouria and the Exchange of Populations Between Greece and Turkey', *Balkan Studies*, vol 27, no 2, 1986, p 310.

10. Ibid., pp 310–11

11. Fischer, *King Zog*, p 148.

12. Unpublished letter from Edith Durham to Dervish Duma, 26 March 1942.

13. Fischer, *King Zog*, p 154.

14. PRO.F.O. 371/37135 196824 101.

15. Carter, F., 'City Profile', *Cities*, vol 3, no 4, November, 1986, p 272.

16. Kontos, *Red Cross, Black Eagle*, p 143.

17. Fischer, *King Zog*, p 104.

18. Roucek, J.R., *Balkan Politics – International Relations in No Man's Land*, New York, 1948, p 128.

19. Cohen, L.J., *The Socialist Pyramid, Elites and Power in Yugoslavia*, Ontario, 1989, p 340.

20. Verli, M., 'The Colonizing Agrarian Reform in Kosova and Other Albanian Regions in Yugoslavia after the First World War,' (statistics used are from M. Obradovic, *Agrarna Reforma i Kolonizacija na Kosovu 1918–1941*, Pristina, 1981), *The Truth on Kosova*, Tirana, 1993, p 155. Other useful studies on the colonization question include M. Verli, *Reforma Agrare Kolonizuese ne Kosove 1918–1941*, Iliria, Bonn/Tirana, 1991; and M. Roux, *Les Albanie en Yougoslavie*, Edition de la Maison des sciences de l'homme, Paris, 1992.

21. More detail can be found in K. Krstic, *Kolonizacija u Juzhnoj Srbji*, Sarajevo, 1928.

22. PRO.F.O. 371/13711 3896 (C9441) 9 Dec 1929.

23. PRO.F.O. 371/15147 C6456/475/90 5 AUG 1931.

24. Armstrong, H.F., *Where the East Begins*, New York, 1929, p 95.

25. Kontos, *Red Cross, Black Eagle*, Foreword by N.C. Pano, pp vii–ix.

26. Ibid., pp vii–ix.

27. Kontos, *Red Cross, Black Eagle*, p xiii.

28. Ibid., pp 121–2.

29. Ibid., p 81.

30. Unpublished letter from Edith Durham to Harry Hodgkinson, 7 January 1938.

31. Robyns, G., *Geraldine of the Albanians*, London, 1987, p 38.

32. Fischer, *King Zog*, p 212.

33. Kontos, *Red Cross, Black Eagle*, p 178.

34. Newman, B., 'The Law of Lek', *The Geographical Magazine*, vol IV, no 2, p 143.
35. Fischer, *King Zog*, p 249.
36. Robyns, *Geraldine*, p 28.
37. Unpublished letter from Edith Durham to Harry Hodgkinson, 28 March 1938.
38. Hoptner, J., *Yugoslavia in Crisis 1934–1941*, New York, 1962, p 126.
39. Robyns, *Geraldine*, p 68.
40. Fishta, I., and Toci, V., *Gjendja Ekonomike e Shqiperise ne Vitet 1912–1944*, Tirana, 1983, p 206.
41. *Count Ciano's Diary 1939–1943*, London, 1947, p 54.
42. Robyns, *Geraldine*, p 88.
43. Unpublished letter from Harry Hodgkinson to Edith Durham, 27 June 1939.
44. Fischer, *King Zog*, p 280.
45. Robyns, *Geraldine*, p 95.
46. *Ciano's Diary*, p 66.
47. Ibid., p 68.
48. PRO.F.O. 371/37135 196824.
49. Fischer, *King Zog*, p 283.

7. The Second World War and the Founding of the Albanian Communist Party

1. PRO.F.O. 371/37144 XC196634 27/9/43.
2. Robyns, Gwen, *Geraldine of the Albanians*, London, 1987, p 113.
3. Montgomery-Massingbird, H. and Watkin, D., *The London Ritz, A Social Architectural History*, London, 1980, p 105.
4. Robyns, *Geraldine* p 122.
5. PRO.F.O. 371/37135 196824.
6. Unpublished letter from Harry Hodgkinson to Edith Durham, 27 June 1939.
7. Rothchild, J., *East Central Europe between the Two World Wars*, New York, 1977, p 366.
8. PRO.F.O. 371/37144 XC196634 27/9/43.
9. PRO.F.O. 371/37144 XC196634 27/9/43.
10. Lendvai, P., *Eagles in Cobwebs, Nationalism and Communism in the Balkans*, London, 1969, p 182.
11. Albanian accounts of the founding of the ACP completely ignore the role of the Yugoslavs. Although after 1948 the official line was that the Albanians founded their own Communist Party, the Yugoslavs were undoubtedly the motivating and unifying force behind Albanian Communism.
12. Stojkovic, J., and Martic, M., *National Minorities in Yugoslavia*, Belgrade, 1952, p 36.

13. Cohen, L.J., *The Socialist Pyramid, Elites and Power in Yugoslavia*, Ontario, 1989, p 344.

14. PRO.F.O. 371/37144 XC196634 27/9/43.

15. PRO.F.O. 371/37144 XC196634 27/9/43.

16. PRO.F.O. 371/37144 XC196634 27/9/43.

17. PRO.F.O. 371/37144 XC196634 27/9/43.

18. For the Yugoslav account of the founding of the ACP see Vladimir Dedijer *Yugoslav–Albanian Relations 1939–1948*, Belgrade, 1984.

19. Hammond, T., *Ingredients of the Communist Takeover in Albania*, p 227.

20. Unpublished letter from Edith Durham to Harry Hodgkinson, 27 June 1939.

21. See Margaret Hasluk 'The Muslims of Albania', *Contemporary Review*, cxxvii, May 1925.

22. PRO.F.O. 371/37144 XC196634. 30 July 1943.

23. Fielding, Xan, *One Man and His Time, The Life of Lieutenant-Colonel NLD McLean, DSO*,   London, 1990, p 43.

24. Halliday, J., *The Artful Albanian, The Memoirs of Enver Hoxha*, London, 1986, p 32.

25. The wartime period is one based on more misconceptions and illusions than any other era in Albania's history. There remains much bitter controversy surrounding this period, not only in Albania but also among the ex-BLOs themselves. It is beyond the scope of this book to discuss these differences.

26. Miladin Popovic met an untimely death in Pristina in 1945. He was most probably killed by the Yugoslavs, due to his intimacy with the Albanian leadership – which, as Dizdarevic says, made dealings with the Albanians at that time difficult. The Yugoslavs, however, claim that he was murdered in 1945 by right-wing Albanians in Kosova.

27. Interview with Nijaz Dizdarevic, *Nin*, 29 January 1989, pp 20–21.

28. Ibid.

29. Ibid. For the Yugoslav account of the plan to merge Albania with Yugoslavia see M. Djilas, *Conversations with Stalin*, New York, 1962, pp 142–7.

30. Interview with Nijaz Dizdarevic.

31. Hoxha, E., *The Titoites*, Tirana, 1982, p 58.

8. 'Building Socialism' under Yugoslav and Soviet Tutelage

1. Armstrong, Hamilton-Fish, *Tito and Goliath*, London, 1951, p 236.

2. Hoxha, E., *Laying the Foundations of the New Albania*, Tirana, 1984, pp 554–5.

3. Pipa, A., *Albanian Stalinism*, New York, 1990, pp 184–5. For further discussion on the Gheg–Tosk language debate see A. Pipa, *The Politics of Language in Socialist Albania*, New York, 1989.

4. *Zeri-i-Popullit*, 17 May 1981, p 1.

5. Ash, W., *Pickaxe and Rifle*, London, 1974, p 143.

6. Lovett, F., 'The New Albania', *National Geographic*, vol XIX, 1946.

7. Hoxha, *Laying the Foundations*, pp 540–41.

8. Djilas, M., *Conversations with Stalin*, London, 1962, pp 129–30.

9. Griffiths, W., *Albania and the Sino-Soviet Rift*, Cambridge, Mass., 1963, p 18.

10. Shnytzer, A., *Stalinist Economic Strategy in Practice; The Case of Albania*, Oxford, 1982, p 10.

11. Logoreci, A., *The Albanians, Europes's Forgotten Survivors*, London, 1977, p 91.

12. Hoxha, E., *The Titoites*, Tirana, 1982, pp 9–14.

13. Ash, *Pickaxe and Rifle*, p 83. Although most Western observers privately agreed later that it was unlikely the Albanians could have laid the mines and considered the Yugoslavs responsible, the fact was not acknowledged for fear of upsetting Tito, who split with Stalin around the time the International Court was delivering its verdict on Albania.

14. In 1948 the Tripartite Commission awarded the gold to Albania, only to annul the decision in 1950. Britain continuously refused to return the gold.

15. Shnytzer, *Stalinist Economic Strategy*, p 11.

16. Ibid., p 10.

17. Dedijer, V., *Tito Speaks*, London, 1953, p 312.

18. Griffiths, *Albania*, p 18.

19. Djilas, *Conversations with Stalin*, p 143.

20. Rusinow, D., *The Yugoslav Experiment*, London, 1977, p 354.

21. Shnytzer, *Stalinist Economic Strategy*, p 12.

22. Rusinow, D., *The Other Albania*, American Universities Field Staff Reports, 1980, p 13.

23. Hadri, A., *The National and Political Development of Albanians in Yugoslavia*, vol 1, Zagreb, 1970, p 551.

24. *Zeri-i-Popullit*, Tirana, 25 September 1949.

25. PRO.F.O. 371/78217 10197 21.10.49.

26. Griffith, *Albania*, p 21.

27. Jelavich, B., *History of the Balkans*, vol 2, New York, 1983, p 380.

28. Ash, *Pickaxe and Rifle*, p 138.

29. Andoni, A., 'Albanian Economy under the Communist Regime 1945–1962', *Albanie*, Published by the Comité National-Democratique 'Albanie Libre', Paris, 1962, p 272.

30. Ash, *Pickaxe and Rifle*, p 121.

31. Skendi, S., *Albania*, New York, 1956, p 296.

32. Ibid., p 298.

33. Ibid.

34. Hoxha, *Laying the Foundations*, pp 31–3.

35. Beeson, T., *Discretion and Valour, Religious Conditions in Russia and Eastern Europe*, London, 1974, p 283.

36. Brogan, P., *Eastern Europe 1939–1989*, London, 1990, p 178.

37. Zischka, A., *The Other Europeans*, London, 1962, p 81.

38. Ibid., p 83.
39. Griffith, *Albania*, p 21.
40. Ash, *Pickaxe and Rifle*, p 184.
41. Ibid., p 189.
42. Biberaj, E., *Albania and China, A Study of an Unequal Alliance*, New York, 1986, p 36.
43. Lendvai, P., *Eagles in Cobwebs, Nationalism and Communism in the Balkans*, New York, 1969, p 192.
44. Griffith, *Albania*, p 23.
45. Logoreci, *The Albanians*, p 122.
46. Lendvai, *Eagles in Cobwebs*, p 193.
47. Halliday, J., *The Artful Albanian, The Memoirs of Enver Hoxha*, London, 1986, p 221.
48. Ash, *Pickaxe and Rifle*, p 156.
49. Adoni, A., *Albanian Economy*, p 276.
50. Griffith, *Albania*, p 29.
51. Halliday, *The Artful Albanian*, p 219.
52. Griffith, *Albania*, p 34.

9. The Retreat into Isolation

1. See 'Albania, An Outcast's Defiance', *Problems of Communism*, vol 11, no 3, May/June 1962.
2. Griffiths, W., *Albania and the Sino-Soviet Rift*, Cambridge, Mass., 1963, p 61.
3. Griffiths, *Albania and the Sino-Soviet Rift*, p 80.
4. Logoreci, A., *The Albanians, Europe's Forgotten Survivors*, London, 1977, p 133.
5. Biberaj, E., *Albania and China, A Study of an Unequal Alliance*, Boulder, Colo., 1986, p 46.
6. Ibid., p 50.
7. Ibid., p 56.
8. *Zeri-i-Popullit*, 1 October 1961.
9. Lendvai, P., *Eagles in Cobwebs, Nationalism and Communism in the Balkans*, New York, 1969, p 196.
10. *Zeri-i-Popullit*, 13 October 1962.
11. Halliday, J., *The Artful Albanian, The Memoirs of Enver Hoxha*, London, 1986, p 13.
12. Andoni, A., 'Albanian Economy under the Communist Regime 1945–1962', in *Albanie*, Published by the Comité National-Democratique 'Albanie Libre', Paris, 1962, p 286.
13. Hoxha, E., *The Selected Works of Enver Hoxha, Vol II*, Tirana, 1974–1982, p 445.
14. Hoxha, E., *History of the Party of Labour*, Tirana, 1971, p 627.
15. Beeson, T., *Discretion and Valour, Religious Conditions in Russia and Eastern Europe*, London, 1974, p 284.

16. Ibid., p 285.

17. Gardiner, L., *Curtain Calls*, London, 1977, p 64.

18. Logoreci, *The Albanians*, p 157.

19. Ibid., p 152.

20. Ibid., p 180.

21. Magas, B., 'Yugoslavia, The Spectre of Balkanization', *New Left Review*, no 174, 1989, p 11.

22. *China Reconstructs*, vol xx, January 1971, pp 45–6.

23. Gardiner, *Curtain Calls*, p 68.

24. Ash, W., *Pickaxe and Rifle*, London, 1974, p 175.

25. Ibid., pp 244–5.

26. Gardiner, *Curtain Calls*, p 14.

27. Ash, *Pickaxe and Rifle*, p 218.

28. Gardiner, *Curtain Calls*, p 15.

29. Halliday, *The Artful Albanian*, p 285.

30. Biberaj, E., *Albania, A Socialist Maverick*, Colorado, 1990, p 26.

31. Biberaj, *Albania and China*, p 121.

32. Halliday, *The Artful Albanian*, p 336.

33. *Radio Free Europe Background Report* 282, December 1979.

34. Ramet, P., *Nationalism and Federalism in Yugoslavia*, Indianapolis, 1984, p 165.

35. Tanjug News Agency, 29 September 1981.

36. *Radio Free Europe Background Report* 215, July 1981.

37. Tanjug, 10 April 1981.

38. Pavlovich, S.K., *The Improbable Survivor*, London, 1988, p 87.

39. *Radio Free Europe Background Report* 142, May 1981.

40. *Zeri-i-Popullit*, 8 April 1981.

41. *Radio Free Europe Background Report* 199, June 1981.

42. *Radio Free Europe Background Report* 326, November 1981.

43. Biberaj, *Albania, A Socialist Maverick*, pp 36–7.

44. For an interesting debate on the subject of Mehmet Shehu's sudden demise see Jon Halliday, 'The Strange Death of Mehmet Shehu', *London Review of Books*, 9 October 1986, and the subsequent series of letters by Professor Frank Walbank and Harry Hodgkinson.

45. Summary of World Broadcasts, EE/7923/B/4, 12 April 1985.

46. Pipa, A., *Albanian Stalinism*, East European Monographs, New York, 1990, p 122.

47. Lendvai, P., 'Traveller in Albania', *Encounter*, May 1985, p 64.

10. The End of Communism and the Path to Democratic Pluralism

1. Albanian Telegraphic Agency, Bulletin, 21–24 September 1988.

2. Biberaj, E., 'Albania at the Crossroads', *Problems of Communism*, September–October 1991, p 4.

3. *Drita*, 19 November 1989, p 5.

4. Hadji-Ristic, P., 'Shaking Albania's Torpor', *Index on Censorship*, 1/1991 p 10.

5. *Report on Eastern Europe*, 26 April 1991, p 4.

6. Reuters Bulletin to BBC, 20 January 1991.

7. *Report on Eastern Europe*, 19 July 1991, p 2.

8. Radio Tirana in English, 14:30 gmt, 1 July 1992.

9. BBC Summary of World Broadcasts EE/1336 B/3, 23 March 1992.

10. BBC Summary of World Broadcasts EE/1332 B/1, 18 March 1992.

11. Szajkoski, B., 'The Albanian Elections', *The Journal of Communist Studies*, vol 8, no 3, September 1992, p 128.

Bibliography

Books

Alcock, John and Antonia Young (eds), *Black Lambs, Grey Falcons, Women Travellers in the Balkans*, Bradford, 1991.

Alia, Ramiz, *Report to the 9th Congress of the Party of Labour of Albania*, Tirana, 1986.

Amery, Julian, *Sons of the Eagle; A Study in Guerilla War*, London, 1948.

Antologji e Letersise Shqipe, Tirana, 1955.

Armstrong, Hamilton Fish, *Tito and Goliath*, London, 1951.

Ash, William, *Pickaxe and Rifle*, London, 1974.

Babinger, Francis, *Mehmed the Conqueror and His Time*, Princeton, NJ, 1978.

Beeson, Trevor, *Discretion and Valour, Religious Conditions in Russia and Eastern Europe*, London, 1974.

Bethel, Nicholas, *The Great Betrayal*, London 1984.

Biberaj, Elez, *Albania, A Socialist Maverick*, Boulder/San Francisco/Oxford, 1990.

—— *Albania and China, a Study of an Unequal Alliance*, Boulder/San Fransisco/Oxford, 1986.

Bogdanovic, Dimitrije, *Kniga o Kosovu*, Belgrade, 1985.

Bridge, F.R., *The Habsburg Monarchy, Among the Great Powers, 1815–1918*, London, 1990.

Brogan, Patrick, *Eastern Europe 1939–1989*, London, 1990.

Cohen, Leonard J., *The Socialist Pyramid, Elites and Power in Yugoslavia*, Ontario, 1989.

Count Ciano's Diary, 1939–1943, ed M. Muggeridge, London, 1947.

Crampton, Richard, *The Hollow Detente, Anglo-German Relations in the Balkans 1911–14*, London, 1979.

Dedijer, Vladimir, *Yugoslav–Albanian Relations, 1939–1948*, Belgrade, 1984,

────── *Tito Speaks*, London, 1953.
Destani, B., *Bibliography on Albania*, Centre for Strategic Studies, Belgrade, 1986.
Djilas, Milovan, *Conversations with Stalin*, London, 1962.
Drizari, Nijaz, *Scanderbeg, His Life, Correspondence, Orations, Victories and Philosophy*, California, 1968.
Durham, Edith, *The Struggle for Scutari*, London, 1914.
────── *High Albania*, London, 1985.
────── *Twenty Years of Balkan Tangle*, London, 1920.
Fischer, B.J., *King Zog and the Struggle for Stability in Albania*, New York, 1984.
Fox, Frank, *The Balkan Peninsula*, London, 1915.
Frasheri, Sami, *Was war Albanien, Was ist Es, Was wir Es werden?*, Vienna, 1913.
Gardiner, Leslie, *Curtain Calls*, London, 1977.
Griffiths, William, *Albania and the Sino-Soviet Rift*, Cambridge, Mass., 1963.
Hadri, Ali, *The National and Political Development of Albanians in Yugoslavia*, vol 1, Zagreb, 1970.
Halliday, Jon, *The Artful Albanian, The Memoirs of Enver Hoxha*, London, 1986.
Helmreich, E.C., *The Diplomacy of the Balkan Wars, 1912-1913*, New York, 1989.
Hibbert, Reginald, *Albania's National Liberation Struggle*, London, 1991.
Hobhouse, J.C., *A Journey Through Albania, Travels in South Albania and Epirus, 1809–1810*, vol 1, New York, 1971.
Hoptner, J., *Yugoslavia in Crisis 1934–1941*, New York, 1962.
Horvat, Branko, *Kosovsko Pitanje*, Zagreb, 1989.
Hoxha, Enver, *Selected Works*, Tirana, 1982.
────── *The Khrushchevites*, Tirana, 1980.
────── *The Titoites*, Tirana, 1982.
────── *The Anglo-American Threat to Albania*, Tirana, 1982.
────── *Laying the Foundations of the New Albania*, Tirana, 1984.
────── *Vepra* (Works), Tirana, 1968–1985.
Huges, Thomas S., *Travells in Greece and Albania*, London, 1830.
Jelavich, Charles and Barbara, *The Establishment of the Balkan National States, 1804–1920*, Washington, 1977.
Jelavich, Barbara, *History of the Balkans, Twentieth Century*, Cambridge, 1983.
Kemal, Ismail, *The Memoirs of Ismail Kemal Bey*, ed S. Stone, London, 1920.
Kiraly, Bela K. and Djordjevic, Dimitrije (eds), *East Central European Society and the Balkan Wars*, New York, 1986.
Knight, Edward, *Albania, A Narrative of Recent Travel*, London, 1880.
Kondis, Basil, *Greece and Albania – 1908–1914*, Institute For Balkan Studies, Thessalonika, 1976.
Konitza, Faik, *Albania, The Rock Garden of Southeastern Europe*, New York, 1937.

Kontos, Joan F., *Red Cross, Black Eagle, A Biography of the Albanian–American School*, New York, 1981.

Kristic, K., *The Colonization of Southern Serbia*, Belgrade, 1928.

Laffan, R.G.D., *The Serbs, The Guardians of the Gate*, New York, 1989.

Lane, Rose Wilder, *The Peaks of Shala*, London, 1923.

Lear, Edward, *Journals of a Landscape Painter in Greece and Albania*, London, 1965.

Lendvai, Paul, *Eagles in Cobwebs, Nationalism and Communism in the Balkans*, London, 1969.

Logoreci, Anton, *The Albanians, Europe's Forgotten Survivors*, London, 1977.

Marmullaku, Ramadan, *Albania and the Albanians*, London 1975.

Miller, William, *Travel and Politics in the Near East*, London, 1898.

Montgomery-Massingbird, H. and Watkin, D., *The London Ritz, A Social and Architectural History*, London, 1980.

McManners, John, *Lectures on European History, 1789–1914*, Oxford, 1977.

Nicol, Donald M., *The Despotate of Epiros 1267–1479*, Cambridge, 1984.

Noli, Fan S., *George Kastrioti Skanderbeg*, New York, 1947.

Norris, H.T., *Islam in the Balkans, Religion and Society Between Europe and the Arab World*, London, 1993.

Odysseus, *Turkey in Europe*, London, 1900.

Palmer, S.E. and King, R.R., *Yugoslav Communism and the Macedonian Question*, Connecticut, 1971.

Pavlovic, Stefan K., *The Improbable Survivor*, London, 1988.

Peacock, Wadham, *Albania, The Foundling State of Europe*, London, 1914.

Pettifer, James, *The Blue Guide to Albania*, London, 1994.

Pipa, Arshi, *The Politics of Language in Socialist Albania*, New York, 1989.

———— *Albanian Stalinism*, New York, 1990.

Pipa, Arshi, and Repishti, Sami, *Studies on Kosova*, New York, 1984.

Plomer, William, *The Diamond of Janina, Ali Pasha 1741–1822*, London, 1970.

Pollo, Stefanaq, and Puto, Arben, *The History of Albania*, London, 1981.

Prifti, Peter R., *Socialist Albania since 1944*, Cambridge, Mass., 1978.

Puaux, Rene, *The Sorrows of Epirus*, Chicago, 1963.

Puto, Arben, *From the Annals of British Diplomacy*, Tirana, 1981.

Ramet, Pedro, *Nationalism and Federalism in Yugoslavia*, Indianapolis, 1984.

Rankin, Lt. Col Reginald, *The Inner History of the Balkan War, Vol 1*, New York, 1914.

Robyns, Gwen, *Geraldine of the Albanians*, London, 1987.

Rothchild, Joseph, *East Central Europe Between the Two World Wars*, New York, 1977.

Rusinow, Denis, *The Yugoslav Experiment*, London, 1977.

———— *The Other Albania*, American Universities Field Staff Reports, New York, 1980.

Rushiti, Limon, *Levizja Kacake Ne Kosove (1918–1928)*, Pristina, 1981.

Shnytzer, Adi, *Stalinist Economic Strategy in Practice, the Case of Albania*, Oxford, 1982.

Shoup, Paul, *Communism and the Yugoslav National Question*, New York, 1968.

Shupp, P.F., *The European Powers and the Near Eastern Question 1806–07*, New York, 1931.
Sufflay, Milan, *Srbi i Arbanasi*, Belgrade, 1925.
Skendi, Stavro, *The Albanian National Awakening*, Princeton, NJ, 1967.
—— *Albania*, New York, 1956.
—— *Balkan Cultural Studies*, Boulder, Colo., 1980.
Stavrianos, Leften, *The Balkans Since 1453*, New York, 1958.
Stojkovic, L. and Martic, M., *National Minorities in Yugoslavia*, Belgrade, 1952.
Sugar, Peter F., *Southeastern Europe under Ottoman Rule 1354–1804*, Washington DC, 1977.
Swire, Joseph, *Albania, The Rise of a Kingdom* (reprint), New York, 1971.
—— *King Zog's Albania*, London, 1937.
Trotsky, Leon, *The Balkan Wars, 1912–1913*, New York, 1980.
Tucovic, Dimitrije, *Serbia and Albania*, Belgrade, 1914.
University of Tirana, *George Kastrioti Skanderbeg, The Albanian–Turkish Wars of the IV Century*, Tirana, 1967.
Vandeleur, Robert, *Albania's Road to Freedom*, London, 1941.
Verli, Marenglen, *Reforma agrare kolonizuese ne Kosove, 1918–1941*, Bonn/Tirana, 1991.
Vukmanovic, Stvetozar, *Struggle for the Balkans*, London, 1990.
Wilkes, John, *The Illyrians*, Oxford, 1992.
Winnifrith, Tom (ed), *Perspectives on Albania*, London, 1992.
Woods, Charles, *The Danger Zone of Europe*, London, 1911.
Zischka, Anton, *The Other Europeans*, London, 1962.
Zürcher, Erik J., *Turkey – A Modern History*, London, 1993.

Articles

Artisien, Patrick, 'Yugoslavia, Albania and the Kosovo Riots', *The World Today*, vol 37, no 11.
Biberaj, Elez, 'Albania at the Crossroads'. *Problems of Communism*, Sept-Oct, 1991.
—— 'Kosovo, The Struggle for Recognition', *Conflict Studies*, no 137, 1982.
Carter, Frank, 'Tirana, City Profile', *Cities*, vol 3, no 4, November 1986.
Dizdarevic, Nijaz, *Nin*, Belgrade, 29 January 1989.
Effendi, Vasa, *La Vérité Sur L'Abanie et les Albanais, Étude Historique et Critique*, Paris, 1879.
Emmert, T.A., 'The Kosovo Legacy', *Serbian Studies*, vol 5, no 2, 1989.
Hadji-Ristic, Peter, 'Shaking Albania's Torpor', *Index on Censorship*, 1/1991.
Hasluk, Margaret, 'The Non-Conformist Muslims of Albania', *Contemporary Review*, CXXVII, May 1925.
Krasniqi, R. 'Persecution of Religion in Communist Albania', *ACEN News*, no 128, March/April 1967.
Lovet, Frank, 'The New Albania', *National Geographic*, vol XIX, 1946.

Magas, Branka, 'Yugoslavia in Crisis', *New Left Review*, 174, 1989.

Newman, Bernard, 'The Law of Lek', *The Geographical Magazine*, vol IV, no 2, 1936.

Oakley-Hill, Darryl, 'The Albanian Gendarmerie, 1925–1938, and its British Organizers', *Albanie*, Published by the Comité National-Democratique, 'Albanie Libre', Paris 1962.

Remington, R.A., 'China's Emerging Role in Eastern Europe', *The International Politics of Eastern Europe*, Ed C. Gati, New York, 1976.

Thornton, T.P., 'The Soviet–Albanian Dispute', *Military Review*, 42, October 1962.

Treptow, Kurt, 'The Albanian Rebellion of 1481', *Albanian Life*, vol 48, no 2, 1990.

Unpublished correspondence between Edith Durham and Harry Hogkinson.

Periodicals and Official Publications

Foreign Office Handbook No. 17, H.M.Stationery Office, London, 1920.

Balkan Studies, Published by the Institute of Balkan Studies, Thessalonika.

China Reconstructs, vol xx, January 1971.

Foreign Office Papers of Great Britain, Public Records Office, Kew.

Great Britain, Foreign Office, Greece, no 1, 1879, *Correspondence Respecting the Negotiations for the Rectification of the Greek Frontier*, London, 1879.

British Documents on the Origins of the War, 1878–1914, ed. Gooch and Temperley, London 1926–1938.

Report of the International Commission to Enquire into the Causes and Conduct of the Balkan Wars, Carnegie Endowment for International Peace, Washington DC, 1914.

Radio Free Europe Reports, 1981–89.

Tanjug, Official Yugoslav News Agency, Belgrade.

Zeri-i-Popullit, Tirana.

Index